PRAISE FOR

ECHOING HOPE

*   *   *

"Does the inevitability of pain rob life of its goodness? Or is it possible for God to redeem pain through Jesus Christ? This is the question addressed head-on in *Echoing Hope*. With the mind of a theologian and the heart of a pastor, Kurt Willems walks us through the problem of pain without resorting to worn-out clichés. This book will help many people."

—BRIAN ZAHND, lead pastor of Word of Life Church in St. Joseph, Missouri, and author of *Sinners in the Hands of a Loving God*

"Kurt takes us on an authentic, vulnerable journey into faith, hope, and love. He translates our deepest pain, confusion, joy, hope, doubts, fears, and emotions in a way that can make us all feel less alone. We'll all be better by not just reading but also meditating on this terrifically genuine, relatable book."

—BEN HIGGINS, star of ABC's *The Bachelor* (season 20), founder of Generous Coffee, and author of *Alone in Plain Sight*

"In *Echoing Hope*, we find a rare and generous invitation into the areas of our own lives where pain understandably raises questions about God's power, love, and nearness. As you dive into your own humanity and vulnerability, you will gently encounter God. As you dive into the humanity of Jesus, you will gently encounter yourself. May this careful look at pain in the context of Jesus's life and ministry open up avenues of discovery and healing."

—MINDY CALIGUIRE, cofounder and president of Soul Care and executive team member at Gloo

"Kurt Willems's book provides an approachable framework for understanding and carrying pain in light of Jesus Christ. I loved the practical invitation to apply and practice Kurt's insights in our own lives through helpful formation exercises. *Echoing Hope* gives us something to hold on to in the midst of suffering."

—SARAH BESSEY, author of *Jesus Feminist*
and *Miracles and Other Reasonable Things*

"More than ever we need the encouragement and insight of *Echoing Hope*. We need enthusiastic reminders of Jesus's humanity and his acquaintance with our vulnerabilities. Every page of this book asks us to ponder, *What if Jesus actually gets it? What if Jesus really empathizes with us because he experienced life just like us?* You can see Kurt's pastoral heart as he invites us into the humanity of Jesus to learn from him and love him anew. This is very good news."

—OSHETA MOORE, pastor and author
of *Dear White Peacemakers* and *Shalom Sistas*

"*Echoing Hope* captures the paradox of the life of Jesus—the God who suffers so that suffering doesn't get the final word. Jesus absorbs the violence of the world to subvert it with love. In Jesus, God leaves all the comfort of heaven to join the struggle here on earth. As a brown-skinned Palestinian Jewish refugee baby, God came into the world. He experienced the pain of the world, from his birth as a homeless baby in a manger until his imperial execution on the cross, where he hung naked and humiliated, crying, 'My God, my God, why have you forsaken me?' (Matthew 27:46, NIV). This is a book about the enduring hope that God is with us . . . no matter how bad it gets."

—SHANE CLAIBORNE, author, activist,
and cofounder of Red Letter Christians

"Kurt has written a hands-on pastoral guide to engaging gospel faith. This book will be of special interest to those who seek entry into the grace-filled wonder of the gospel and those who yearn to grow in their faith. Kurt is in deep touch with the pain that marks our world and sees the way in which Jesus is present amid that pain in his transformative humanity. This work is an important corrective to faith that lives in an innocent bubble of otherworldliness. Readers who hope for more from the gospel will be informed and empowered by this generative rendering of the truth of Jesus."

—WALTER BRUEGGEMANN, professor emeritus
at Columbia Theological Seminary

"The question of pain has long stood as one of the great challenges to understanding the meaning of our human experience. What am I to do with the hurt, loss, and tragedies of life? Kurt Willems offers us a gift in this book. Rather than giving trite answers, he guides us with care and precision through beautiful storytelling, rich yet accessible theology, and a captivating vision of hope. This is a book for any and all who've tasted the bitterness of pain and long for the sweetness of hope."

—JAY Y. KIM, pastor and author of *Analog Church*

"Spend time savoring this book. If you do, *Echoing Hope* will change you. Kurt Willems's heart is on every page, gently teaching us the important truth that there are no silver bullets in this life but only the gradual transformation of ourselves into Christlikeness. Let this be a guide that brings you closer to life in all of its fullness."

—BRUXY CAVEY, teaching pastor at the Meeting House
and author of *The End of Religion* and *Reunion:
The Good News of Jesus for Seekers, Saints, and Sinners*

"Often, I'm overwhelmed with the simple truth that God came to us. God didn't just fix things from afar. He connected with us here on earth. I'm so thankful for Kurt's ability to help leaders grasp the importance of Jesus's humanity and the role it plays in our day-to-day faith! *Echoing Hope* is such a crucial work for the season we are living in today!"

—TYLER REAGIN, author of *Leading Things You Didn't Start*
and *The Life-Giving Leader*, founder of the Life-Giving Company,
and cofounder of 10Ten Project

"In *Echoing Hope*, Willems deftly weaves together theological ideas and biblical teaching with personal experiences and historical realities to invite us to trust our whole selves to a Savior who gave his whole self for us. Because Jesus is fully human, he is our reliable source of hope. Having served as a pastor for many years, witnessing the trials and triumphs of hundreds of people, I believe that *Echoing Hope* will be a needed balm, a prophetic push, and a practical theological guide for many."

—DENNIS R. EDWARDS, associate professor of New Testament at North Park Theological Seminary and author of *Might from the Margins*

"Kurt Willems represents a new generation of theologians who dare to let their own vulnerability, courage, and pain inform their beliefs about God. *Echoing Hope* is no exception. As Willems leads readers into clearer understandings of ancient Jewish customs and culture, his pastoral roots gently usher in an embrace of the subversive power of Jesus's true nature. I've no doubt Kurt's words will change the way readers interact with themselves, with their neighbors, and with the God who stands in solidarity with them all."

—CARA MEREDITH, author of *The Color of Life*

"Nothing is as transforming as entering into the experience of Christ in his context and finding our own healing in his presence. *Echoing Hope* helps us do that!"

—JAN JOHNSON, author of *Abundant Simplicity* and *When the Soul Listens*

"*Echoing Hope* is integrated and honest, attending to both the inward and outward dimensions of faith. Willems weaves theology with spiritual practice in ways that beckon the reader to bring their own pain and hope into a living conversation with Christ."

—MEGHAN LARISSA GOOD, teaching pastor and author of *The Bible Unwrapped*

"In this book, Kurt generously and vulnerably invites us into his own pain to illuminate the healing hope of a God in Jesus who doesn't dismiss our pain but accompanies us in the midst of it. In rare form, *Echoing Hope* weaves history, theology, story, and practice into an accessible guide for reframing our scars from reminders of pain to signposts of God's restoration."

—JON HUCKINS, author and cofounding
director of the Global Immersion Project

"Shockingly few books truly illuminate the humanity of Jesus. But Kurt Willems has given us a rare gift—a beautifully written account of Christ's humanity and also a tender, vulnerable account of Kurt's own. This brave book gives us permission to be fully human both in the most fragile and most high, holy senses of the word, in all the ways Jesus was and told us we could be. To read *Echoing Hope* is not only to go deeper into Christ's story but also to go deeper into yours."

—JONATHAN MARTIN, author of
How to Survive a Shipwreck and *Prototype*

"Bookstore shelves are lined with rarely kept promises for making our pain disappear. But Kurt doesn't make promises he can't keep. Instead, he leans into the inescapable reality of sorrow in life to point us toward the only One who can truly heal our pain and wipe away our tears. This meditation on the life of Jesus shows us a better way forward to become the hope-filled, hope-spreading followers of Jesus we were created to be."

—ZACK HUNT, author of *Unraptured:*
How End Times Theology Gets It Wrong

"As Christians, many of us can be quick to affirm that Jesus was fully human and fully divine. Yet from that point, we tend to almost exclusively focus on Jesus-the-divine—and rob ourselves from the invitation to have a life-changing encounter with the Jesus-like-me. This book came at a time in my life when my own pain and grief were hindering me from connecting with the Jesus-who-just-wouldn't-understand, and it reintroduced me to the Jesus-who-knows-how-it-feels. If you're longing to connect or reconnect with Jesus on a deeper level—one that is real and authentic and doesn't dismiss or gloss over the pains of life—you need to read this book . . . I did."

—DR. BENJAMIN L. COREY, author of *Unafraid: Moving Beyond Fear-Based Faith*

"Pain and despair have gripped the hearts, minds, and bodies of countless humans who have traveled across time. It's not if but when we endure pain. As one who has navigated his own trauma and heartache, Kurt Willems writes for the hurting, lifts the eyes of the questioning, and points to the hope woven and soaked in the gospel. Every pastor must have multiple copies of this book on their shelves to offer to the despairing in their midst."

—TARA BETH LEACH, pastor and author of *Emboldened* and *Radiant Church*

"As a speaker, writer, and speaking coach, I've tried for twenty-five years to help church folks see and hear the women and men in the Scriptures for who they are—real women and men. Our forerunners in faith struggled with the same anxieties and exhilarations as we do. Kurt Willems is out to do the same, not only with our fellow sojourners but also with our Savior. *Echoing Hope* draws Jesus near—in his humanity, pain, and purpose—without losing Jesus's divinity in the process. Kurt brings his own stories of healing and hope to the feet of an accessible Jesus, so that we readers can bring our own."

—SEAN PALMER, author of *40 Days on Being a Three* (Enneagram Daily Reflections) and *Unarmed Empire,* speaking coach, and teaching pastor at Ecclesia Houston

"I admire Kurt Willems's accomplishment in writing this book. It will deeply bless many readers. Willems sensitively and openly reflects on his own memories and relates them to Jesus's life of suffering and teachings about forgiveness. Willems invites readers to realize that Jesus himself experienced our pain and gives us guidance to walk in his steps."

—LOIS TVERBERG, author of *Reading the Bible with Rabbi Jesus*

ECHOING HOPE

ECHOING HOPE

HOPE

HOW THE HUMANITY OF JESUS
REDEEMS OUR PAIN

KURT WILLEMS

FOREWORD BY SCOT MCKNIGHT

WATERBROOK

For Chloe Margaret—

You bring contagious joy to our family. You are bold, loving, funny, and adventurous. May you discover your identity comes not just from Mommy and Daddy but also from a wonderful Creator in whose image you are made. You are a masterpiece, my dear, worthy of a love so profound that it can only be described as divine. I'm honored to be your daddy each and every day. Please never stop taking me by the hand and guiding me wherever you want us to go together.
I love you, Chloe-girl.

For Lydia Kimberly—

You bring a sense of magical wonder to every moment with us. You are courageous, compassionate, creative, and a companion to all. May you continue to open yourself up to the overwhelming goodness of Christ so you will know—before anything else—that you are worthy of the greatest Love in the universe. You are fearfully and wonderfully made: may all your identity be rooted in the God who sees you.
Being your daddy is truly a gift, kiddo. I love you, Lydi-bug.

For my dearest, Lauren—

You are God's gift to my life. I've written about sixty thousand words in this book, none of which come close to describing how grateful to the Lord I am for you: my best friend, partner, and travel companion. Making memories and creating a future with you bring me more joy than I knew was possible. Thanks for fostering the space for me to be my full, vulnerable, weird self—and thanks for returning the favor. May you continue to "know the love of Christ that is beyond knowledge so that you will be filled entirely with the fullness of God" (Ephesians 3:19). I love you, beautiful.

FOREWORD

* * *

I grew up in a kind of Christian faith that almost completely ignored Jesus.

We learned Jesus stories, to be sure, mostly in Sunday School classes, where we drew figures, colored inside the lines, and put images on flannel boards. But the "big people's" gatherings were all about the apostle Paul, the Bible and theology, and fundamentalist commitments to certain behaviors, such as not smoking, chewing, or "going with girls that do." These teachings focused on either abstract propositions or legalistic instructions. I would later understand that the Christian faith I was exposed to as a boy was not focused on Jesus as we find him in the Gospels—Jesus the *person*.

Later I began to discover that Jesus. That journey began in my first class in seminary, when my professor, Walter Liefeld, taught Synoptic Gospels in a way that put Jesus on center stage and God's grace for us on full display. I was beginning to see Jesus the *person*. Sure, we talked kingdom theology and Matthew's theology and all that academic stuff. But Jesus lurked in that classroom as a real presence. As someone who lived and died. As someone who was (and is) *real*.

He was like us in so many ways. But better yet, *we are like him in so many ways*. That's why we need Jesus—a real human person who shows us how to live in a real, painful world.

Violence and pain are two of the oldest stories, and many people connect them to redemption in far too casual of a manner.

Redemption doesn't permit us to pretend violence and pain aren't real. Neither does it excuse those who want to diminish or deaden the reality of the violence and pain by appealing to too-easy sentiments, such as "But I got saved! I got through it!" Worse yet, we can begin to believe the idea that "God did the violence and caused my suffering for my redemption."

In *Echoing Hope,* Kurt takes us into moments of pain and violence from his own life, but he does so with Jesus ever-present. Jesus's presence did not remove the pain, and it didn't provide a new method for living happily. Instead, Kurt shows us how it was about Jesus's presence in our pain, about God with us, and about our suffering with Jesus in his pain.

Reading Kurt's book means encountering pain—not good pain—but real, bad, awful, inner pain. When pain is caused by violence and injustice, the word *good* doesn't belong with the word *pain.* This book is not about how violence redeems, but about the redemption on the other side of violence.

We need Jesus to redeem Christian theology from abstraction. We need Jesus not only for what he accomplished—on the cross and through his resurrection and ascension—but also for all of who he was and is.

The real Jesus was rejected, accused, made fun of, yelled at in public places, exhausted, beaten, bruised, scratched, and humiliated on a cross, and then he died. No doubt, this bloody man likely suffocated to death in full view of his haters, friends, and followers. His mother was accused, his father seemed to be absent, his brothers didn't like him, and all the "righteous people" seemed to think he was nothing but trouble. They must have said aloud, "If he's not careful, he'll get us all in trouble and he'll get himself killed." Jesus knew pain and rejection throughout his life, which eventually culminated in the crucifixion.

We need that real Jesus because we, too, suffer. We need a God who knows our suffering, not one who knows *about* our suffering but one who knows what it's like to feel it—a God who *knows* our suffering. Without that God, our pain is remote from our Creator. We become an abstraction from a God who only knows us in the way a drone peers into something out of our range. But because of the real, human Jesus—the one who suffered—God knows our pain firsthand.

Jesus stands with us in our suffering. Sometimes he's clearly present, and at other times he's not. But he's there because our suffering is his and his suffering is ours. When we hurt, we draw closer to Jesus—perhaps more than we realize, but we do. God loves us and knows our anguish because the Son, Jesus, suffered and God knew him in that suffering. Our grief is *personal* to God.

In Jesus's suffering there is hope. Why? Because we know what happened beyond the hideous cross: Easter happened and Easter still happens. Yes, in my life and Kurt's and yours.

Easter happens in this book.

Read it.

—*Scot McKnight, professor of New Testament, Northern Seminary*

CONTENTS

* * *

JESUS, PAIN, AND BECOMING HUMAN

* * *

Echoes reverberate from an empty grave. Like a shout reso-nating from a canyon floor, sound waves bounce from stone walls in vacant caves back out into the world. Reflected noises resound, reminding us of the vast beauty of creation or the void of isolation. The hardened empty space required for echoes to exist keeps us in awe or fills us with dread. There is power in an echo: to inspire or overwhelm us. Echoes, depending on our per-ception, are filled with wonder or are signs of our desolation. Imagine the lost wanderer yelling for help but hearing only his own voice in response or, by contrast, the adventurer backpacking to a cliff of serene beauty and shouting for joy upon her arrival at the summit. We experience echoes differently depending on the position from which we hear them. In my childhood, the echoes were often hollow, fearful, and disorienting.

On a Sunday morning about two thousand years ago, a hollow tomb became a chamber of echoes. An empty tomb isn't usually good news. From ancient times, thieves have robbed burial sites. Think of royalty buried with their riches or enemies being dishon-ored even after death by the removal and desecration of their corpses. To remove a body from its sacred resting place dehuman-izes the memory of the deceased.*

---

* I'm aware of a practice in the nineteenth century in which medical students would go body snatching and steal the remains of African Americans for ex-periments. *Detestable* doesn't begin to describe such a practice.

Jarring is the moment in the Gospels when women arrived at the tomb of Jesus to find that he had gone missing. The alarm the women at Jesus's graveside experienced at the words "He is not here" (Luke 24:5, NRSV) matches what many of us feel. The phrase brought dismay rather than hope. Jesus was gone in a moment when they needed him most. For those of us who believe—or who want to believe—in God, pain echoes at a decibel loud enough that we can become clouded with doubt. No wonder, when the disciple of Jesus ran into the tomb, the gospel of John says that he "believed . . . [but] didn't yet understand" (20:8–9). Even today hope eludes when we consider many things in our world that reek of death:

Cancer	Losing a job
World hunger	Homelessness
Abuse of the vulnerable	HIV/AIDS
Student loan debt	Gun violence
Mental illness	Social inequity
Racism	Viral pandemics
Slavery	Wars and rumors of wars
Conflict with loved ones	Natural disasters
Patriarchy	Divorce
Child soldiers	Gravesides

And we're just getting started. (Feel free to take a deep breath if you need one.)

Amid the pain and suffering that will come into our lives, how can we learn to love and live well? Actually, you are already acquainted with pain and suffering. This isn't a theoretical exercise but involves a series of intimate hurts. We each hold them in our own way, but often our way doesn't cultivate a holy and life-giving relationship to and through our pain. But when we look at Jesus, we see the one human being whose relationship to love and pain is worthy of imitation. (But probably don't try that execution part.)

Dietrich Bonhoeffer once wrote, "Human beings become

human because God became human. . . . In Christ the form of human beings before God was created anew."¹ God created us as humans, and when we look at Jesus, we see the prototype for what all humans are designed to become. As we look at the life of Jesus, we see someone who experienced joy and pain and everything in between. He was "impressed" (Matthew 8:10), "deeply grieved" (26:38, NRSV), and "deeply disturbed" (John 11:33), and he "overflowed with joy" (Luke 10:21). In two situations, once at the death of a friend (John 11:32–35) and another upon gazing at a soon-to-be destroyed Jerusalem (Luke 19:41), he was brought to tears. Jesus lived in the real world as a real person, showing us the kind of human we are all designed to become.*

This book has two main objectives. First, I want to invite people to truly lean into the tension between pain and hope. Pain is real. Hope is a necessary gift only as long as hurts exist. It serves to keep us going, trusting that the world will be healed and whole one day when God gets God's way. Pain isn't going anywhere until that happens. Jesus did not whisk it away, and neither can we. We can take cues from Jesus's life, teachings, and effect on those around him for how to step into the highs and lows of our own lives. He didn't shy away from pain. He didn't allow the risk of pain to keep him from love.

My second goal is to offer a bit of a manifesto on the life and teachings of Jesus, focusing on his *humanity*. I want this to be a book that anyone—including a non-Christian—can pick up and ask, *Who is Jesus, and does he have anything to contribute to my life—especially when everything is falling apart?* The humanity of Jesus, although acknowledged by Christians, seekers, and skeptics alike, often isn't taken as seriously as the New Testament writers would invite us. I mean, think about it. Jesus was born just like all of us. He went through every phase of life, from infant to grown-up. (Although he never made it to middle age. So, if you have made it past thirty-three, congrats—you beat Jesus at something.) But seriously, Jesus is presented in the Bible as the fully human

---

* In case you are wondering, I affirm the full divinity of Jesus. I'm a Trinitarian.

one who perfectly models being an image bearer. He is the human that the story of Eve and Adam hoped for. He is the human who enacts what all of us are designed and destined to live. The human who shows us what God would do when faced with the mingled love and pain of life in the real world.

When we look at Jesus, we see what God always wanted for all of us: a life in tune with our Creator, one another, the earth, and our unique selves. Jesus is the image of God (Colossians 1:15–20), showing us simultaneously what God is really like and what truly being human is all about.

The humanity of Jesus is also about his posture in the world. Christ *has humanity* as he steps into the pain of others—just as he did when he bore his own suffering. His humane compassion informed every action and reaction in the Gospels. Of course, limited as he was by time and space, he could be present only to those around him. When he saw that someone was sick, he healed. When someone was overwhelmed by demonic evil, he liberated. When someone was hungry, he multiplied resources for the masses. When enemies bound, whipped, and executed him, he responded with forgiveness rather than vengeance. These individual examples of his compassion, love, and sacrifice show us his deep love for people. He invites his disciples to follow his example, beyond the small bit of real estate he occupied during his three short years of ministry. We can have humanity too.

As I bring these themes together, my goal in *Echoing Hope* is to create a space to explore the life of Jesus through the grid of pain to empower us to step into the challenges of life just like he would. The humanity of Jesus shows us a path through our challenges that ultimately redeems our pain. And here's the thing: we all have pain. This book isn't only for those grieving a recent loss; it's for anyone who lives in a world where pain is real. That's all of us.

There is no doubt in my mind that I come at the topics of pain, hope, and becoming human like Jesus in my own particular way. I'm a white, able-bodied, middle-class, theologically trained pastor, young father, and husband, who is Christian and male. Being human involves so many other perspectives besides my specific lens, which is shaped by my culture and experiences. This book is not an attempt to capture *everything* it means to become human like Jesus. My hope is that I share my reflections in ways that build bridges toward others with gracious space for our differences and enthusiasm for how the transformation process invites all our stories.

This book is raw at some points. I'm vulnerable about my own hurts. While this is by no means a memoir (nor are my personal stories in any sort of chronological order), I do share moments of both childhood trauma and pain experienced in adulthood. I've tried to be sensitive about each memory shared, as some of what you will read may open up wounds that still need some tender care in your own life. If your trauma still needs to be processed, especially if it pertains to abuse, I encourage you to discern whether or not to read this book with trusted friends, faith leaders, or counselors. (What I share here will not be overwhelming for most, but it is heavy at times.)

My hope is to challenge readers to hold their pain in light of the life and teachings of Jesus, but I don't want to heap "sorrow upon sorrow" (Philippians 2:27, NIV). If you decide to step into the first chapter and beyond, you will discover a Jesus who experiences our despair and invites us to see the beautiful potential of our lives as we discover that resurrection is real and that sometimes our emptiness allows hope to echo all the louder. To help process what you're reading, I've included formation exercises for you to engage as well.

This book is broken up into four parts. Part 1 will explore the kind of world Jesus entered as a human, especially with regard to the human experience of suffering. It will launch us into parts 2 and 3, which take us on a journey through the Gospels (Matthew, Mark, Luke, and John), beginning with the birth of Jesus. This will lead us to part 4, which explores the latter part of Jesus's ministry: his agony over the coming destruction of Jerusalem, his arrest, his death, and his resurrection.

Jesus's empty tomb is where the book will begin and end because I am convinced that resurrection is the most human thing of all—it is a final act of God's grace that makes a person fully human forever. Only then will we be free of pain. And until then, we look for Jesus when life hurts and try to uncover how to become an echoing hope to the world that he so loves.

Part One

AN ECHOING PAIN

There is no doubt—things in this world aren't as they ought to be.

No matter our experiences, we're invited to step into our broken world with Jesus. Jesus—God become human—offers us a model for how to live in this sort of world. Finding God in a world tattered by evil seems impossible in many circumstances. Rather than explain those experiences away, what if we named the fact that Jesus goes missing once in a while? What if when we admit that we can't see him, we're primed to find him in a new way?

CHAPTER 1

WHERE IS JESUS?

* * *

The problem of pain meets its match in the scandal of grace.

—PHILIP YANCEY, *What's So Amazing About Grace?*

J oy and pain aren't enemies. They're companions. The highs and lows of life dance together more often than we'd like to admit. When life graces us with contentment, we may feel enticed to ignore hidden layers of struggle. When stress bombards our momentary happiness, it's as though those gifts that energized us are now elusive, like oil through our fingers. Joy and pain, hope and anguish, stability and disruption—these stand shoulder to shoulder in the real world. As a generally optimistic person, it's taken me years to see that my positive outlook was directly shaped by an insecure childhood. But it wasn't all bad.

In 1994, I was a lanky fourth grader with two front teeth that hardly fit my face and unruly hair that was either styled as a flattop or forced to succumb to Grandma's Wahl clippers. Yet I was a generally cute kid according to most of the pictures.

California's Central Valley was home. Sunshine and outdoor play, rec league sports, playdates (we didn't call them that back then), the churning of Grandpa's homemade ice cream, trampoline dunk contests with uncles and cousins, occasional trips to the mall's toy store, and swimming pools to cool me down—these frequently cultivated joy and grit in me as a child.

My parents divorced when I was a toddler, and in the years after, Mom had primary custody and Dad cared for me every other weekend. Not an ideal arrangement for any child, but having both parents in your life—even if not in the same household—is a gift that not all share.

On New Year's Day of my fourth-grade year, Dad remarried and asked me to be his best man. Although we were somewhat deprived of time together, we had a great relationship. At home with Mom, joy and pain coexisted in a more obvious way. With a new boyfriend entering our lives when I was about four, the joy she brought to me as a nurturing mother was intertwined with the pain of abuse. There was fear. There was joy. The greatest blessing during those years were the gifts of a younger brother and sister. Many of my early memories involve us being silly or having adventures together. My brother and sister are six and eight years younger, so being "Bubba" to them was a role I took pride in.*

I'd later learn that my brother and sister didn't show up on our doorstep as gifts from a stork. They were the beautiful gifts that came from a tragic relationship. From about 1989 until 1995, Mom endured an abusive relationship. I doubt it started that way, but I can't recall a time when he felt like a safe presence. With him, my primary emotion was fear. Numerous times, Mom was abused physically and verbally in front of me. I saw it all. I experienced his violence directly at times as well.

One situation shortly after Dad's wedding sticks with me, and it isn't unlike other stories of abuse from those years. I can describe it from the perspective of all five senses because that's how vivid this memory is to me. (Even now as I type, tears are starting to well up.)

Recalling the place and time in my mind, I can *feel* it. The fear sweeping over my body as I lay in my lofted bed as a fourth-grade kiddo. The feeling of being smacked in the face about three times as I lay helpless.

The memory is also something I can *see*. The flash of light—

---

* My siblings have their own stories. I won't share theirs, except in generalities like this. When I share about Mom, it's only as part of my story and not to carelessly share hers. Mom eventually left the abusive boyfriend, got a restraining order, and moved on. She gave me permission to write these stories down. My desire is to honor my family in every way possible.

although difficult to describe—that seems like it happened milliseconds before the hand impacted my face. The wall of my bedroom that I faced to try to escape the danger. The blurs fading in and out as tears clouded my vision. The window in my room that faced the street, perhaps the next level of escape if I dared try.

I can still *hear* this moment of abuse. The screams of my mom pleading with her boyfriend to stop hitting her and to leave me alone. The shaming yell of being called a bastard. The slamming of a treasured picture frame containing a recent image of me and my dad posing, as groom and best man, for the wedding album. The shredding sound of the photo being ripped into pieces.

The *smell* stays with me as well. The musty scent of an old pillow as I buried my face to protect myself from a possible second wave of violence.

I also *taste* the intensity of this moment. The salty drizzle flowing down my cheeks toward my mouth. The bitter flavor that comes when you've been force-fed an overdose of trauma.

I remember how it ended each time too: with the loud roar of a motorcycle driving away. I was safe, for now.

As much as I have wanted to forget that moment when my mom's long-term boyfriend came home drunk and beat her and smacked me, it lingers. The scars are real. They will always be there, no matter how much the wounds might heal. Pain and joy didn't coexist in that moment. Only pain that echoed in my inner emptiness. My helplessness. Fear. Anger. It was like my home life was a dark cave from which escape was momentary, only to be confined to the darkness again and again. I knew Jesus when I was at church, but did he know me when I was at home? Many times I felt all alone, wondering if my vacant cries for rescue would be answered.

Your Pain Is Real

Where is Jesus when life hurts? Where is the echoing hope that interrupted reality two thousand years ago? Pain reminds us that hope brings a longing for what isn't healed yet. No matter your context in life, you have pain. Challenges in life are inevitable. I've faced anguishes that look quite different than yours, and vice versa. Comparing pain is like comparing our worst injuries. Both situations leave us with broken bones. Nothing is fixed by such a contrast.

Sometimes we use our pain to compensate for our insecurities *(The reason I'm not like her is because I had this disadvantage and she didn't)* or to boost ourselves up as the underdog *(I had it hard and I'm winning anyway!).* We might minimize our struggles in comparison to the "real issues" of the day *(Well, my struggles really don't matter since there are people in the world who don't have enough food to eat).* Our pain might even attract attention by making others feel bad for us *(My boss is so horrible; look at how he treats me).*

Pain is contextualized by the privileges (or lack thereof) that we are born into, but the truth is that seemingly hopeless circumstances eventually present themselves to us all. Owning our pain (ideally within the context of a supportive community) is the first step toward healing. In my journey, after neglecting my struggles—or rather, after having become as healed from my past wounds as I could be with the spiritual and emotional resources I'd attained up until then—I came to a tipping point. Pain presented as anxiety. I didn't know what to do. Most of my life I have struggled with anxiety, but I'd either muscle through it or ignore it. I couldn't ignore it any longer. I needed help and longed for wholeness. Therapy was the next step.

LOOKING FOR JESUS IN PAIN

In a ten-by-twenty room on the fourth floor of yet another expression of Seattle construction, I confronted insecurities, blind spots, and unhealed wounds. Every other week I opened up to the deeper parts of my story—those wounds that I believed were already miraculously healed but which festered just below the surface of my consciousness. That room proved to be sacred space, where my therapist (who also had training as a spiritual director) mediated God's love for me through just the right mix of invitation and challenge.

In our modern world, the imagination is often dismissed as childish. What a mistake. I've discovered that it's powerful. In fact, imagination gives us the space we need to reconsider the past, reimagine the future, and reclaim the present. The imagination is a place where we can attune our hearts to the deepest realities of our lives with God.

In our modern world, the imagination is often dismissed as childish. What a mistake. I've discovered that it's powerful.

In the Christian tradition, there's a set of spiritual growth resources that was popularized by Saint Ignatius of Loyola, who founded the Jesuit order. Ignatian contemplation encourages readers to step into a biblical story and imagine the scene with all five senses. He invited his students to "compose the place" in their imaginations so they could experience the story with Jesus in a deeper way. Sometimes you might find yourself relating to a character in the story; at other times perhaps you are watching from the gathered crowd. But in the imagination, something profoundly real takes place: you can experience Jesus in ways that are experientially more concrete.[1]

Another way this devotional practice can be applied is to take a memory from one's life and "compose the place," inviting God to breathe fresh insights into our souls. James Martin, SJ, said, "God may invite you to remember something that consoles or delights you. What is God saying to you through those consoling memories?"[2] Some use a version of this practice to pray through painful memories.

With this framework, when the time was right, my therapist suggested a spiritual formation exercise. Just like the suggestion to go the gym and exercise, I thought about it long before I ever acted on it. One day when I was at home, during a moment of quiet inspiration, I thought, *Let's give this a go.*

The story of abuse that I shared a bit ago kept coming up as a connection point to many of the challenges I was facing. Could I step into that memory with a contemplative posture to allow its full weightiness to be touched by Jesus? To simplify the process of prayerfully composing the place, my therapist provided guiding questions: *Where was Jesus in the room when this horrible situation took place? What if you went back into that space and asked Jesus to be real and present to you in that scene—what would you see?*[3]

COULD I FIND JESUS?

The memory I was invited to explore hurts. Even now. To write this chapter, I had to compose the place afresh. For a long time, it was a source of shame for me. That no longer is the driving source of pain. A sense of injustice toward that little boy—me—brings more sadness than should be humanly possible to feel.

The injustice also brings an awareness of other children in the world who face neglect, abuse, slavery, and every other sort of evil imaginable. And then it translates right down to my two precious daughters. My oldest is near the age I was when the abuse started. I can't even . . .

Stepping into deep pain with open eyes is one of the hardest things we can do. As I sat at my townhouse kitchen table listening to the midmorning Seattle traffic buzz by, I centered myself on Jesus. I prayed. I invited the Spirit of God to be present and active so that with Jesus's help I'd see something beautiful in the midst of the pain. I needed hope. I longed for healing. I wanted to know that Jesus was there, even in that dark hour of my story.

> *Stepping into deep pain with open eyes is one of the hardest things we can do.*

As the scene came into my heart and mind, all my senses drew me back to that moment. The place was composed. I began to look for Jesus. Where was he going to be in the room? My beliefs about God include a deep conviction that God is in solidarity with us in our suffering, not distant from it. He had to be in the room. *Fourth-grade Kurt needs you, Jesus!* I couldn't find him. Frustrated, I looked some more. Jesus was nowhere to be found. I wanted more than anything in that moment to see Jesus and to allow him to bring great healing to this wound. Instead I had to sit in the anxiety and the pain.*

When Jesus Is Missing

The moment when Jesus went missing in the gospel accounts is perplexing. This isn't a surprise to the reader because of the way the author composed these stories. But to the people living within that space and time—people like Mary and her friends, the disciples, and the many others mourning the death of Jesus—despair was real. Jesus was gone for good.

John's version of the story begins in a garden area with tombs. Mary arrived at the garden tomb, and the stone was rolled away (John 20:1). She was already mourning the loss of Jesus; now he was literally lost! Who would do such a thing? Didn't the grave robbers have any respect? Didn't they know who he was?

Mary was persistent. She remained at the garden of tombs (verse 11) on what the text twice tells us was the "first day of the week" (verses 1, 19). She wept, believing that her world was broken and hopeless. Mary's despair seems beyond repair. And to add insult to injury, a random gardener showed up and asked her why she was weeping. She said, "They have taken away my Lord, and I don't know where they've put him" (verse 13). The empty tomb's echoes brought a reverberating dread.

Later in the same chapter, we encounter another disciple of Jesus, Thomas. At this point, all the close disciples of Jesus had seen him except for Thomas, who apparently forgot to RSVP to his Evite. This story is so well known that we sometimes label a person a "doubting Thomas." One dictionary says that a doubting Thomas is "a person who refuses to believe without proof; skep-

---

* I'll come back to this exercise later on in the book, but for now I want to say that processing a traumatic memory like this is best done in the context of a support group, therapy, or spiritual direction. It took an extended period of personal work before I was ready to step into this version of Ignatian imaginative prayer. I suggest starting with a gospel story rather than negative personal memories.

tic."[4] Although this has become a bit of an insult, I think Thomas offers us a profound gift in the story.

Thomas helps us see Jesus's marks on his hands and side as symbols of our own lives (more on that in a bit). After being told by the other disciples, "We've seen the Lord!" Thomas wouldn't have it. He told them he'd believe only if he saw "the nail marks in his hands" and put his "finger in the wounds left by the nails" (verse 25).

Thomas needed to see Jesus's scars. If he could see them—if we can see them—then a great hope might actually be true: *even our pain is redeemable by God.* Thomas wanted to know whether the pain that thrusts itself at us—the grave disappointments—is redeemable by the God he'd come to know in the face of Jesus. Sadly, all this had come into question with Jesus's execution. Thomas desired for the rumors to be true. But desire alone doesn't always lead us to what we hope for. Thomas couldn't find Jesus.

Does Jesus Even Care?

Many times when I looked for Jesus, I couldn't find him. There are few things more frustrating than submitting your life to a God who doesn't want to be found. This is like Mary in John 20. Jesus transformed her existence. She knew pain but in him found hope beyond anything she could dream up on her own. Yet instead of finding Jesus's resting place ready for a fresh bouquet of flowers, she discovered a rolled-away stone. She couldn't take it.

It's the same with Thomas, who wondered if the so-called miracle being described was that his friends got ahold of some more of that "good wine" Jesus had made out of water (2:10). Thomas needed something he could touch and see to assure him that it wasn't all a hoax or a group hallucination. He missed the party. Now Thomas longed to see the scars on Jesus to know that he truly was raised from the dead.

Look at your own story. In a meditative posture, perhaps you can discern your connection with Jesus or what the image of an empty tomb brings up for you. Perhaps you've looked and have yet to find him. You like him as a teacher and guru but not as a personal expression of the God of the universe. Or could it be that Jesus is real to you but mostly as a belief system? This is true for many Christians I've met.

Maybe Jesus is present to you, but when it comes to your deepest hurts, you haven't been able to pinpoint where he fits into all of it. Like Mary, could you be truly seeking Jesus and feel surprised that he's not where you expect him to be? Like Thomas, do you need something experiential to break through the pain, to remind you that God is still on the move to bring healing and hope?

I needed Jesus to be in the room with fourth-grade Kurt. I needed him, like the disciples claimed to experience, to mysteriously appear with me without needing the front door. I had composed the place and he was nowhere to be found in my moment of great need.

Where is Jesus? I couldn't see him. At least not yet.

FORMATION EXERCISE

When we look around us, we know something isn't right. You may not have any major pain points right now, but we all face challenges in our journeys. When we have seasons when God feels distant, it's natural to wonder if we've done something wrong or even to feel disappointed or angry. Choose one or more of these prompts to take a step forward in engaging your pain with open eyes.

Consider a time in your life when God has seemed absent. Maybe it's a situation you are experiencing right now. Don't try to fix it or reframe it. Simply be honest. See it.

Scripture: Read Psalm 22. What do you notice about how David expressed his dissatisfaction with God's seeming distance?

Reflect: How does this psalm relate to your experience of God's absence?

Journal: How does your experience of God's absence shape your openness to Jesus? Address your questions, challenges, and desires to Jesus honestly in prayer.

CHAPTER 2

JUST IN CASE YOU HAVEN'T NOTICED, SOMETHING'S WRONG

* * *

Shalom is God's dream for the world as it should be: whole,
vibrant, flourishing, unified, and yes, at peace. Shalom is God's
dream for his love to bring wholeness and goodness to the world
and everything within it, including you and me.

—OSHETA MOORE, *Shalom Sistas*

Sometimes we can't find Jesus in the emptiness. We may long to hear the echoes from the empty tomb, but what we experience is silence as our pain drowns out any reverberation of hope.

And by the way, just in case you haven't noticed—something's wrong with the world.

I remember a day that still shocks me to the core, even as I write: December 14, 2012. On that Friday morning, I learned there had been another shooting of some sort. Due to the flow of the day, I had no more information than that until after a staff brunch when I got in my car to make my forty-five-minute commute back home.

After our previous car decided to blow up on the freeway (perhaps a bit dramatic, but you get the idea), we purchased a used Prius that came with a free trial of satellite radio. I could listen to CNN, Fox News, MSNBC, and other television channels, without the picture. Upon tuning in to CNN, I learned that this shooting had turned into an absolute nightmare. At that time, the report stated that eighteen young children had been killed (twenty when the report was updated).

I reacted with a surprising surge of emotion. On the highway I pounded my steering wheel while yelling out in agony, "Eighteen little kids! No f—ing way! It's so wrong! How can this be, God? How can this be?"*

Tears welled up in my eyes. As I listened to the reports about what had happened, layers of questions and emotions stacked up. I imagined it was the school where my wife teaches. I pondered the reality that those little kids were not too far removed in years from the baby we hoped to have in the near future. I questioned God, ultimately coming to terms with the fact that this was not the will of the Divine. Evil always occurs outside the will of God. This was another moment when I had to ask, *Where is Jesus?*

Something is profoundly wrong. Jesus goes missing way too often.

Shalom

In one of the Bible's creation stories (Genesis 2–3), God roams the garden with humans. A moment we might not expect happens after Eve and Adam eat the forbidden fruit: God can't find them. Sometimes God looks for us.

Wow. God seeks out the humans who have hid themselves in their shame. God pursues them, even when they are in shameful flight from their Creator. This sort of shameful hiding is a picture of what it looks like when *shalom* (the Hebrew word for "complete peace, wholeness, harmony") is disrupted. Our shame hides us from God, who comes looking for us anyway.

But that doesn't mean everything is fixed. I have often wondered where Jesus is when I need him the most. Yes, even after he found me. This is part of each of our spiritual stories. And it's not just you and me. It's *all* of us.

---

* My apologies to those offended by coarse language. I chose not to omit the word because, in the context, it portrays the authentic emotion I was experiencing in that moment.

FOUR RELATIONSHIPS

The early chapters of Genesis have several ways to describe that the world as it is isn't the world as it should be. Scot McKnight pointed out that humanity was created as image bearers to live in four harmonious relationships: *to God, others, self, and creation.*[1] The world is as it ought to be when these relationships are free of any sort of friction, usually caused by sin.

As God looks after us, we look after the world, and in so doing we align ourselves more and more with God's design. Genesis tells of a world unhindered by evil, which is how the world ought to be. However, we know what happens: we end up in a state of shame, and God comes looking for us. Shalom gets disrupted. God looks for us. Sometimes we also look for God.

> *As God looks after us, we look after the world, and in so doing we align ourselves more and more with God's design.*

DISRUPTED

Sin is a word that we struggle to define. If you find it helpful, think about sin (both its personal and systemic dimensions) as the disruption of shalom. If humans were made to reflect God's love to the world and if this is carried out through four harmonious relationships (to God, others, self, and creation), then sin is what happens when alienation exists in any of these relationships. As the reformed theologian Cornelius Plantinga Jr. observed, sin is the "culpable disturbance of shalom."[2] Sin is *shalom disrupted.* Sin is a betrayal of the full humanity Jesus reveals to us. Contrary to what many of us feel, sin is *against* our humanity, not part of it.

> *Sin is shalom disrupted. Sin is a betrayal of the full humanity Jesus reveals to us.*

When twenty little kiddos are mercilessly executed, the disturbance of shalom overwhelms us with sorrow. *Where are you, Jesus?* we ask. Most of us come up short for satisfying answers.

Where is Jesus when shalom is disrupted? It's difficult to say. When we pursue things that bring suffering, God pursues us anyway. Yet when the wrath of a despairing world imposes itself upon us, sometimes finding Jesus seems impossible. This was true for Mary in John 20. She wanted to mourn the loss of a dear friend and teacher. Then his body was lost, as were her hopes and dreams. This was true for Thomas in the same chapter of John. He missed Jesus's "welcome back" party and couldn't believe Jesus was present until he could see the marks on his hands and side.

Finding Jesus with Scars

When Mary came to the place where Jesus had been buried, all her deepest desires were contradicted by what she believed to be true: Jesus was *dead*. In the ground. In that tomb lay all the hopes and dreams she had invested into this *almost* messiah. But now, those buried hopes had gone missing. His body was gone. And it was the same for Thomas just hours later as he (naturally!) doubted that a dead man could come back to life. They wanted to find Jesus in their most painful of circumstances.

Eventually, Mary found herself in conversation with a gardener. This gardener asked her, "Why are you crying?" (John 20:13). At first she was nearly offended by the question, but her guard completely dropped when her heart was opened to the fact that it was the resurrected Jesus who was speaking with her. Anguish was forgotten. Hope was actualized.

Eventually, Thomas found himself in the right place at the right time. It apparently took Jesus eight more days to show up magically inside a locked room, but there he stood. Jesus said, "Peace [shalom] be with you. . . . Put your finger here. Look at my hands. Put your hand into my side. No more disbelief. Believe!" (verses 26–27).

In the midst of his doubts and despair, Jesus gave Thomas exactly what he needed, tangible expressions of Jesus's personhood: scars. Jesus's scars show us that all pain is seen—but never directly caused—by a God of redeeming and unrelenting love. For Jesus, love looks like solidarity with the outcasts of this world. In his experience as a marginalized man in a militaristic empire, Jesus chose solidarity with the powerless and poor first. They are for all of us a reminder that God feels the pain of the world with us, while giving us hope for a shalom-shaped world that God is birthing in the midst of this one. Jesus's scars show us that our stories matter, even the painful ones.

SHIFTING GEARS

Some of the heartbreaking stories I will share throughout this book involve the worst of my childhood, but let me tell you that even with the struggles we had, Mom was so much fun. As we kids got older, she found ways to play with us. She was always down to shoot hoops in a game of H-O-R-S-E. She took a genuine interest in the cartoons and movies I liked. Her sense of humor brought safety and hilarity to us. She let us play in the mud. Mom *still* knows how to have a good time.

One of the coolest things she did for me was teach me how to drive a stick shift. No, she didn't let me full-on drive as a fifth grader, but she taught me how to change gears in our car. I would sit in the passenger seat, and she would hit the clutch and yell, "Shift!" It was a blast every time. I have fond memories doing this out on country roads, with the windows down and kids' music playing for my siblings. I may have painful memories, but the scars don't hide the great ones. Both are part of my story.

Both scars and resurrection were part of the experience of the disciples as they encountered Jesus's empty tomb. Beauty existed in the scars, not only because Jesus rose but also because, with Jesus, the disciples knew both the incredible memories and the tragic ones.

Jesus Feels Pain with Us

Our pain, evidence of the disruption of shalom, is real. Jesus endured the full weight of a world broken by evil as he willingly died for even his enemies. His empty tomb and scars display loud and clear that there is a profound hope that can accompany pain. Resurrection is not merely a one-off thing that God did with Jesus to prove that he is God. Resurrection is the hope that God freely offers humankind. Our future resurrection will be the ultimate reclaiming of shalom by Jesus for us, when our world is restored and saturated by God's eternal gifts of justice, peace, joy, and love.

Jesus's scars stand in the intersection between our pain and the actualization of our hope. As followers of Christ, we trust that Jesus feels our pain deeply and has a hope-filled plan to bring heaven to earth on that day when he returns to judge, purge, heal, resurrect, and reclaim every square inch of the cosmos. Our pain is *real*. But the gospel says it is not *permanent*.

Our pain is real. But the gospel says it is not permanent.

All that feels dandy, doesn't it? At least on paper. But discovering Jesus in our real pain, here and now, is often much harder. Hope can seem like lofty idealism when what is real is tragic. Twenty precious kiddos found that out in a school on December 14, 2012.

I can only imagine what Jesus was doing when those babies were being shown no mercy: weeping. He wept over Jerusalem, knowing that the Romans would come in the near future and flatten the city. He wept after learning that his dear friend Lazarus was dead. And he wept on December 14, 2012. Jesus is the God who cries when children die.

In his book *Lament for a Son*, Nicholas Wolterstorff described his journey of losing his son to an accident. Beyond recommending it as a resource on grief, I want to share something that affects me to this day. Wolterstorff said,

> Every act of evil extracts a tear from God, every plunge into anguish extracts a sob from God. . . . God's work to release himself from his suffering is his work to deliver the world from its agony; our struggle for joy and justice is our struggle to relieve God's sorrow. . . .
>
> Until justice and peace embrace, God's dance of joy is delayed.[3]

God, according to both Testaments, isn't exempt from sorrow. God's Spirit groans in the midst of our broken world (Romans 8:18–28), as did the Hebrews under slavery to Pharaoh (Exodus 2:23–24; 6:5). As early as the flood story in the first book of the Bible, God is said to be "heartbroken" (Genesis 6:6). God doesn't always get what God wants because God has created a world with free will. Suffering is never God's will for humanity.

God is, in fact, *for* us all, even when the evidence seems to point to the contrary. "Evil extracts a tear from God" every time. The task of bringing this world to its hopeful destiny of ultimate liberation from sin and perfect union with heaven is driven by God's own desire to be free from sorrow, as well as to free us from ours. Jesus isn't missing when things go wrong. Jesus is weeping with us every time shalom is disrupted in our lives.

Where is Jesus? Here. Even if it doesn't feel like it.

MAKING SENSE OF JESUS'S NEARNESS

But there's a problem. This reality that Jesus is present in our pain can turn into an empty platitude. It can become another pious saying that means nothing. It makes a decent bumper sticker but holds no comfort. In my own life, as I go back into the darker moments of my story, knowing that Jesus isn't distant from my pain but is in solidarity with me reframes my trauma as a shared agony with him—even if he's hard to find sometimes.

Maybe you have past wounds that fester constantly just beneath the surface or pain that is buried so deep inside that numbing it has been your way of coping. Take a breath if that just described you. Seriously, inhale deeply for four seconds, hold the air for four more, and slowly release it for six. Now give yourself some grace. We all have pain that we haven't fully processed. Shalom will always be disrupted in our world and lives in ways that will take a resurrection to fully heal.

Now, what about those deep wounds, those sins done to us or by us? How does God's solidarity in our suffering help us experience some redemption from our pain? I continue to search for that answer, but hopefully I can point you in a direction to explore. In the process of writing this book, I came back to my first memory of when the violence all started.

JESUS AND PAINFUL MEMORIES

"*Mijo,* he is drunk. When you get into the car, I want you to sit in the back seat and close your eyes. Be quiet so that you don't get hurt. He is probably going to hit your mom, but you close your eyes and try to sleep."

At the age of five, this is my earliest memory of domestic violence. We had spent the afternoon and evening in a town about twenty minutes from our home in Dinuba, California. That's where my mom's boyfriend's older brother lived with his family. They were always kind, and my "cousins" were fun to play with. I remember all of us jumping on a bed and me being the ringleader as I taught them a silly song, "Entertainment Tomorrow." I can still remember the tune and inflection I used as we sang, giggled, and jumped. (Yes, it was inspired solely by a vague awareness that there was a show on TV called *Entertainment Tonight.* Kids are awesome.)

My "uncle" pulled me aside, with my mom's knowledge, and gave me that talk after a day of fun. He and my mom's boyfriend had drank throughout the day, but clearly his little brother was inebriated. We got into the car, an old Oldsmobile that we called "the boat," and all that he predicted came true. From the middle of the back seat, I watched him yank my mom by the hair. Hit her in the face. Slurred his words as he called her a b—. All this while she was driving the car.

While I don't recall whether he hit me that night, the images from the back seat are forever burned into the vulnerable parts of my mind. No child should be subjected to violence and fear. Nor should any human being for that matter. Finding Jesus in these moments is one of the greatest challenges life presents to us.

So what's needed? To see how Jesus—in all the complexity and beauty of his humanity—teaches us how to live as people in this world full of pain, this world aching for God's original shalom. Seeing Jesus in his whole and completely perfect humanity is our best shot at moving closer to healing as we tap into the echoing hope of his resurrecting love.

Was Jesus in the car with me that night? I sure hope so. Does this take away the pain? Nope. But there is something transformational about opening up my story to the "God of all comfort" (2 Corinthians 1:3), who weeps and desires nothing more than that shalom be restored. God doesn't always get God's way in the moment, but the echoing hope will one day crescendo when God "will wipe away every tear from [our] eyes" (Revelation 21:4). Perhaps in wiping away our tears on that last day, Jesus will wipe the final tear of compassionate agony from his own face. Until then, we sit with the disruption of shalom and partner with Jesus—by becoming like him—to become people who allow God to hold us in our tears and empower us in holding the pain of others. Trauma will not get the final word.

> *Perhaps in wiping away our tears on that last day, Jesus will wipe the final tear of compassionate agony from his own face.*

Just look at the first disciples of Jesus, for example. They experienced so much joy in learning from Jesus, which was then contrasted with both his prediction of his death and the event of his death itself. They were on their way to Jerusalem, and Jesus said,

"The Human One* must suffer many things and be rejected—by the elders, chief priests, and the legal experts—and be killed and be raised on the third day" (Luke 9:22). Writing about Jesus and trauma, Dawn Eden said, "It was *traumatic*. . . . Hearing him predict his own death was as though they were hearing their own father tell them he would be beaten, humiliated, and killed. . . . So . . . they blocked it out."[4]

This might explain why when Jesus was crucified, they were shocked. They had pushed that terrifying prediction so deep into their subconscious that they had no hope for his resurrection three days later. But then, through an angel, God brought the full memory back to the surface: "'He isn't here [trauma], *but* has been raised [hope]. Remember what he told you while he was still in Galilee. . . .' Then they *remembered* his words" (24:6, 8).

Where the first half of the sentence briefly adds insult to injury, the *but* interrupts the echoing heartache of the previous two days with an invitation to remember. Jesus predicted not only his suffering and death but also that he'd conquer the powers of sin and death by being "raised on the third day." In blocking out the cryptic, traumatic prediction Jesus made concerning his death, the disciples—these women and men who had dropped everything to follow their beloved teacher—also blocked out the saving grace of the moment: his resurrection.

So often hope and pain come in the same messy package. Jesus predicted both his death *and* resurrection, yet so disturbed by the bad news, the disciples couldn't hold on to the good news. When shalom is disrupted, the only way to access the beautiful things is through the complicated mess caused by the darkness.

Sometimes we just have to go through our challenges to discover Jesus on the other side. (And sometimes we find that Jesus is guiding us through them.) We don't get a choice in the matter.

---

* Don't you just love how the Common English Bible renders "Son of man"? It takes some getting used to, but it really amplifies the meaning of this title that Jesus uses of himself. He is the one full human who represents God to the world perfectly. He is, as Paul says elsewhere, "the last Adam . . . that gives life" (1 Corinthians 15:45).

No perfect world exists where we are insulated from the hurts of life. Trying to take a detour from pain is like asking to get off the roller coaster just as it reaches the peak on the track before the massive drop. There's no going back. You can't ignore the drop. No matter what you do in that moment, it won't change the sensation that your stomach is falling at a much slower pace than the rest of your body. You can close your eyes to cope with the coming rush, or you can face its terror with eyes wide open.

Jesus wanted his disciples to have access to all that is good, but this is possible only through cognitive dissonance—a willingness to hold hope with pain. By blocking out their pain, they missed out on the hope when they needed it most. In a move of grace, God brought back those memories, reframing Jesus's traumatic words in light of a hope that they could understand only on the other side of his resurrection.

The truth is, you and I have baggage in our stories—both past and present—that Jesus is ready to help us unpack. He hates that we have pain. He by no means causes it. But Jesus understands it, not only as the all-knowing God of the universe but also as the Human One who suffered in the worst way imaginable on our behalf. If we will take the risk to learn from his example, if we will give ourselves to the path that allowed him to lean into the tension of pain and hope, then we can slowly grow in our capacity to discover the heavenly that exists alongside our personal hells.

And even though we'll never (in this life) fully overcome the pain we walk through, we can step *into it* and *through it* in a different way. *That* is what Jesus ultimately offers us. Not easy answers or quick fixes. And definitely not absolute protection from the evils of a broken world. But a promise to abide with us, to open us up to the possibility that with him as our guide, we have all we need to walk the road of suffering while echoing hope to ourselves and others. Jesus embodies an empathic humanity for those who suffer or feel exposed. He is closer than we realize and wants you and me to know that we are never alone in our pain.

FORMATION EXERCISE

Sin is the disruption of four relationships: with God, others, self, and creation. Most of us can quickly think of a time when one of these relationships broke down.

Reflect: Do you have a particular memory that is representative of an ongoing challenge in your life? (As a caution: Please do not tap into traumatic memories without proper supports in place, such as a therapist or another trusted counselor.) If not a memory, perhaps you are currently facing a challenging situation that represents shalom's disruption in your life.

Scripture: Read John 20:24–29 once all the way through to get an understanding of the story. Then read it again—slowly—two more times. Prayerfully take note of a word or phrase that stands out to you.

Journal: Is there a connection between your memory or current situation and the word or phrase that stood out to you from the story? Be creative and open. Use whatever comes to you as an opportunity to pray and listen for God's still, small voice.

CHAPTER 3

HUMAN . . . LIKE JESUS?

* * *

Jesus is . . . the blueprint for the genuine humanness which is on offer through the gospel. . . . Jesus is himself the one "in whom" we are called to discover what true humanness means in practice.

—N. T. WRIGHT, *Paul for Everyone: The Prison Letters*

I 'm only human." We say this to comfort ourselves when we have failed at something, hurt someone, or experienced challenging circumstances. It might be the sort of thing we say to someone during a pseudo-apology ("Give me a break! I'm only human.") or something we tell a friend struggling with the various battles of life ("Don't let it get you down. You're only human."). These three words give voice to more than solace in difficult times. "I'm only human" is the anthem of resignation. It also might be the greatest lie we've ever told about ourselves.

If during my life I've had reason to utter this phrase beneath my breath, it was while writing this chapter.* My older daughter—a kindergartner—caught the flu. Normal. It happens. But we also had a brand-new baby girl in our home who weighed in at 7.1 pounds and was about 19.5 inches. With our kitchen as a natural barrier, I lived in the guest room next to my sick kiddo's room; Lauren (my wife) kept our baby mostly in our room, which is in the other half of the house.

---

* As a reminder, the writing process for this book happened over a couple of years, so my daughters' ages will vary some. This particular story took place in the first part of 2019.

Halfway through the week I had cabin fever (of course, I didn't know what *real* cabin fever was, as this was before COVID-19). Oh, I failed to mention that one of the few brief moments I left the house was to see a urologist, who told me I had a prostate infection at the ripe ol' age of thirty-five! I was poppin' antibiotics like Skittles and awaiting a medical procedure involving a long and narrow camera. (Which eventually happened. Fun, right?)

No doubt, more than once my dad and husband credentials were tested, and I failed. I lost my patience at times. I also was tired and feeling sick to the point where I wasn't thinking straight. *Woe is me* became an easy refrain as I questioned my life's calling, dad skills, and general success at being human. No one would fault me for thinking in these moments, *I'm only human.* But there's got to be a better posture to face life with! Could *human* be the description of the best version of ourselves instead of the worst? Let's see whether Jesus has any clues to offer us.

FYI: *Jesus Was Human*

When we talk about the empty tomb echoing hope throughout the ages, we are talking about a human being who walked out of it after he had died. A resurrected human being is the center of hope in a world filled with pain.

In the gospel of Matthew, the writer tells us a series of stories that give us a glimpse into Jesus's humanity. After what amounted to being one of the worst weeks of his life—so far in the story—Jesus took time away by hopping in a boat. Imagine being so popular that the only way to get alone is to do a solo sail! As he was on retreat, crowds started to follow him along his route. Eventually Jesus accepted that his short-lived retreat was over, joined the people, and ended up multiplying fish and loaves to feed them all. But even the act of retreating begs the question, Why did Jesus seek a space to be rejuvenated?

The week or so leading up to the famous "Feeding of the Five Thousand" story wasn't nearly as miraculous. Jesus had to have been at the point of utter emotional and physical exhaustion by the time he stepped into that boat. His body was human just like ours. He had a brain, heart, lungs, muscles, and skin. Pushing any person's body through emotional experiences takes a toll on its cooperation with whatever is coming next. At some point, our bodies need recovery time. Jesus's opportunity to restore himself was interrupted. I can relate to this.

Before boarding, Jesus had a few difficult moments. He visited Nazareth and was mocked by the locals because he was the home-town kid (13:54–58). Can you imagine Jesus feeling that rejection from the community that raised him? Then he got the news that his cousin, ministry companion, and friend, John the Baptizer, was beheaded by Herod the tetrarch (14:1–12). From an attack on his identity to an unthinkable loss. No wonder he needed to create some space for himself. While I haven't had a week exactly like that, if I were holding half the pain and loss that Jesus did, I'd be ready for some time alone.

Jesus made a healthy choice—one that many of us often need and rarely act upon—to stop everything he was doing. He needed to decompress, to process all that he was experiencing. Retreat rhythmically created the space he needed to reenergize and recover. Yep. The Son of God needed to have his tank re-plenished. As we know, this rest didn't last long. The plan basi-cally failed. His "deserted place" (verse 13) to relax was invaded by crowds of people until he canceled his retreat and offered them compassion.

From this one sequence of events, you can see a glimpse into the humanity of Jesus. We have to take this seriously because the Bible takes it seriously. Here's how I might summarize Jesus's hu-manity: the New Testament portrays Jesus—everything he says, does, and teaches—as the pattern for the type of humans we all can become. I'm not saying we will become *just* like him in this life, but Jesus invites us to become *more* like him as we journey *with* him. Jesus is what it looks like when God is human. Jesus invites us to follow his way of being human. So if we become like

Jesus, in a mysterious sense, we become more human like God.*
Yes, my mind is blown too.

> *The New Testament portrays Jesus—everything he says,
> does, and teaches—as the pattern for the type of humans we
> all can become.*

When Jesus did anything special in the Gospels, it had less to
do with proving that he is actually God (which I fully believe he
is) and more to do with demonstrating that he is the human that
God has always wanted for God's world.[1] Only God in the flesh
could show us how best to be image bearers! We must remember
that *many* of the prophets did miracles as well, and of course, they
didn't get divine status. Jesus's miracles amplified his genuine humanness, his stewardship over a world destined for shalom.[2]

Underhumanizing Jesus

While *overdeifying* Jesus isn't possible, since as a Christ follower
I'd rather not rob God of any glory, it's increasingly clear to me
that many Christians *underhumanize* him. Christians often talk
about *flesh versus spirit* as though this one image in the New Testament is meant to split physicality from spirituality. I've heard
sermons and read books and blogs that talk about "the flesh," re-
ferring to our bodies (and sinful desires) as what we will leave
behind for brand-new spiritual bodies in heaven.

Sometimes we get the impression that our human bodies will
not be redeemed in the end, that we'll be ghostly. No. The body is
good. *Very* good. Its impulses and lusts ("the flesh") must be trans-

---

*I'm not promoting certain versions of kenotic Christology that go so far as to
claim that all Christians *can* do everything Christ did on earth, especially miracles. I have yet to see that. Nor am I promoting views of kenosis that claim
Jesus was less than God. While accommodating to human limitations so that
he could fully enter into our situation, Jesus modeled what it looks like for a
human being to depend on and operate in the full power of the Holy Spirit.

formed for the good life Jesus offers. These impulses, of course, are often the inversion of healthy desires (lust is rooted in a desire for intimacy, for example). But the point is that the human body isn't disposable; it's redeemable. The imaginations of the writers of the New Testament were always informed by the idea that spirit and matter are deeply intertwined. When did we lose this?

Some Christians believe that our humanity will be shed in eternity. But if we are invited to become like Jesus, why would we desire to escape the humanity he willingly put on himself? Jesus was and is human. So are we.

DON'T DISMISS HALF OF JESUS'S SIGNIFICANCE

Dorothy Day once said, "Don't call me a saint. I don't want to be dismissed so easily." True, countless Roman Catholic sisters and brothers hope she is declared a saint one day for the great work she did during her lifetime. But while she was alive, she wanted people to see that as soon as you call someone a saint, you put her in a do-good class that allows all of us nonsaints a pass. When we overspiritualize our heroes, it ironically makes them *less* heroic, *less* able to influence our lives through their examples. The pedestals we put people on rarely help us follow them.*

Think about it. When we see someone doing something great, something beyond what we could imagine our lives being like, we idolize him. Be it an inspiring activist (Dr. Martin Luther King Jr. or Mother Teresa), an amazing athlete (Michael Jordan or Bo Jackson), an Oscar-winning actress (Viola Davis or Julie Andrews), a Grammy-winning singer (Beyoncé or John Legend), a world-changing entrepreneur (Mark Zuckerberg or Elon Musk), or a famous politician (Abraham Lincoln), giving someone a saintly or superhuman label separates him or her from the rest of us common folks.

But here's the thing. Jesus doesn't want to be your idol. Because

---

* My friend Jason Ekk, when I was talking with him about this chapter, suggested the Dorothy Day quote. It made this idea come alive in a fresh way for me.

he is God, we worship him, no doubt. Yet when we look at Jesus's humanity, he pushes us to see the implications for our own lives. At one point he went so far as to tell his disciples, "Whoever believes in me *will do the works that I do.*" Did you catch it? Jesus said you can do what he did. Not just the miracles but also the lifestyle of love. You can do it! And then he dropped a more shocking truth, which keeps us from making him an unattainable divine "other": "[Believers] will *do even greater works* than these because I am going to the Father" (John 14:12). Whether *greater* means more things or better things, the point is well taken: disciples can live like Jesus! Jesus is both worthy of worship and possible to imitate (even if imperfectly).

Saints can be dismissed. Idols are adored as the unattainable "other." For some reason, we've allowed Jesus's saintly—rather, divine—status to give us an out, and we give mere lip service to his human status. We've dismissed half of Jesus's significance!

WE CAN RELATE TO JESUS'S HUMAN LIFE

We miss half of Jesus's significance when we miss his humanity. I'm not talking only about cognitive beliefs about him (most people believe Jesus was a human). Instead, we *experientially* neglect his humanity. In a strange way, lots of us want to primarily associate Jesus with the God "up there" so that we can keep him at a safe distance from the muck and mess of our daily lives. He's in the sky somewhere when we need him for a crisis or when we're feeling connected to God because we're having a good day. (I want more of Jesus than this.)

Honestly, I've had seasons when going to church to worship Jesus on Sunday gave me just enough to get through the struggles of the upcoming week. Church can become a means of spiritual survival to remind us of a God out there who helps us. The rest of the week we sprint from work, to day care, to car pool duty, to soccer practice, and eventually to bed, only to start the marathon all over again the next day. Jesus the human being shows us that a more truly human life is possible. In short, Jesus gets it.

Paul the apostle recorded a powerful hymn about how God in Jesus emptied himself of his divine advantages. In his letter to early Jesus-followers living in the city of Philippi, he wrote,

Adopt the attitude that was in Christ Jesus:

Though he was in the form of God,
    he did not consider being equal with God something to
        exploit.
But he emptied himself
    by taking the form of a slave
    and by becoming like human beings.
When he found himself in the form of a human,
    he humbled himself by becoming obedient to the point of
        death,
    even death on a cross.
Therefore, God highly honored him
    and gave him a name above all names,
so that at the name of Jesus everyone
    in heaven, on earth, and under the earth might bow
    and every tongue confess
        that Jesus Christ is Lord, to the glory of God the Father.
                                                (Philippians 2:5–11)

In humbly giving himself to the task of becoming human like us, Jesus gave witness to the definitive revelation of God's self-offering, humble nature. What does this mean? If we take Paul's words seriously, everything we read in the New Testament about Jesus's earthly life and ministry should alert us to his humanity while simultaneously inviting us to discover God's true character. Even where a passage highlights Jesus's divinity, it also speaks volumes about his humanness.

Here we see that God didn't so much give up something by becoming human, but showed us the definitive character of God—especially in going so far as being executed on a cross! Jesus experiences a full humanity, which although out of step with what we might expect of God, is in perfect stride with the core truth of who God is: self-offering love. This is the love that image bearers are designed to reflect. In Jesus, we have both the reality of God and the perfect image of God, all in one person.[3] Jesus reveals that God is relatable to us. The writer of Hebrews spoke to this reality:

> Let's hold on to the confession since we have a great high priest who passed through the heavens, who is Jesus, God's Son; because we don't have a high priest who can't sympathize with our weaknesses but instead one who was tempted in every way that we are, except without sin.
>
> Finally, let's draw near to the throne of favor with confidence so that we can receive mercy and find grace when we need help. (4:14–16)

This changes everything about how we suffer. Did Jesus experience the same sort of human struggles that we face in a messy world like ours? Yes indeed. In fact, the challenges of life often propelled Jesus into a therapist's office. The difference being, of course, that therapy for Jesus was connecting deeply with his heavenly Father. Think about it. When Jesus was on his way to be betrayed and eventually crucified, he agonized and prayed while sweating drops like blood (Luke 22:44). The crisis of being human in the real world overwhelmed Jesus with anxiety. But rather than act out of step with his humanity, Jesus embraced the pain of humankind by taking on our suffering through the solidarity of crucifixion. He gave himself to the will of God, enduring the cross, which gave humanity the greatest example of love we've ever seen.

Become Human Like Jesus by Being with Jesus

In my own journey, anxiety is a real struggle. It has been for as long as I can remember. For a long time, I simply tried to ignore it—to distract myself until it went away. Maybe you've been there too. As I look at the human Jesus, sweating out his stress and asking God to take away his cup of suffering, I see my own life. But here's the key point. Where I want my anxiety to simply disappear— and let's keep it real, so did the Lord—Jesus owned the fact that it wouldn't be that simple. He chose to endure the anxiety (and suffering) and courageously held all that stress as he carried his cross to the deadly hillside. If that is what Jesus had to do with his anxiety, rather than stuff it inside or make it magically disappear, then maybe there's freedom in walking through it rather than around it. I'm finding that there exists a freedom *through* anxiety rather than a freedom *from* it. Jesus taught me that.

I remember one moment when I needed to leave the house but was feeling anxious. I stepped outside and prayerfully asked Jesus, *Can you take away my anxiety?* I sensed he responded with a kind and compassionate grin, playfully saying, *Nope. But I'll walk with you through it.* Allowing this sort of anxiety to affect me—although not always the remedy I want—has transformed my posture toward Jesus and loved ones while giving me courage to walk through it (at least on my good days).

Look, it would be easy to let a lot of this divinity versus humanity stuff stay in the abstract. Shoot, the early church had to host multiple ecumenical councils (gatherings of bishops and theologians) to settle what the Bible teaches: in Christ are two perfect natures. I'm not stepping into that argument. It was settled a long time ago. So then, what's the payoff, really, for you and me? At the end of the day, Jesus offers us example after example—through teaching and lifestyle—of what we humans should do when we encounter situations similar to those he did.

- Need to deal with an enemy—you know, that annoying person at work? (Matthew 5:43–48)
- Need to know how to courageously step into a situation where you or another person is unjustly treated? (Luke 7:36–50; John 8:2–11)*

---

* In both these situations, Jesus elevated the status of women. He stepped into the tension, told the truth, and de-escalated with firm love.

- Exhausted from the chaos of normal life and need permission to take a nap? (Mark 4:35–40)
- Ever been betrayed by a friend? (compare John 18:15–27 with 21:15–19)
- Want something that isn't yours to have? (Luke 4:1–13)
- Struggling to manage money? (Matthew 6:19–24; Luke 16:9; 18:18–27; 19:8–9; 21:1–4; Acts 20:35)
- Want to know how to enjoy a good party? (Matthew 22:1–14; Luke 7:36–50; John 2:1–11)
- Want a solid summary of wise human ethics that pretty much covers everything? (Matthew 5–7)

Taking note of Jesus's humanity is very practical for us.[4] We don't always want to follow his example or teachings. Some of them feel too dang hard. But he displays the kind of person we all are invited to become. Yeah. That's daunting. And no, none of us will get there in this life. That is why we need a resurrection too!

Jesus shows us how to be human while also giving us a front-row seat to the heart and character of God. We see a God who becomes like us—in all humility and without sin. Jesus took on our nature *so that we might take on his.* This mystery is at the center of the gospel. The Eastern Orthodox Church often refers to the process of becoming like Jesus as theosis: the process of growing in the divine nature as humans. One Bible scholar, Michael Gorman, reflecting on theosis, said, "To be fully human is to be Christlike and thus Godlike."[5] Becoming human like Jesus is to become human like God—thus we become *like* God by our participation in the life of God through Christ as human image bearers. Yes, there's a lot in that sentence!

Notice that the story of Jesus on earth doesn't begin with resurrection and ultimate heavenly enthronement. It begins with the raw reality of being human. Resurrection is what happens when God makes someone fully human forever. According to the New Testament, this is the hope of humankind. I'll say a bit more on resurrection in following chapters. For now, notice how resurrection is also a very human thing: it is the fullest experience of personhood, beyond what we could even imagine.

Think about this for a second. Jesus's body—that same body raised from the echoing, empty tomb—bore the scars of his suffering. He carried the marks of whips and nails with him. What does that say about the power of God to redeem, not erase, our deepest marks of pain and trauma in this world? God may not erase all the sources of pain in our lives, but wow . . . God does everything possible to repurpose our pain as a platform for our potential.

Maybe you are thinking, *Okay, Kurt. Sure. God redeems suffering. Jesus is with us as we suffer. And when we step into suffering like Jesus, we become more human like him. Great. But. Why? Why does that stuff happen in the first place? Wouldn't a good God fix it?*

Now you're putting me on the spot, aren't ya? In the next chapter, I'm going to give some informed guesses about the "why" questions. You might agree. Or not. Ultimately, the one thing that isn't up for debate is *what* happens. Suffering. Pain. Broken relationships. Loss. Death. Mosquito bites. Country music (too far, Kurt!). The cause of pain is worth exploring. We'll spend a whole chapter doing that. Being curious about how to posture ourselves with the resources of Jesus in the midst of suffering, now that's the point of this whole book.

I've been put to the test many times when it comes to my posture toward my problems. Before COVID-19 hit us in 2020, I was ready for the crapfest (sorry, that's the technical theological term) of 2019 to end. (Of course, there were some pretty awesome things sprinkled in there too.) So many times, I wanted to let go of the hope Jesus offers me in those challenging moments. At the beginning of the year, I was diagnosed with a prostate infection, thirty years too early. Near the end of the year, I contracted hand, foot and mouth disease, thirty years too late! Many other struggles sandwiched in between those two illnesses. Moments came up where "I'm only human" could have defined my reactions to those struggles. But again and again, I am confronted with the reality that if Jesus is human, I've got to embrace it for myself: all the pain and joy and everything in between.

So we've got a job to do if we're going to take Jesus seriously.

The world needs more people who take the human nature of Jesus as a foundation from which to echo hope. We've neglected the lived ramifications of this part of him for too long. I can imagine Jesus saying something like this to us: *Don't call me God until you also see the depths of my humanity. I don't want to be dismissed so easily.*

Jesus wants us to see him. *All* of him. This means we have to look closely at his humanity. The Incarnation—God taking on human flesh and experience—is what makes Christianity so compelling. God in a body. That body means God is human. Jesus is what it looks like to perfectly live as an image bearer. We could learn a thing or two by watching how he does it.

FORMATION EXERCISE

When God becomes human, Jesus is what it looks like. We are invited to become human like Jesus: human like God! This may seem daunting, but what if it's also liberating? Think about the disciples and how much they grew as a result of knowing Jesus. Becoming like Jesus doesn't happen by following a set of rules. It happens in the context of relationship with him and with a like-minded community of friends.

Reflect: When you think of Jesus, what character traits come to mind for you? How does Jesus inspire you? Can you list several examples?

Scripture: Read 2 Corinthians 3:12–18. Paul said that as we look to the Lord, we transform "from one degree of glory to the next degree of glory" (verse 18). Jesus removes the veil from our eyes so that we see him with greater clarity. We become like the One who is glorious so that we can become more human like him. (By the way, some traditions call this sanctification.) As you read the passage, pray that God will open you up to see Jesus in a fresh way.

Reflect some more and/or journal: What character traits (or virtues) from your list do you desire Jesus to grow within you?

Imagine: Close your eyes and imagine your life as you are energized by Jesus to lean into these new character traits. What changes in your heart? How does your posture and attitude transform as you confront daily challenges or deep hurts?

CHAPTER 4

WHY SUFFERING?

* * *

What is the purpose of lament? It allows us to connect with and grieve the reality of our sin and suffering. It draws us to repentant connection with God in that suffering. . . . Lament seeks God as comforter, healer, restorer, and redeemer. Somehow the act of lament reconnects us with God and leads us to hope and redemption.

—LATASHA MORRISON, *Be the Bridge*

Each day you make 35,000 decisions (according to some sources).¹ I just scratched my head. *Decision.* I decided to write about scratching my head. *Decision.* All the micro-choices that led to those decisions should be accounted for here too. We constantly make choices during our waking hours. While I'm neither a scientist nor a mathematician (no, I don't want to talk about my GRE scores in math—they compare to a fifth grader's), I find this daily number fascinating even though it is debatable.

Consider the number of people in the world. A round estimate gives us: 7.8 billion.² That is a lot of people making 35,000 choices per day! It gets interesting when we do the math. That adds up to 273 trillion choices that are made among humankind each and every day!³ Of course, other beings such as angels, spiritual powers, rulers, authorities, the satan,* and demons exercise free will as

---

* I plan to avoid *he* for the devil/satan. This is more of a title than a masculine name. *The* satan is *the* accuser who is a subpersonal being. Very real, but let's put the devil in its place!

well. We add this to the trillions of choices made by humans every day, and the world becomes a complex place.

This complexity of human choice, as we know from experience and observation, leads to beauty and death each day. The pain in our lives is a result of this web of free will, and we cannot escape its wrath. Naturally, we come up with explanations for why bad things happen. Ultimately, we know that any idea about the cause of evil comes up short.

What we do know is that choices—our own and those of other people—can lead to both wonderful and horrible outcomes. How are we to make sense of this? And how do we live with faith and hope in a world where life is just a few bad choices away from going tragically wrong?

Yeah, Jesus, but Why?

For some of us to experience the echoing hope of Easter, we need to explore why bad things happen in the first place. That's the reason I put this chapter in the book. With that said, you might not resonate with this issue. Or you might not agree with my particular perspective. That's okay too. These next few pages are for those who wrestle with why a good, loving, and powerful God allows suffering.

We aren't the first to ask questions about suffering. Surprised? I doubt it. However, a story from Luke is often overlooked that gives us some important reflections from Jesus about the hurts of his day. Jesus was told about how Pontius Pilate, a client ruler, had executed Galileans while they were sacrificing to God. I imagine those present had many questions about the nature of evil, which is likely why they wanted Jesus to comment on the situation. In Luke 13:2, Jesus responded, "Do you think the suffering of these Galileans proves that they were more sinful than all the other Galileans?" He asked a similar question about "eighteen people who were killed when the tower of Siloam fell on them" (verse 4). He answered both rhetorical questions with an emphatic "No . . . but unless you change your hearts and lives, you will die just as they did" (verses 3, 5; this sort of change is translated as "repent" in most Bibles). I can imagine asking Jesus for his answers to the questions raised by 9/11, COVID-19, or drone strike victims. We have the same curiosities two thousand years later! *Jesus, why?*

Notice what Jesus did for us. It's not the precise, scientific answer we might want. Instead, he said that evil happens and it isn't because the victims did good or bad things. Pilate was a jerk, consumed by power. He was no friend to the Jewish people.[4] He did something evil, and this wouldn't be the last time.

Later in Luke 13, Jesus healed a woman "bound by Satan for eighteen long years" (verse 16). Jesus shows us that human choices intersect with those of the spiritual powers of evil, creating the conditions for suffering—far beyond our ability to choose. There is a web of free will at work in the world, and those 273 trillion daily human choices, along with the choices of invisible beings such as angels and demons, leave humankind victim to evil every single day.

Jesus has a remedy. It won't rid the world of pain. But his remedy will allow his followers to position themselves to be able to respond to suffering like he would. *Repent.* Go a different direction. This is an important word for Jesus. What we will discover is that in many of his warnings, Jesus had in mind a day when the Romans would destroy Jerusalem (we'll talk more about that, but it happened in 70 CE within the generation of his disciples). A collapsing tower was a mere shadow of the devastation to come when the temple itself would fall. Jesus wanted them to make the right choice now. Choose justice and peace. Choose a path that leads to wholeness rather than destruction.[5]

But really, we don't get as clear an answer as we want from the Bible. Sure, there are helpful clues. Ultimately, "why" gets sidelined for "what" and "how"—*what* is true in the world and *how* we are to respond. *What* is true is that suffering is inevitable. *How* we are invited to respond to suffering isn't primarily by seeking theological answers but rather the biblical practice of lament. This is the practice of calling upon God, as we see in Psalm 35:17, where David wrote, "How long, O LORD, will you look on?" (NRSV). The

Scriptures teach us that when we suffer, we should push harder into God by naming evil and suffering and calling upon God's justice, mercy, and kindness.

Now let's take some time to examine *why* we suffer. (By the way, I don't expect to get this all the way right. But I'll give it a shot.) Then I'll follow this up by inviting us to find God in our suffering, especially through the biblical practice of lament. My goal is to offer ideas that will produce fruitful contemplation and dialogue with others. In the next few pages, I want to offer some introductory-level reflections on three common Christian assumptions about suffering. It might feel a bit dense at times (seriously, this is a *huge* issue I'm tackling in this chapter), but if you hang in there with me, hopefully you'll discover a nugget or two that will help you discover God in the midst of your pain.

(If "why" questions aren't something you're curious about, you have my blessing to skip ahead to the section titled "Suffering Can Make Us Human Like Jesus" on page 47.)

ASSUMPTION #1:
GOD CONTROLS EVERYTHING THAT HAPPENS

To say that God is in control is to speak something that begs several questions. What is the nature of this sort of divine control? Does God control even evil things that happen? What about Auschwitz or atomic bombs (to name some extreme examples)?

From the onset, I want to be blunt: God *could* be in control if God wanted to be, *but apparently God didn't set up the world that way.* As soon as you challenge the idea that God is in meticulous control of everything, many Christians are tempted to jump to the conclusion that the idea of God's sovereign power is being attacked. But, as I'll suggest, this isn't the case. This reaction happens because the idea of God's control is ingrained in some of us from a young age.

No matter where you fall on this theological debate, just for the sake of argument, let's suspend the idea that God is orchestrating everything that happens. What might this mean? First off, we'd be able to account for the 273 trillion human choices (plus nonhuman) each day. These choices, then, become *actual choices*—not preprogramed into God's software system for running the world. If free will is real—conditioned as it is by circumstances and cultural realties that shape us without our even knowing it—then these decisions are not controlled by God. For those who are open to it, God's Spirit certainly is at work to influence us, but almost never to coerce us to choose a particular path.[6]

The other part of this has to do with God's knowledge of our future choices. But look, before I go any further, I want to again say that I'm fully aware that you might not share my opinion. If a lot of this is new to you or if you flat-out disagree, there's still plenty of room for you in this book. Besides, it's always good to know how other Christians think so you can both challenge and firm up the perspective that you find most helpful. In my own work to make sense of how God relates to our pain, I've had to consider all viewpoints, and I think this one best guards God's character and glory while being consistent with our real experience of life. So, let's get back to looking at God's knowledge of the choices we will make in the future.

If our choices are truly free, then the future has some flexibility built into it. A choice that hasn't been made yet consists of things that may or may not happen. Even an all-knowing God would have perfect information only about things that exist. The outcomes of certain choices do not yet exist because they are contingent on human choice. God is infinitely wise and able to see all possible paths forward in our web of choices (trillions!). In many cases free will means that although nothing surprises God, certain information about the future exists only as possibilities rather than certainties. God knows every single possibility. This isn't about God having less knowledge but way more!

God knows every single thing that could happen and how it would play out. This is an *infinite* number of possibilities, all known perfectly by God. My view at the moment is that God experiences human free will as *possibilities* usually, *probabilities* sometimes, and *certainties* rarely. While the future is not completely open ended, it is partially so.[7] Otherwise, how would our prayers effect change? If prayer changes things, then it seems things must be capable of actual change.* At least that is how many of us pray in the midst of our pain. Right?

ASSUMPTION #2:
SUFFERING IS PART OF GOD'S WILL

Some Christians believe that suffering is part of God's will and plan for the world. I've heard this explained by the idea that God's ultimate goal is to have God's glory revealed. Sometimes, in this mode of thought, suffering points to God's glory (even if mysteriously), so God causes it for that aim. Others disagree that suffering is part of God's *actual* will but believe that in a world of free choices, it is inevitable. For these Christians, God may know all aspects of the future but typically doesn't violate free will to stop suffering from taking place. Free will is God's will for the world, even if the suffering that results breaks God's heart. These two contrasting views are usually held by proponents of Calvinism and Arminianism. Likely, you've heard one or both of these perspectives and may even hold to one of them yourself. We are all trying to figure this out.

If we table (even if temporarily) our assumption that suffering is part of God's will, we then return to the 273 trillion human choices with multiple options. These choices are neither predestined by God to reveal glory and a greater good (Calvinism) nor the regrettable outcome of God's limited control (Arminianism). Rather, these choices are *real choices* made by agents other than God. In fact, when we look at Jesus through a divine lens, we see that Jesus is the God who weeps over evils like the premature death of his friend Lazarus (John 11:1–37) and the impending destruction of Jerusalem (Luke 19:41–44). God grieves, authentically

---

* A helpful example is how Moses pleaded with the Lord and thus changed God's mind in Exodus 32:11–14. God also regretted that things didn't work out as hoped (Genesis 6:6; 1 Samuel 15:35), asked non-rhetorical questions about future events (Hosea 8:5; Numbers 14:11), made statements about what may or may not take place (Jeremiah 38:17–18; Ezekiel 12:3), and expressed surprise at outcomes not anticipated (Jeremiah 3:6–7, 19–20).

feels the pain of the world, and is actively working to bring about good wherever possible.

So, God isn't the source of evil in the world except insofar as God created a world that was truly free to choose love or to choose evil. The Christian hope is that when God determines the time is right, Jesus will return to earth—bringing heaven with him!—to judge, heal, purge, resurrect, and renew all things. Romans 8 says that creation is currently in a state of groaning (like the groans of the slaves in Egypt under Pharaoh) but "that the creation itself will be set free from slavery to decay and brought into the glorious freedom of God's children" (verse 21). However, until that day, God's influence is the primary means that God has to deal with evil. God deeply experiences pain and is in solidarity with us image bearers through it all. God's empathy is better than God's control.

No, God didn't cause the suffering in the Auschwitz Nazi concentration camp or a tower to fall at Siloam. Nor does God cause humans to detonate atomic weapons. Evil grieves God, but God is committed to a world that is truly free. So, when something happens to a loved one, I never will say that all things happen as part of God's will. I won't claim that God is in control (if by this I'm implying that God caused suffering as part of a greater good). God knows that many bad things will likely or possibly happen. Bonnie Kristian summarized this perspective by saying, "God never makes evil things happen, and in this perspective, he is actively working, in real time, to prevent evil as much as possible without overriding our free will. . . . When evil does occur, God does not want it."[8]

ASSUMPTION #3:
GOD CAN ALWAYS INTERVENE

Keeping all that I said in the previous two sections in mind, what if we reverse this assumption? What if God *can't* always intervene? *Can't* needs to be qualified by saying that God, in theory, *can* do anything. However, if God made a free world with real choices and actual possibilities, then there are times when God *cannot* get in the way of evil.

We see this clearly in the life of Jesus. If Jesus wanted to, he could have leaned into his divinity and never failed at a miracle. However, when he visited his hometown of Nazareth, Jesus "was unable to do any miracles there, except that he placed his hands on a few sick people and healed them" (Mark 6:5). His intervention was limited by the postures of the people in that town. Realizing that I can't have my cake and eat it too, I know it isn't completely fair to use this example since I've emphasized that Jesus did miracles mostly as a result of his full humanity empowered by the Holy Spirit, not primarily as a result of his divinity. But it paints the picture well, consistent with the dynamic relationship God has to humans.

C. S. Lewis, in *The Problem of Pain,* made a point about the nature of God's intervention in the world:

> Christianity asserts that God is good; that He made all things good and for the sake of their goodness; that one of the good things He made, namely, the free will of rational creatures, by its very nature included the possibility of evil; and that creatures, availing themselves of this possibility, have become evil. . . . It would, no doubt, have been possible for God to remove by miracle the results of the first sin ever committed by a human being; but this would not have been much good unless He was prepared to remove the results of the second sin, and of the third, and so on forever. . . . [This] would have been a world in which nothing important ever depended on human choice, and in which choice itself would soon cease.[9]

What Lewis makes clear is that human freedom, not God, is the source of evil in the world. The problem with the question of suffering is that often a detached yet controlling God is ascribed as its source. Biblically speaking, God is not directly the source of evil but rather created the potential for evil in giving humanity free will. If God created humanity in any other fashion, we would be the equivalent of robotic androids preprogrammed for obedience to God. This would indeed have been a world in which choice and freedom are nonexistent.

To take this issue to the practical level, we can examine one of the greatest evils in modern history, the Holocaust. Did God know with absolute certainty that Adolf Hitler would murder millions of people? If we answer yes, we direct the blame on God: free will did not cause this atrocity; rather, God's predetermined will did. If such a theology leads to the belief that there is a reason for everything, then it follows that God had a divine purpose in the execution of millions of innocent people. Try having this discussion with a non-Christian; God inevitably comes out the bad guy.

If we believe that God knew only of the possibility that Adolf Hitler would choose an evil path, then God is not directly to blame. God's resources are infinite, but God chooses not to coerce human free will. As a result, this leads to the natural consequences of rebellion. And this isn't just about one person named Hitler. There were hundreds of thousands of soldiers who enlisted and took part in a system of oppression. What about the massive popularity of Hitler among the general population? What about the anti-Semitism that already existed when Hitler was voted into power? He was the angry ball of energy that gave people the space to carry out evil. Their web of choices is as much to blame as Hitler himself. This is a systemic and a personal issue. God is committed to a free humanity, and sometimes the natural outcome of those choices is great devastation. God certainly heard the cry of the victims and felt the pain of those who were burned in the furnaces of Auschwitz.[10]

In my own journey as I've asked "why" questions, the conviction that God didn't cause my suffering is powerful. The purpose of my hard childhood wasn't to teach me things. It wasn't to punish me. It wasn't for some greater good. The abuse I experienced caused God sorrow. No wonder the psalmist wrote that "the LORD is close to the brokenhearted" (Psalm 34:18). God isn't distant, orchestrating pain to create some sort of good. At least that's not my perspective any longer. God is in the mess—with me, with you—when everything hurts, redeeming as much as possible from the evil we experience and redirecting it to bring about something good: our transformation.

Suffering Can Make Us Human Like Jesus

Here's what we can actually know: We know that pain is real and doesn't magically go away. You can't usually pray pain away (sometimes prayer can lead to healing, but not always), and God isn't a magic genie waiting for us to rub our Bible like a lamp so our wishes may be fulfilled. We know that our choices stem from a web of free will that can contribute to systems that oppress some and elevate others. We know that God is love. We know that somehow all these truths intersect but that mostly the problem of evil is a mystery we will never be able to fully solve.

God may not cause pain, but pain is no less real. God meets us in time and space, in *our* space of anguish. Whenever we hurt, God hurts with us. God borrows the context of that hurt, without causing it, to redeem something from it, if at all possible. Jesus knows best that pain, which was meant for evil, can be redeemed for our ongoing healing as we become more human like him.

My spiritual director shared some helpful reflections on suffering that resonate.[11] There are three postures that we often have when facing pain. First, we may say,

Jesus, you fix it.

We direct everything toward God. Then, we may say,

Jesus, join me in my suffering.

Finally, we might learn to join Jesus in his suffering, which connects us to the pain of others. We may say,

Jesus, I want to experience your pain, which includes mine and the suffering of others.

At this stage, we've moved from a focus on personal problems to joining Jesus in his own pain as he holds the pain of the world. Jesus steps into the mess and invites us to find counterintuitive hope and healing as we meet him there.

I find comfort in knowing that God doesn't want us to suffer. God is guiding us to the ultimate destiny of all things—new creation—but the path to getting there is not easy. We won't make sense out of all the things that go wrong in our lives, but we can give ourselves to the possibility that what was meant for evil can bring about something good. This never dismisses or minimizes the losses we face but considers that even when God doesn't step in to fix something, God's influence is always working for our good.

TO LAMENT IS HUMAN

Now, we could stop on that comforting point, or we can do something with it. The echoing hope of Jesus isn't just a lofty idea; it is experiential—an embodied experience in the face of pain. This brings me back to the practice of lament. Jesus lamented—even wept. In times of suffering, the people of God developed a tradition that gave them space to name suffering (sometimes caused by their own sin and other times caused by evil done to them). Psalms, for example, sway to and fro from praise to lamentation. David could, in one breath, say "How long, O LORD?" (35:17, NRSV) and "O Lord, do not be far from me!" (verse 22, NRSV) and in the next breath say, "Great is the LORD, who delights in the welfare of his servant" (verse 27, NRSV).

Lament is an act where we name reality, what is actually happening—all the crap flinging in ten different painful directions—and we also name our longing for God to step in. Reflecting on the Psalms, Walter Brueggemann wrote, "While we all yearn for [equilibrium], it is not very interesting and it does not produce great prayer or powerful song."[12]

Soong-Chan Rah said that "laments are prayers of petition arising out of need. But lament is not simply the presentation of a list of complaints, nor merely the expression of sadness over difficult circumstances. Lament . . . is a liturgical response to the reality of suffering and engages God in the context of pain and trouble."[13] It's a lost art for many Christians I know. Lots of us prefer the feel-good praise, the happy clappy, the slightly sappy, and the not so crappy. That might be overstating it, but sermons on lament are rare in many churches, and prayers of lament are needed now more than ever.

With people facing illness, violence, loss, and injustice, we need an outlet that allows us to offer our pain to God. That's the brilliance of biblical lament in the first place. In the practice of lament, we name something God has named since shalom was first disrupted: things aren't the way they ought to be. In fact, things aren't the way God wants them to be. But when the web of free will brings suffering, God invites us to bring it all to the cross of Jesus, where he himself once cried out in forsaken lament (Matthew 27:46; Psalm 22).

> *We need an outlet that allows us to offer our pain to God.*
> *That's the brilliance of biblical lament.*

Another example of lament comes as a response to the Babylonian Exile. In 587 BCE, Nebuchadnezzar captured King Zedekiah (2 Kings 25:1–7). He had his general take into exile most of the population, excluding the poorest citizens, some of whom were left behind to fend for themselves. The first temple, the one built by King Solomon, was flattened to the ground.[14] Psalm 137 depicts the laments of their new reality:

Alongside Babylon's streams,
　　there we sat down,
　　crying because we remembered Zion.
We hung our lyres up
　　in the trees there
　　because that's where our captors asked us to sing;
　　our tormentors requested songs of joy:

"Sing us a song about Zion!" they said.
But how could we possibly sing
    the LORD's song on foreign soil? (verses 1–4)

Israel legitimately desired to be back home, restored with the fullness of human dignity. So they lamented. So should we. Even if we think we've figured out why suffering is possible in our world, that doesn't take it away. Yet the gracious God who Jesus perfectly reveals says, "Come to me, all you who are struggling hard and carrying heavy loads, and I will give you rest" (Matthew 11:28). Jesus invites us, mess and all, to come to him and seek rest in him. Rest comes when we acknowledge that our loads are indeed heavy and painful. We lament on behalf of others. We lament ourselves. Rest comes when we name what is real and then bring laments before God.

FORMATION EXERCISE

Lament is the language of those in pain, who don't box it up but bring the truth of their hurts before God. We won't ever have fully satisfying answers about why we suffer, but we do have an invitation in the Scriptures to do something with our pain. Lament is essential in the journey toward the redemption of pain.

Scripture: Read Psalm 13 (it's only six verses—short for a psalm if you compare it to 119!). After reading through it slowly a couple of times, see if you can identify these parts of it:

- Acknowledge—God is here even when it seems otherwise
- Complain—Lament the painful circumstances
- Ask—Petition God to bring wholeness
- Praise—Offer trust in God and in God's solidarity with you

Journal: Grab a pen and write down your own lament psalm, using these four bullet points as headings. It doesn't have to be poetic, just honest. Focus on either a personal or a systemic lament. (Or do both!)

Reflect: Are you walking through a personal hurt? Is there a systemic injustice that you want to lament? Write it down.

Do you desire to trust God more but need to know that Jesus is still at work to transform you? Petition God. Tell Jesus what you want.

Then listen for a still, small voice that may speak back to you. Even if you hear nothing, how might you declare your trust in God anyway?

Part Two

FINDING JESUS IN THE ECHOES

While the pain in our lives shapes us, it doesn't have to define us. As difficult as they are, pain and suffering help us grow into our God-given belovedness, our deepest image bearer vocation. If we can come to a place where we realize how loved we are, how like Jesus we are, we will be able to step into the challenges of life with courage, vulnerability, and abundance. We will be able to step into pain in a totally revolutionary way.

Jesus shows us what it's like to step into hurt with a core identity saturated with the love of God. We are loved. But now our challenge becomes clearer—how do we live in the fully human holiness of our identity in Christ? Fortunately, Jesus's life and teachings show the way.

CHAPTER 5

VULNERABLE COURAGE

* * *

The idea that God, if there is a force of Love and Logic in the universe, that it would seek to explain itself is amazing enough. That it would seek to explain itself and describe itself by becoming a child born in straw poverty. . . . Unknowable love, unknowable power, describes itself as the most vulnerable.

—BONO, *Bono: In Conversation with Michka Assayas*

Seminary was finally coming to a close. Five years of hard work and sacrifice led me to this moment: I would defend my final project and paper. A frequent procrastinator, I turned the paper in to my professors and readers with moments to spare. The previous night, the oral presentation and defense preparation had come together. I felt like I was in the zone—not only with my academic career but with life.

A family of churches was preparing to send us to Seattle to start a church. Lauren and I were ready to start a family. The Sunday prior to my oral presentation, we announced to the small church family we were part of that we were expecting a baby. Truly, life was disorienting but leaning toward several positive next steps. I felt joyfully energized.

On what would have been an exciting and emotional day all on its own, something unexpected happened. We woke up that morning and began getting ready. Suddenly, Lauren called to me, "Kurt—I'm spotting." Everything stopped. Those three words disrupted everything.

The rest of the day was a blur—call the doctor, go, have Lauren give a blood sample, drive to the university to deliver my presentation, give said presentation with my mind reeling, everything that had happened in the previous few hours running in the background of my mind, *somehow* manage to do a decent job defending my argument, pass, walk outside to a picnic table, and sit, stunned, as Lauren received a call from the doctor: "We are so sorry . . ."

She was having a miscarriage. Shock is an understatement of what we felt. We didn't believe that God was making this happen, at least not rationally, but emotions betray beliefs when life's deep hurts crash in.

It never really registered for us that between 10 and 20 percent of confirmed pregnancies end in miscarriage.[1] We were a statistic, yet we were not alone. We learned of several friends who had suffered this grief in silence. In the moment, we felt betrayed— *betrayed*—by God and didn't know why we should hold on to hope.

So, in the aftermath of the loss, I held Lauren. A lot.

She held me.

Jesus held us both.

It sucked.

As spontaneous as miscarriage itself, waves of grief rushed over us in unexpected moments. Yet God's compassion was gracious. Jesus's love undeniable. His offer of hope increasing. Vulnerability growing within us. Even with an empty womb, we were sustained by the empty tomb's echoing hope.

Beautiful Vulnerability

As I think about that memory of loss, I'm astounded that God would become a baby. It's incredible that the God of the universe entered our reality through the same pain-filled and vulnerable path that all the rest of us do: childbirth. Each of us is born into a complex system of choices and circumstances. Pain starts at birth, before we have any power to take care of ourselves.

Mary's strength and resolve coupled with Joseph's steadfast support led to the safe delivery and rearing of our Savior. Jesus entered our world vulnerably, via a process that doesn't always end positively after nine months, and matured into the great teacher from Nazareth. God became human in every single way possible: without sin. That's because sin isn't a natural characteristic of being human but a distortion that dehumanizes us. God invites us to become vulnerable, like Jesus, to allow the Holy Spirit to open gracious space within us which can increase our capacity to echo hope to others.

The word *vulnerability* can be used in multiple ways. I'm going to borrow Brené Brown's helpful definition:

> Vulnerability is the birthplace of love, belonging, joy, courage, empathy, and creativity. It is the source of hope, empathy, accountability, and authenticity. If we want greater clarity in our purpose or deeper and more meaningful spiritual lives, vulnerability is the path.[2]

Sometimes I find it helpful to swap out the word *vulnerable* for *insecure* (or *susceptible*) when it's used to describe people in difficult situations.* We may be food insecure, financially insecure, emotionally insecure, socially insecure, and so forth, but in these circumstances we can discover a creative love that resists focusing on our lack. Pain can show us what we lack—physically, emotionally, spiritually, and so on—but vulnerability exposes us to Jesus's "power [that] is made perfect in weakness" (as Paul said of his own experience of pain in 2 Corinthians 12:9).

And even though so many of us act as if we're invincible, it's when we embrace the radical vulnerability of simply being human that we find ourselves empowered to become more like Jesus. He can't teach us to be strong until we know how weak we really are.

---

*I don't always swap these out. I'm bringing this up for the sake of clarity in this particular chapter.

A Subversive Birthday

Weakness isn't something we naturally attribute to strength. That goes against the grain of common experience, which is perhaps one of the reasons the message of Jesus is so compelling. Christmas is the birth announcement of a humble King, who beckons us to reorient our lives toward sacrificially loving humanity well. Jesus offers us a life to be lived for the flourishing of others.[3]

Jesus offers us a life to be lived for the flourishing of others.

We see Christmas as a holiday and easily ignore its deeper levels of meaning. The Christmas story might be one of the most revolutionary pieces of writing from the ancient world. Perhaps *ever.* Charlie Brown[*] doesn't *quite* give us the prophetic edge to the story, but Luke certainly does, when we listen for it. Luke wrote,

> In those days Caesar Augustus declared that everyone throughout the empire should be enrolled in the tax lists. (2:1)

This one verse gives us access to a whole world of insight that Luke's gospel is inviting us, as readers, to enter. Not only does the mention of Caesar Augustus serve as an important time stamp for the birth of Jesus, but this earthly emperor frames the entire story. Into the world's system of power and pain and struggle, a baby is about to be born. A baby who will change everything. What is the message hidden in Christ's manger? *Power is not what you think it is.*

What is the message hidden in Christ's manger? Power is not what you think it is.

---

[*] Linus's monologue in *A Charlie Brown Christmas* is basically on point, though.

WHO WAS CAESAR AUGUSTUS?

Caesar embodied the dominant idea of power. In the early years, Caesar Augustus was known as Octavian, the great-nephew of Julius Caesar (who would adopt the boy as his son and heir). After the assassination of Julius, Rome was left in civil war. Octavian won this war in 31 BCE and eventually became the sole ruler (authorized by the Senate) of the Roman Empire. By ending war through victory, he was hailed as a peacemaker. Coins and inscriptions declared him to be the "son of god" (especially since he was now considered the son of Julius, who had been deified as a god upon his death). By 27 BCE, the Senate would bestow on him a new name, Augustus, which loosely means "venerable one" or "one worthy of worship."

His military might brought a state of general prosperity to Roman citizens and a subjugation of conquered nations that became part of the Roman Empire. Themes of freedom, justice, peace, and salvation permeated Augustus's reign, which when proclaimed in a public setting were part of his "good news" or "gospel" (yes, the same word Jesus used).*

But the gospel of Caesar Augustus was good news only for the elite. It was sort of okay news for those willing to fall in line with the power structures that trickled down from Rome. It was quite bad news for anyone else—resisters or the poor. It certainly wasn't good news for non-Romans in the empire, specifically the Jewish people who longed for liberation.

JESUS WASN'T BORN IN ROME

We are going to continue diving into the deep end for a few more pages. Hang with me. According to Luke's birth narrative, Caesar Augustus issued a decree that the entire Roman world would be counted. This was so that the emperor would be able to tax the people with greater accuracy to fund the military and building projects and to enhance overall imperial control. Those in Judea

---

* I'll show you an example of this in a bit.

and surrounding areas found themselves either as part of the aristocracy (the minority, of course) or in poverty. If you weren't a Roman citizen, you were a target for exploitation. So it comes as no surprise that a random baby born in a marginal town like Bethlehem wasn't on Rome's radar.

Think about this. God's kingdom* didn't enter at the centers of power and wealth (Rome) but at the margins of insecurity (Bethlehem). Jesus had no interest in the sort of power celebrated by the Romans. Instead, he humbly became human among the marginalized and embraced vulnerability, not just in how he was born but throughout his life, teachings, death, and resurrection. Jesus is for all of us, but his birth story and overall life show us that Jesus started with insecure communities to model the power of vulnerability.

Jesus's embodied vulnerability, like the luminous star that guided sages to the young Jesus (Matthew 2:1–12), shined a light on the unjust suffering the Jewish people faced. In a place where the rest of the empire saw obscurity, the wise men found the light. In the midst of our own struggles, finding the light of hope may seem impossible. This is why I'm thankful Jesus wasn't born in Rome—he relates to pain in a much more profound way. It helps his light shine into our darkness.

Sunlight doesn't come easy in Seattle. Yet anytime the rays make their way through the clouds and into our home, my dog Mylee will be there. It could be the smallest sliver of winter light; she *always* finds it.

---

* It's important to name something here: the kingdom metaphor in the New Testament can trip modern people up. For one, no kingdom in history has ever avoided patriarchy. What kind of good news is it if it is another version of that? Secondly, Jesus connected the metaphor of kingdom to a party. If you find it hard to connect with the image of a kingdom, perhaps do a reframe in your mind to replace *king* with *host* and *kingdom* with *party*. Lastly, I know some people have tended to move to the use of *kin-dom* to remove fully the patriarchal connection and emphasize the togetherness of the Jesus community. I respect this approach a lot, yet I choose to stick with language Jesus himself chose to use, even if it has to be unpacked—especially since there are important historical connotations to this term within the biblical tradition.

I can't think of a better image for what Christmas is. It is the light breaking through. When I think of the hurts we face, it is as though Jesus always desires to help us find his light. Looming clouds conceal the light, but the sun's powerful beams eventually break through the troposphere, bringing warmth to all they touch. The sun, like Jesus, is the more powerful force, even when depressing cloud cover is all we see. There is something delightfully subversive in finding the light on a dark day. And this is the hope that the weakness and seeming foolishness of God-as-a-baby can bring into a world system of hard power and into our own stories of pain.

> *When I think of the hurts we face, it is as though Jesus always desires to help us find his light.*

CAESAR VERSUS JESUS

Jesus's birth story eventually leads to the pasture where shepherds watched their flocks. While doing a job beyond the pale of honor for Romans, they found themselves surrounded by angels. This sort of angelic glory was a spectacle Augustus's money and power could never buy.

Augustus wanted everyone to know just what a big deal he was (or thought he was). Coins made his divine status clear. Slogans assured the world that only "Caesar is Lord." He was the "son of god," worthy of worship as part of the gods of the imperial machine. When Caesar came to town, you bowed in adoration. He even had writers come up with hymns and declarations of his greatness.

There's an ancient inscription from 9 BCE that gives us clues to how Caesar Augustus was understood. He was "divine" and considered "equal to the Beginning of all things."[4] This should remind us of Mark's gospel, which opens, "The beginning of the good news about Jesus Christ, God's Son . . ." (1:1). The world was in chaos—all hope was lost—and then ~~Caesar~~ Jesus appeared.* The inscription goes on to say, "All the cities unanimously adopt the birthday of the divine Caesar as the new beginning of the year." This was Augustus's birthday announcement! He is called "Savior" and the one who "put an end to war." His Roman-style peace "has fulfilled all the hopes of earlier times" and thus "the birthday of the god [Augustus] has been for the whole world the beginning of good news."[5]

We won't believe the hype, though, am I right? Augustus was glad to be "divine" because it legitimized his terrible treatment of people. His propaganda was a cover-up for the pain he perpetuated. He wanted taxes, so he reminded the world of how great things had become since he was in charge. Augustus offered poetic gimmicks to mold the minds of subjects, kind of like trying to use Photoshop to make a bad image pretty. No matter how much you try, the picture will be covered up so much that it becomes something entirely different.

Was it good news that Caesar was running the world? Only for those with money, power, and citizenship. But those who saw through the flashy rhetoric knew the truth: his propaganda was designed to conceal the pain of the masses and to mold an empire into a machine producing goods and services that ultimately benefited the few. Covering up pain doesn't heal it. It conceals it until it builds up enough steam to explode. (This explosion came into clear view when Rome flattened Jerusalem in 70 CE.)

Although the sources of our pain differ from those living under the Roman regime, we still deal with pain. Augustus used propaganda to make suffering seem more palatable. In today's world, other forms of propaganda seek to convince us that a particular product, activity, allegiance, or relationship is all we need to find happiness. We feel weak, so we need this product, this opportunity, this set of skills, or this political party. Then we will be able to get past our struggles. Quick fixes to patch up our pain won't work.

---

* The strikethrough is a playful way to say that Caesar Augustus claimed something that has only ever been true of Jesus. Also, I blogged for years before writing a book. Clearly old habits die hard.

Or maybe you've had someone try to minimize your struggles at some point. Here's a classic line: "It's no big deal. Look at the bright side." While a good reframe from time to time is good for the soul, hiding behind the framing can set us up to ignore legitimate challenges. Propaganda, whether we try to sell ourselves on the idea that things are great or we try to do this for others, gives us the counterfeit to the real thing we are longing for—every single time. Augustus wanted everyone to buy what he was selling. The Jesus story entered stage right and upstaged that gimmicky plotline altogether.

VULNERABLE SUBVERSIVE POWER

Hopefully you see the parallels to the Jesus story emerging here. Jesus, the antigimmick from the margins of Rome's vast empire, was the prophesied, long-awaited one too. This begs the question, Who gets to truly be both Savior and the Son of God? Who really brings peace to the earth? Whose birthday truly transformed the cosmos? Should we celebrate September 23 (Caesar's) or December 25?* Luke 2 tells us the Christian response to empires that exploit the vulnerable:

> But the angel said to them, "Do not be afraid; for see—I am bringing you *good news* of great joy for all the people: to you is born this day in the city of David a *Savior,* who is the Messiah, the *Lord*. . . ." And suddenly there was with the angel a multitude of the heavenly host, praising God and saying,
>
> "Glory to God in the highest heaven,
>   and *on earth peace* . . . !" (verses 10–11, 13–14, NRSV)

In a world where Caesar was the undisputed lord of all, where his good news—a royal gospel announcement—proclaimed him to be the great savior, and where his violence brought about an

---

* And yes, I'm making a point here. I am fully aware that we have no evidence historically for when Jesus's birthday actually took place.

intimidating peace, angels announced to poor shepherds that Augustus was a counterfeit! A vulnerable baby, born in vulnerable conditions, to be reared by vulnerable parents, is the most powerful Lord and Savior the world has ever known. This baby is the Prince of Peace (Isaiah 9:6). This helpless child, the embodiment of Israel's God, will sit on the throne of the universe.

Augustus was anything but vulnerable, but hey, angels never sang his praises on a mountainside either. The God of all power, the Creator of the universe, became human to show us how to live and love without being slaves to shame and guilt. Jesus embraced vulnerability's subversive power. We are invited, no matter our position in life, to do the same.

As we look to the life of Jesus, and here his birth, the vulnerable path God used to show us how to be fully human makes perfect sense. Had Jesus been born in Rome, he would have played into the power grabs that dehumanize so many. A Bethlehem birth shows us that the world's true King turns the idea of rulership upside down. This King is a servant of all. This King knows weakness, helplessness, and oppression. Jesus, from the beginning of the story, entered our reality of pain. Rather than let vulnerability ultimately crush his identity, it was a foundational space from which he modeled unconditional love, contagious joy, admirable courage, profound empathy, and creative power.

What impresses me about Jesus is *he never forgot his roots.* For his entire ministry career, he focused on people who, like him, were susceptible to the abuses of society. One of the best lines in the whole Bible is "This man welcomes sinners and eats with them" (Luke 15:2). How dare Jesus be so inclusive! He didn't merely reach out to social outcasts, but as we will see, he taught a courageous vulnerability as both an inward disposition of the heart and an outward expression of love. He went so far as to call his disciples to love enemies and pray for persecutors (Matthew 5:43–48). You can't love people who hate you and not be full of courage and vulnerability.

This was put on full display when Jesus stood before the Roman prefect Pontius Pilate. It's like Jesus couldn't stop being the contrast to the Roman way of running a kingdom! Instead of cowering down, even though he stood before a ruler with the power to have him crucified, Jesus engaged Pilate directly with words of truth, that he was, in fact, a king. He told him, "My kingdom doesn't originate from this world" (John 18:36), meaning that his kingdom's capital city is in the heavenly realm, which he previously prayed would come "on earth" (the Lord's Prayer). He added that if it did originate in this world, "My followers would be fighting to keep me from being handed over" (verse 36, NRSV).

What Jesus was saying was, *If my kingdom movement were part of this system—the Roman Empire system or any other system that has ever been created—then my followers would pick up swords and fight back. I would not be here in chains. I'd be fighting. But that's not the kind of thing we do. My kingdom is an upside-down kingdom, where love, generosity, equity, and peace are values—not violence and oppression for the benefit of the few.* Jesus lived out courageous vulnerability, even though it took him to a Roman cross.

Courageous Vulnerability

I have a friend named Ben Higgins, who in an interesting turn of events, became a well-known reality TV star.* He's a follower of Jesus and continues to discern ways to use his platform to reflect the love of Jesus. I admire the courage it takes to navigate all the complicated forces involved in a public life like his.

As I was in the thick of writing this book, I asked him for some advice. This is the first book I've ever written, and for some reason, I sensed that God was inviting me to be raw and open, especially with several painful stories from my journey. At times, the idea of putting this out there for public scrutiny terrifies me. I asked him, "Do you have any advice for how to handle being vul-

---

* For those of you who enjoy a glass of something special while Chris Harrison guides people into love, my friend was the star of *The Bachelor* (season 20 in 2016). He's the real deal.

nerable in front of so many people? How do you do it? I have lots of personal stuff in this book, and to be honest, it kind of scares me to put it out there."

Ben responded with how his vulnerability used to feel like a weakness. Articles criticizing him, even minor things, would hurt and overwhelm him once in a while. But one night he had an encounter with God where it became clear that his platform was about someone bigger than himself. He came to recognize that vulnerability is a source of power and strength. He realized not only that his platform is a gift to be stewarded wisely with Jesus but also that in being vulnerable he can influence others. Vulnerability is a source that empowers my friend to empower others. As Brené Brown said, "Courage starts with showing up and letting ourselves be seen."[6]

Maybe that is partially why Jesus came in such an unexpected fashion. He wanted to show us that vulnerability is a different kind of power than ancient and modern-day caesars have to offer. With all the shame many of us hold, Jesus teaches that we can be truly free from the power brokers, influencers, systems, and stories we narrate to ourselves that tell us we aren't good enough. That sort of vulnerability—the type Lauren and I began to discover in the pains of miscarriage—midwifes hope, creativity, and a new way to step into love.

Do you feel insecure in some way? This can be emotional, but perhaps other forms of insecurity are real for you. Financial troubles, social struggles, and inequities are only a few things that perpetuate pain in our lives. Like Jesus *showed up and let himself be seen,* not from a place of power but of humility, we can discover how Jesus offers us a courage that replaces insecurity with a holy vulnerability. Pain when processed with Jesus finds redemption as we allow our truest image-bearing selves to take the lead through all of life's challenges and joys.

FORMATION EXERCISE

We can find strength in sharing our stories of pain and loss, rather than worrying about the reactions of others. When pregnancies end due to miscarriages, when dreams don't come to fruition, when circumstances press in on us, we can show up authentically and discover a love powerful enough to hold us in the midst of it all. Jesus shows us that vulnerability is subversive power, which is ultimately love.

Reflect: Where are you dealing with insecurity right now (emotional, physical, economic, social)? Can you identify any false stories that circulate in your mind and reinforce shame? With the power of Jesus's subversive love, can you imagine ways in which that insecurity could awaken vulnerability, leading to courage, strength, and creativity?

Look beyond yourself: Where do you see insecurities in people or communities that differ from yours? Be careful. This isn't a space to start judging others. Rather, where does your empathy come into contact with Jesus's solidarity with others?

Pray: How might your pain and challenges open you up to courageous vulnerability in how you step into life and relationships? How might Jesus invite you to see your vulnerability as a space of openness and a platform for strength?

Share: Find someone you trust who is accompanying you on your journey with Jesus. Are you holding something that you need to give voice to? Ask this person to sit with you and listen. Sometimes we need someone to remind us that we aren't alone.

CHAPTER 6

EMBRACED AND EMPOWERED

* * *

No matter who you are, where you've been, or how long you've been avoiding the River, Jesus is standing waist deep and calling to you in this very moment. . . . So here you are, listening to Jesus calling you to a baptism that terrifies and delights you. Could the invitation really be as good as it sounds? Or maybe you felt as if you had already answered the invitation, but now you realize you were simply splashing around in the shallows.

—AARON NIEQUIST, *The Eternal Current*

In the fall of 2006, Lauren, my girlfriend at the time, picked me up from the home next to the church that had been converted to office spaces. I hopped in her little blue Hyundai Tiburon, and before we had pulled out of the driveway, my pocket began to vibrate. My close friend Derrick,[*] who's always up for an adventure, enthusiastically spoke to me over the phone: "Bro, guess what. Because I'm a firefighter in San Diego, I was given four free passes to take a hot air balloon ride. Would you and Lauren be interested in coming with us?"

I'm not a fan of heights. I'm not . . . *not* a fan of them either. Mostly, I don't look for opportunities to experience the sensation of falling from high things. Planes? I'm good as long as the turbulence is down to a minimum. The Space Needle? Dig it. Rappelling or a high-ropes adventure course? Nope. I'm *selectively* afraid

---

[*] By the way, if I lived in San Diego, I'd definitely check out Makers Church with Laurel, Derrick, and the crew.

of heights. But after discussing the idea, Lauren and I decided this was too big an opportunity to pass up.

So, a couple of weeks later we went down to Pasadena (where our friends lived at the time), but when we got there, we were met with some disappointing news. We were greeted by Derrick's wife, Laurel (also a good friend), who had a somber look on her face. Derrick was in the living room ironing his fireman's uniform, and he had a sad look as well. He shared that just minutes before we arrived, he'd found out the department needed extra firefighters to work overtime shifts the next couple of days. He couldn't get out of it. It was his first year at the department. Derrick and Laurel insisted we take the balloon ride and said they'd do it some other time. We were disappointed but still excited for the opportunity.

The next morning we arrived just before 6:00 a.m. We helped fill the balloon and set up the basket. Then, after some instruction from our balloon pilot, we were ready to fly. Just before takeoff, we stepped inside the basket, and the pilot took a souvenir picture of us with a Polaroid camera that we'd be able to take home with us. We still have that memento. It marks something that was surreal. Sure, our nerves kicked in as we made the vertical assent. But it was totally worth it.

I never imagined that I'd get to ride in a hot air balloon, let alone with the love of my life. The closest I planned on getting was being fortunate enough to watch them from the ground. Yet here I was—no longer on the earth's surface as a spectator but up where the action happens, soaring for all to see.

Preparing for Liftoff

Faith sometimes feels like that, doesn't it? Getting an unexpected invitation to step into something transcendent is how many people's journey with Jesus begins. Likely, we didn't start our faith with liftoff but took several steps of preparation (maybe you experienced a conversion or baptism or committed yourself in an act of renewal to God, for instance).

But those high-flying moments came as the result of ground-work. You may have observed others soaring in ways that made you curious. Perhaps it took time to move from spectator to getting in on the action, so to speak. Or perhaps you are still in a place of curiosity as you read this book. To be honest, it's possible to be all in when it comes to Jesus and to go through seasons where we are willing to step into the basket but feel there isn't enough spiritual heat to lift off. But moments will arrive, perhaps as a shock to you or others around you, when you will be invited to get in on the action: to take the next step in your journey of becoming human like Jesus.

> *Moments will arrive when you will be invited to get in on the action: to take the next step in your journey of becoming human like Jesus.*

Even Jesus spent time as a spectator (yes, metaphors eventually break down, but go with me for a moment). We know next to nothing about his life between his birth and baptism. We know that at the age of twelve, Jesus's parents couldn't find him until they discovered him three days later at the temple, sitting at the feet of the great teachers of the Torah (Luke 2:41–50). His holy curiosity lured him into his "Father's house" (verse 49), where he had been "listening to [the teachers] and putting questions to them" (verse 46). He was a spectator in one sense but also doing the hard and holy work of preparation for the day when he would be called into the action itself.

Being a spectator isn't a problem. In fact, it is part of the process of preparing for the next phase of our journey with God. Preparing well sets us up for those surprising moments when it's go time. Jesus modeled this for us in the years prior to his baptism. He "was obedient to them [Mary and Joseph]" and "matured in wisdom and years" (verses 51–52). Jesus waited until it was time to move from spectator to contender—from preparation to inauguration.

Surprising Waters

In the story of Jesus's baptism, crowds of people had been flocking to John the Baptizer at the Jordan River. In spite of his weird clothing and food choices, he drew an audience. Those who repented of the sins that held them back from fully representing the God of Israel were baptized, which expressed their repentance.

The surprise in the story comes when Jesus, who John proclaimed to be "the Lamb of God who takes away the sin of the world" (John 1:29), asked to also be baptized. John responded, "I need to be baptized by you, yet you come to me?" (Matthew 3:14). Jesus was like, *Yep.*

If I were John, I would respond to Jesus with an emphatic no as well. In what universe does the Son of God need to *repent*? John said at one point that he wasn't worthy to even stoop down and tie the sandals of Jesus (Mark 1:7), and here Jesus was asking to be baptized? At this point we note that the universe doesn't make sense. For Jesus, however, this was the inaugural moment for his public ministry. The time for him to begin his real work was *now*. The story continues,

> When Jesus was baptized, he immediately came up out of the water. Heaven was opened to him, and he saw the Spirit of God coming down like a dove and resting on him. A voice from heaven said, "This is my Son whom I dearly love; I find happiness in him." (Matthew 3:16–17)

Jesus stepped out of the waters with the greatest of affirmations: God the Father spoke pure love and delight over him. In the gospel of Mark, the Father's words were spoken *to* Jesus ("*You* are my Son . . . ; in *you* I find happiness" [Mark 1:11]). God's overwhelming love as heavenly parent poured out on Jesus. He had done what must be done to "fulfill all righteousness" (Matthew 3:15), and God the Father delighted in the Son as the Spirit filled him up afresh. With spectators surrounding the scene, there was no doubt: the Father's affirmation and the Spirit's fire empowered Jesus to soar.

We're still left wondering, *But why? Why did Jesus get baptized?* There are several points to consider. First, the fact that humans were being called to baptism means Jesus was included in this number. Jesus modeled his human solidarity by doing what every Christian is invited to do. In the ancient context, it was more specific than Jesus's being human, however. Jesus enacted what can only be considered *a baptism of repentance on behalf of all Israel.* Since the Babylonian Exile and return, the Jewish people had attempted to answer questions about their identity in the world. As empire after empire took over their land, they wanted to figure out how to get God on their side again.

That is the wrong question.

The United States, for instance, has a stream of history when they sought to use God as the justification for national interests. From the genocide of Indigenous peoples, to the enslavement of persons from the African continent, to Jim Crow, to the ongoing systemic racism facing Black, Indigenous, and People of Color, Americans have falsely used God to justify their profit and power. And we are still doing it today. No wonder peaceful protests erupt as videos continue to surface showing how Black people face brutality even now. These injustices flow from a long history of evil on what is now considered US soil. How often has our generation asked how to get God back on "our side" as our culture changes? Again, *wrong question*! Having political power and financial privilege over others is not what it means to have God on our side.

When we feel that life is out of control, our human questions are often about power. But the question Jesus started with was, How can I show my submission to God? His path to power began with surrendering to the greatest love in the universe. This love empowered him to be the kind of human being who *had humanity* for everyone he encountered, especially outsiders. We can learn to surrender to God's love, purging ourselves from manipulative power games in favor of vulnerability, because Jesus showed us how.

Repentance and Being Jewish in the First Century

The truth is, we all want people to fall in line with our best understanding of the world. As religious people, we often try to figure out which version of God we like and how to live in light of what we have come to understand. In the first-century world of Jesus, not unlike ours, God's chosen people—the Jews—weren't united on how best to live as worshippers of their Lord. Yet each group shared one basic goal: get God back on the side of Israel again.*

The *separation* approach was embodied by groups like the Essene sect that likely gave us the Dead Sea Scrolls of Qumran (one of the most important discoveries about the history of the Jewish people). This approach held that the wickedness of Israel was such that starting over was the only way forward.

The *compromise* approach, often attributed to the Sadducees (some Pharisees) and figures like Herod the Great, sought to build up a life within the pagan systems of Rome. At least they could have access to privileges and power this way.

The *purification* approach of the Pharisees sought to cleanse Israel through radical obedience to the Torah (Law), so much so that they had oral rules about the written rules contained in the first five books of our Bible. This wasn't about earning salvation by doing good works (a huge misconception!) but an attempt at a Jewish revival so steeped in religiosity that Jesus called some of these leaders out for the heavy burden they placed on people.†

The *nationalist* approach of the Zealots, which may have loosely included sympathizers of various sorts, centered its activity around taking back the glory of Israel by force. The nationalist approach of violence conflicted with Jesus's core message of

---

* I wonder if they had a slogan, like God on Our Side Again. Maybe GOOSA hats? It doesn't matter what your party affiliation: that's funny!

† Bible nerd alert: Look up covenantal nomism and E. P. Sanders for more. I have an episode of *Theology Curator* (podcast) called "What Is 'Covenantal Nomism' and Why Does It Matter?" that you can look up too.

love for enemies and personal character formation, as we will see later.

So, with all these approaches for how to get God back on the side of Israel, Jesus stepped in and said that they needed to get back on the side of *God*. Think about the radical nature of that teaching for a minute! It turned accepted wisdom upside down and therefore was deeply offensive to the key religious leaders, who had built a whole platform on the exact opposite of what Jesus had begun to preach.

To repent, in the ancient world, simply meant to go a different way by turning to an alternate path.[1] Jesus, from the start of his ministry in the waters of baptism, invited the Jewish people into a radically different option of living faithfully for Israel's God. That path is no less radical today.

But what can we learn about it as we seek to live with faithful hope? I want to suggest that the *active peacemaking* approach of Jesus (a fifth option) centers his disciples on being liberated from shame and the powers of evil by empowering them with God's relentless love. This love, although not always nice, is offered to anyone willing to repent—to actively contend for justice-shaped peace in our lives, relationships, and world.

Beyond Shame

In showing Israel, and eventually all Christians, that they needed to repent—to change their path of life—to step into the full humanity God had for them, Jesus was also demonstrating that he was the world's true King. This was his royal inauguration ceremony. The waters anointed Jesus, the one from the line of King David, as the ruler of Israel—and, by extension, the whole world. Messiah wannabes tried to take Israel back by force. No one expected a king like Jesus, a peacemaker rather than a warmonger.

So far we've noticed that Jesus was baptized to *repent on behalf of all Israel* and as an *inauguration as the rightful messianic King.* Those first two points are important, but this third one changes

everything: *Jesus's baptism marked the foundation of his identity*—he is loved. Before anything else, at the core of who he is,
Jesus experiences love with a capital *L*. As 1 John 4:8, 16 proclaims,
"God is love." Love like this—this perfect, unending love of
God—is a catalytic force with the potential to transform us. I can't
imagine hearing the words "You are my Son, whom I dearly love;
in you I find happiness" (Mark 1:11) and remaining the same.

Jesus experienced what we all are invited to know: that God is
love. Love marks the Messiah, and that same love marks each one
of us. Just like Jesus, we need reminders of our intrinsic worth.
The tomb that Jesus would conquer through resurrection reflects
the same love of God for the whole world. Through the distortion
of a love-challenged world, if we listen closely, the faint echoes of
hope that remind us we are fundamentally lovable invite us to step
into the next moment more fully human than we were in the one
before. A helpful reflection comes from N. T. Wright in his commentary on Mark's version of the story:

> The whole Christian *gospel* could be summed up in this
> point: that when the living God looks at us, at every bap-
> tized and believing Christian, he says to us what he said to
> Jesus on that day. He sees us, not as we are in ourselves, but
> as we are in Jesus Christ. It sometimes seems impossible,
> especially to people who have never had this kind of sup-
> port from their earthly parents, but it's true: God looks at
> us, and says, "You are my dear, dear child; I'm delighted
> with you." Try reading that sentence slowly, with your own
> name at the start, and reflect quietly on God saying that to
> you, both at your *baptism* and every day since. . . .
>
> Look at this story, he says, look at this life, and learn to
> see and hear in it the heavenly vision, the heavenly voice.
> Learn to hear these words addressed to yourself. Let them
> change you, mould you, make you somebody new, the per-
> son God wants you to be. Discover in this story the nor-
> mally hidden heavenly dimension of God's world.[2]

In college, I used Wright's *Mark for Everyone* for my devotional practice before bed most nights. When I came to this story, God used this quote to speak to the core of my identity. I took the suggestion seriously, meditating on these words as if they were addressed to me. As I prayed, a point came where the words were no longer my adapted recitation but God's own. In that moment, a love washed over me, immersing my whole being with the cleansing waters of God's utter delight. I've often come back to this passage, and the same holds true: God the Father sees us just as Jesus was seen on that day two thousand years ago.

What if God's words to Jesus are God's words to us? Could it be possible that you are, as a renewed image bearer, the subject of God's incomprehensible love? Shame's voice has been silenced by the thunderous heavenly voice breaking through the barrier of reality to whisper words we all long to hear: *I love you.*

With a shame-defying affirmation, Jesus was ready to transition into one of the hardest seasons of his life: forty days in the desert with the devil. He was armed only with his baptism and the Holy Spirit as he faced the world's greatest foe.

Empowered by Love

So what does this all mean for *us*? Everything. If the world's system of power is a facade and if we find true strength by joining Jesus in humility, then all of who we are and all of what we do must start and stop with a deep awareness of the love of God. Not only do we need to know about love, but we need to invite it to wash over us again and again and again—even after it prepares us to step into a life modeled after Jesus's. This love prepares us as spectators and also sustains us as we soar, keeping the balloon powerfully hovering toward the next destination of the journey with the Spirit. God's love prepares us, sends us, and gives us the space to rest when being in the action becomes tiring.[3]

Love is powerful. God's love is the most subversive force in the cosmos. As image bearers of God, we adopt more of Jesus's humanity when we listen for the voice of Love and reflect that love back to God, the world, and our relationships. Shalom surprises us as it heals our pain and empowers us to love like Jesus.

Sometimes it's hard for people to take this idea of love and translate it experientially. Love is risky and, when not reciprocated, hurts badly. Relationships are an example of this. So many of us have expressed love to someone else and been told, "You are great, but I just don't feel that way about you." Some people fear love's humble power to open them up, so they push it away. Others fear offering love, ultimately believing the lie that they are unlovable. Honestly, I've felt many of these things when it comes to love. Love is a risk.

It is sort of like our experience of flying in a hot air balloon for the first time. Sure, there was some prep work. We planned. We drove. We helped inflate the thing. We took the brief safety course with our pilot. We'd had numerous moments as spectators from the ground, so we knew what we were getting into as we cautiously stepped into the giant wicker basket. But eventually we had to take the risk, squeezing each other's hand as we lifted off, so that we could be in on the action.

After ten minutes or so, we shook off our nerves and began enjoying the flight. At that point, our pilot handed me the souvenir— a Polaroid in a folded paper frame. After looking at it, I handed it over to Lauren. She opened up the photo card and looked at the image with a bit of confusion. Before she could figure out what was going on, she looked my direction, only to find me on one knee with a little black box displaying something shiny inside it.[*]

She teared up as I asked her to marry me, up high in the clouds. The picture, of course, was all part of the plan. It said "Will you marry me?" on the outside of the basket, but she hadn't seen it until she read it on the photo. Everything that culminated in that single moment had been prepared to a T, from the initial phone call from Derrick, to his "getting called into work" (wow, my friends are good liars . . . hmm), to the Polaroid picture, to the

---

[*] Jeff Zimmerman hooked me up with his ring guy a few weeks earlier. It's always good when you know a guy who knows a guy, you know?

proposal itself. All this spectator preparation led to the one moment when I declared my intention to love Lauren for the rest of our lives. With nowhere to go but up,* my risk of love was reciprocated. She. Said. Yes.

And look, it is totally possible that she could have said no. It's not the easiest thing to do when you are both trapped in a flying basket, but it's certainly possible. Human love, as much as it is informed by God's love (which is perfectly modeled to us by Jesus), is not perfect. She could have said no. People in our lives *will* say no. Loving others is risky. It's a costly love that Jesus certainly understands. (Just think about Judas betraying him or Peter denying him.)

However, there is a Love that *never* says no. A Love so perfect, so selfless, so profound, so compelling, which was expressed by thunderous echoes from the God who is so intimate and near that Jesus described God as his Abba—a term of endearment (Mark 14:36).

Because of Jesus's encounter with the identity-shaping, shame-defying love of God, he stepped into the next moment, forty days in the desert, with the power to persevere. He knew who he was and whose he was, no matter the pain or challenges that came his way. He shows us that a foundational way God redeems our pain is by immersing us in the waters of a new love-soaked identity so we can step through challenges with courage and compassion.

FORMATION EXERCISE

To step into our pain differently, we can rest in the fact that above anything else, we are beloved by God. We are worthy of that love, just like Jesus at his baptism. Let's soak in that truth right now.

---

* Yes, that line makes me think of the wonderful film *Mary Poppins Returns* (Disney, 2018).

Scripture: Open your Bible to Mark 1:9–11 and read the story of Jesus's baptism. Then reread it . . . slowly. On the third round, focus only on what God the Father said about Jesus.

Reflect: After reading those words slowly a few more times, perhaps memorizing the verse in the process, imagine that those words are not only for Jesus but also directed toward you. Let them wash over you.

Keeping those words at the front of your attention, close your eyes and imagine it is your own baptism and God is speaking those words over you to empower you for whatever comes next. Reflect on that as long as you'd like.

CHAPTER 7

GOD IN THE DESERT

* * *

Vulnerability sounds like truth and feels like courage. Truth and courage aren't always comfortable, but they're never weakness.

—BRENÉ BROWN, *Daring Greatly*

When I was a kid, things were hard. I felt alone, vulnerable, and weak. Growing up in my situation was like being stuck in a desert without adequate supplies. I had enough support from outside my immediate circumstances to survive, but no matter the hopeful oasis of support that surrounded me—Dad, Grandma and Grandpa, aunts and uncles, people from church, parents of friends—I'd still end up back in the desert, forced to fast from the temporary safety they provided.

Looking back, it honestly felt like I lived in two different worlds. One was full of pain and vulnerability. Abuse could happen at any moment. Another was free from fear. When I was with my grandparents, my dad, or even my mom (when her boyfriend was out of sight), I had nothing to fear. Mom was fun and compassionate. She did all she could to ensure that I had opportunities to thrive. We attended church each week with my grandparents, and I was involved in the midweek youth program. I participated in sports— something Mom always supported. We laughed a lot because of her awesomely quirky humor. We spent lots of time at family gatherings playing volleyball (Mom loved playing), basketball, mushball (which is like baseball with a gigantic softball), and card games like BS (but we called it "I Doubt It" *because of Jesus*). She did all she could to expand my world beyond the fear.

Even when things were hard, when she felt powerless, Mom never relented in loving me. Fortunately, as our family grew with the birth of two wonderful siblings, the abusive boyfriend no longer lived under our roof. So I only had to worry if I heard a loud motorcycle heading in our direction. As I got older, I began to truly understand how unjust my situation was. I knew that he shouldn't have power over my life, but I was small. How could I fight back? How could I defend my dignity in those dehumanizing moments of painful abuse? I didn't know, but I knew that I wanted to stand up for myself.

Occasionally, we'd go to his place. I remember when I was about ten years old (a year or so before a final climactic episode of abuse forced him out of our lives for good), we visited his mobile home. It was at the edge of town. A few kids from my school lived there, so once in a while I'd have kids to play with. It was good unless it got bad.

One time when I was on the front porch, he came out of the house from behind me. There were a few steps to get down to ground level. As I headed down the first stair, he apparently thought I was blocking his path. Out of nowhere, as if punting a football, he kicked me from behind directly in the rectum with his steel-toed boot. This hurt not only my body but also my pride. Upon impact, I quickly stumbled down the steps to get out of harm's way. I was tired of being treated this way. So I turned around, stared my abuser in the face, and yelled, "A—hole!" Taken aback, he responded with some sort of verbal threat but quickly went back inside as Mom rushed out to comfort me.

This is one of the times in my life when I related to Jesus's experience in the wilderness. By this age, I knew not only that God loved me but also that others believed in me. Jesus, having been empowered by the words of his Father, stepped into forty days of physical deprivation. His experience of the Father's love prepared him to cease eating for over a month. Jesus's fast from food and comfort was an abundant feast on God's loving presence. The devil had no hope after waiting forty days. Jesus's scarce access to physical nourishment amplified the abundance of being alone with the Father and "full of the Holy Spirit" (Luke 4:1).

Although I was kicked that day, starved for physical safety as I was, my youthful understanding that I mattered, that I was a child of a loving heavenly Father, empowered me to respond from a strength of spirit. Scarcity met its foe: an evolving awareness that being dehumanized by an abuser is never okay. Abundance was sneaking into my life, and I didn't fully know it. Jesus didn't call the devil an a—hole, but he put the devil in its place. Jesus knew *whose* he was, so scarcity in the desert transformed into profound abundance. Dallas Willard once wrote, "The 'wilderness,' the place of solitude and deprivation, was actually *the place of strength and strengthening* for our Lord and . . . the Spirit led him there—as he would lead *us* there—to ensure that Christ was in the best possible condition for the trial."[1] You may think the suggestion that the desert was a good experience for Jesus comes off as counterintuitive. I agree.

The Desert Is Where Jesus Is Strong

After a powerful experience at his baptism, Jesus was "led by the Spirit into the wilderness" (Luke 4:1). He went without food for forty days. At this point, "Jesus was starving" (verse 2). On the one hand, Jesus went to the desert to be tested. He was tested to make certain he truly was the faithful human being for God's mission in the world. Just like God needed to know for sure that Abraham would be the right person to carry the redemption of the world forward, even if it meant a horrible test for him (Genesis 22:1–19), the Father needed assurance that Jesus would pass the obedience test. On the other hand, Jesus went to the desert to be alone with God (where the devil can also tempt).

Here's what is so fascinating. What we naturally label scarcity, Jesus shows us is abundance. No doubt about it: Jesus was weak in that moment. But, oh, he was strong! Dallas Willard said, "The desert was his fortress, his place of power."[2] He practiced the presence of God for forty days straight. Who was the disadvantaged one, really? Certainly not Jesus. Hungry? Sure. Tired? No doubt about it. Weak? Hardly. Jesus trained for that moment when he faced the devil. As you likely know, the training paid off.*

Jesus shows us that it's entirely possible to step into scarce circumstances and overcome them with abundance. That isn't to say scarcity is eliminated. It's not. But we can step into it differently and choose not to let it define us. We are loved by the triune God of the universe, so when it comes to our worth in the world, we lack nothing.

How does scarcity show up in our lives? Not many of us spend over a month in the wilderness without food. Scarcity is, at its core, an affront to our God-given image-bearing identity. Scarcity tells us we *are not enough* and *will never have enough* to *be enough*. Every day we have a growing list of aspirations and obligations, many of which are never quite done. Many of us feel underrested, underpaid, underappreciated, inadequate, insecure, insignificant, and yet aspirational. Those beautiful aspirations, those dreams of what could be, often elude us because scarcity tells us we can't possibly have what it takes, given all the limitations and constraints. Thus, we feel like we are never enough. We begin to define each day by our scarcity rather than our belief that we, as human beings made in God's image, are in and of ourselves enough and are worthy of love.[3]

Facing the Devil While Feasting with God

Jesus found himself, having been affirmed in his beloved identity by God and empowered by God the Spirit, living out a reenactment of the story of Israel as he was tested in the wilderness.[4] The

---

* Matthew 4:1–10 (the parallel passage) puts the three temptations from the devil after forty days of fasting. Luke 4:2 says, "He was tempted for forty days by the devil," yet places the interrogation at the end of the period as well by saying, "Afterward Jesus was starving. The devil said . . ." (verses 2–3). Even though the devil was present in some way during the forty days, God was with Jesus too, which made him ready for the final interrogation that we'll explore here.

themes of exodus and exile are all over the place in this story. We recall the story of Eve and Adam, where the serpent said, "Did God really say . . ." (Genesis 3:1). The devil-snake whispered lies to rationalize poor choices, which mirrors the story of ancient Israel, who at times chose in opposition to God. All the old stories take on new meaning as we see their themes resurface in the experience of Jesus.

It was now day forty. Jesus was starving, yet he was well fed. Feasting on God was the fast he'd chosen. Now he faced three lies, which at their core attempted to convince Jesus that he really should pay attention to the scarcity of his situation. Each time, Jesus appealed to the abundant identity he has as God's true image bearer.

LIE #1: YOU DON'T HAVE ENOUGH BREAD

Jesus was told by the devil to prove he's God's Son by turning a rock into bread to eat. This would have ended Jesus's fast before the Father on terms other than his own. So Jesus rebutted by quoting the Scriptures: "People won't live only by bread" (Luke 4:4). The devil attacked Jesus's identity, countering the Father's words from the previous scene: "You are my Son, whom I dearly love" (3:22). The accuser tried to get Jesus to fall into the trap of having a disordered sense of self. But Jesus knew exactly who he is. The devil had no chance. Jesus, the beloved Son, is abundance embodied! Forty days earlier, God the Father had made this perfectly clear, and Jesus had all this time to feast on that declaration.

This fast wasn't merely a move of piety. Of course, Jesus is pious. But Jesus also sought to identify with the poor and hungry people living under Roman occupation. He showed that under the worst of circumstances, where scarcity is the only thing being force-fed, there exists a glorious identity that undercuts any claims to the contrary, be they by the devil, the Romans, or the religious elites. In knowing himself, Jesus modeled the personal aspect of the four relationships of shalom we discussed earlier (God, others, self, and creation). At the same time, he refused to exploit creation to make his situation more convenient.* In the midst of this trial in his life, Jesus knew who he was because he knew whose he was.

LIE # 2: YOU DON'T HAVE ENOUGH POWER

Jesus was told a second lie: you don't have enough power. This lie disrupts shalom since it offers a disordered relationship to other people. Throughout history, men have compromised for political power and have caused great suffering on the earth. Jesus knew that his power comes only from his intimacy with God Almighty. This all-powerful God flexes that strength by serving others and modeling sacrificial love.

Sadly, professing Christians don't always get it, even today. Besides a history of owning and abusing slaves, wars against others (including against fellow Christians) for national interests, genocide against Indigenous peoples (and similar atrocities in other places), and abusing women and children, Christians continue to maintain their privilege in society by using power and rhetoric to push others into the margins. Many fail to see that our sole allegiance belongs to God's peaceable kingdom of love, not to the pursuit of power (which is really driven by a mentality of scarcity).

The devil made a claim, which Jesus never corrected as wrong: "This whole domain and . . . all these kingdoms . . . [have] been entrusted to me and I can give it to anyone I want" (Luke 4:6). Even the best political situations are under the influence of the devil.[5] "The evil one" (Ephesians 6:16) is at work in governmental systems through the influence of demonic angels that the Bible sometimes calls rulers, authorities, powers, and elements. This is why it is so important that our political ideology never comes before our biblical theology! The powers of evil are at work when a liberal *or* a conservative is in power (for my fellow US residents).

---

* To which you might rightfully say, "But who cares about a rock?" Fair enough, but hopefully you get the deeper point: stewardship over creation is our vocation as image bearers.

No wonder fearmongering works so well each political cycle. Convincing people of their lack wins votes.

This doesn't mean that we must *never* engage in politics—especially when matters of human rights and equity are at stake—but that we should keep our ideas in their proper place in light of the demonic nature of systems of rule. All politics, although needed to minimize evil, are grabs for power by someone. Our allegiance, if we are to follow Jesus, must be only to the world's true Lord: Jesus himself![6]

The whole Mediterranean world was under the charge of the Roman Empire during Jesus's time (Luke 2:1; 3:1), but it was the devil who got the credit for having the ultimate authority. When, rather than giving in to the scarcity lie, we realize that our value comes intrinsically as image bearers, then lusting for power no longer appeals. We don't have to make the world more to our liking, but we can come alongside those whom the world's systems push to the side.

Of course, the desire for power tempts us in other ways: seeking corrupted pleasures, coveting likes on Instagram, cutting corners at work, and so much more. Power itself isn't the deepest issue but the quality of that power. Power over others seeks to mold things into our own image. Power under others seeks to use our influence in ways that look like the self-offering love of Jesus.[7]

LIE #3: YOU DON'T HAVE ENOUGH SECURITY

This third lie also reflects the disruption of shalom by offering a disordered relationship to God. Bread and power relate directly with a scarcity mindset about security. I'm not saying security is never important—quite the opposite. But what is the *nature* of our security? From where does it come? We almost never ask that important question, but that is precisely what was contested in the desert between Jesus and the devil. Jesus was told to prove his Sonship by jumping off the temple to see whether God would send angels to save him. To this, Jesus rebutted, "Don't test the Lord your God" (4:12). For Jesus, God has nothing to prove. God is faithful—full stop.

Joel Green, in his commentary on Luke, showed that Jesus won't be distracted "from his single-minded commitment to loyalty and obedience in God's service." He "interprets the devil's invitation as an encouragement to question God's faithfulness."[8] Green added that "the devil fails to recognize an even deeper mystery, known already to the believing community of which Luke is a part, that divine rescue may come *through* suffering and death and not only *before* (and *from*) them."[9]

God's faithfulness persists even through suffering. Suffering may feel like scarcity but in fact may also be an opportunity for intimacy with God. To be clear, I'm not saying that intimacy with God is the *purpose* of suffering, but it can be the *outcome*.

Lacking Nothing in the Desert

When we discover our value—that God sees us and names us as enough—we no longer need to worry about not having enough. Jesus knew exactly who he was and *whose* he was after a powerful moment at his baptism. The question of whether Jesus was enough had already been answered by the heavenly voice that said, "You are my Son, whom I dearly love; in you I find happiness" (3:22). For forty days, Jesus savored those words as he continued to feast with the Father. Even when tempted, Jesus was feasting as he resisted the lies of scarcity that sought to disrupt shalom in his life. Jesus was powerful, not weak, when the devil tempted him. Where we see Jesus having to overcome scarcity in the desert, Jesus shows us that even in physical deprivation, abundance is ours.

In the story that began this chapter, I felt powerless in one sense. I didn't have enough, and shame told me it meant I wasn't enough. However, I had a growing sense of abundance that the Spirit was cultivating in me. So, when an abuser sought to kick me down, I stood up to him. Although it may not be the most Christlike response for an adult, responding by shouting "A—hole!" was the holy rebuttal of a child needing to assert my full humanity in that moment. Slowly I would learn to feast with the Father, who sees me and delights in me. The same is true for you. God sees you, and you are delightful.

Scarcity starves us of abundance. Forming a fresh understanding of abundance—not that of resources, power, or security but of our identity in God and our belovedness—can transform how we step into the deserts of pain, struggle, and temptation.

In my own life, I struggle with scarcity. One way this shows up is that I have a tendency to look to the grass that's greener on the other side. To flee from the challenges of the present, I tend to dream about what could be. I look forward to what might happen to avoid what is happening, especially when it's painful.

Something that helps form a sense of being enough and having enough is the practice of gratitude. I find that the more I purge myself of a scarcity mindset, the more grateful I am for the small blessings in my life. When I'm sticking to my daily routine (I'll keep it real—this comes and goes), part of my spiritual practice each morning is to thank God for three things or people that make me grateful and then to write them down.

This practice of gratitude invites my heart and mind to come into alignment with the good things God is up to in the here and now. It brings perspective to my pain without ignoring it. God's delight. God's joy. God's goodness and invitation to feast. All these gifts bubble up as I invite Jesus to show me signs of abundance, even when the voice of the accuser shouts to silence gratitude.

You are truly enough. Let God remind you of this fact every single day.

FORMATION EXERCISE

Jesus stepped into the desert, a place of scarcity, but feasted on the abundance of God's love. Even when he was physically weak from forty days of fasting, his power to stand up in the face of evil shows us that we can find strength in our challenges as well.

Scripture: Take a moment to read Psalm 23. Pay attention to the clues that this psalm wasn't written by someone who had it all together. Things weren't easy, yet David said we can step into even the "darkest valley" (verse 4) with the abundance of God's love. Sounds a lot like Jesus in the desert, doesn't it?

Now reread it one verse at a time. Pause after each verse, keeping the main images at the front of your mind, and imagine walking with Jesus through each scene. For example, if you read, "The LORD is my shepherd. I lack nothing" (verse 1), you can picture yourself walking with the Lord as a shepherd. Be imaginative and open to the creativity of the Holy Spirit.

Don't rush this process. Stay with the imagery as a form of prayer for a few minutes per verse (as you feel led).

Reflect and/or journal: Reflect on any meaningful moments by writing in a journal or sharing your experience with a friend.

CHAPTER 8

NORMAL ISN'T NEGATIVE

* * *

*I am a Christian . . . because the story of Jesus is still the story
I'm willing to risk being wrong about.*

—RACHEL HELD EVANS, *Inspired*

Normal isn't the most helpful label since it easily boxes people into the molds of others. Sometimes *normal* holds power over people who are different. Normal is what we want to be when shame narrates our inner world. It is a word of negation—of what we believe we don't measure up against. Kids tell other kids that they are not normal and thus weird. Adults isolate themselves with peers who think, vote, pray, and look like them—in other words, who are "normal." This dehumanizing use of the term needs to die.

However, *normal* can have a different slant as well. It can be a term of solidarity. "Normal people" are folks who, like me, are down to earth and experience life in the real world. I think this is the best sense of the word. *Normal* means that we are in this together. We get it. We likely aren't the elite in the eyes of a celebrity-obsessed culture; we are regular folks.

The New Testament tells the stories of normal people as well. Naturally, we want to idealize people like Peter, James, Paul, Mary Magdalene, and Mary the mother of Jesus. The truth is that each of the characters in the Gospels, Acts, and the letters of the Bible—at least the ones we are tempted to idealize—were regular human beings. They didn't have holy halos on their heads like their old-school religious art portrayals may suggest. Peter denied

Jesus and regularly put his foot in his mouth. Jesus even called him the satan once (Matthew 16:23). Paul dealt with a circumstance he called "a thorn in my body" (2 Corinthians 12:7), which reminds us that he suffered greatly. For all their positives, we must remember that the biblical characters were too similar to us in their humanness to be made up. They were normal people, but they stepped into callings that transformed the world.

Self-doubt turns normal into a negative. But when we let normal lead us to authenticity, we step into the depths of possibility. We who don't have it all together, who are trying to do all we can to lead lives of honesty and kindness to others, who struggle to make ends meet at times, who shuttle kids from school to practices to friends' parties, who cry real tears at the loss of a loved one, who do all we can to lean into the gift of today—we have much in common with the earliest followers of Jesus. We are living out our lives.

> *Self-doubt turns normal into a negative. But when we let normal lead us to authenticity, we step into the depths of possibility.*

Jesus's crowd were the common folks, not the elite. When he got an audience with the power brokers, it usually was from a place of critique. One such audience led to his execution. Naturally, when Jesus began his public ministry, he decided to reach out to some fishermen. These ordinary young men were likely reared to follow in the footsteps of family members who ran the family business, a path distinct from becoming a great religious teacher of the Torah. Sure, they would have committed much of the Hebrew Scriptures to memory, but they ended up not as sages but as sardine catchers.

When pain intersects with normal life, we easily buy the lie that we don't have any options for finding wholeness. *Life is what it is, so I guess I'll deal with it.* Jesus steps in and says, *Being normal isn't a negative. You can become like me, pain and all.*

Fish for People

If you grew up in the church, you've heard Jesus's words to the first disciples: "Follow me and I will make you fish for people" (Mark 1:17, NRSV). What an odd thing to say. I've been fishing only a few times in my life. Sometime around fifth grade, our extended family camped near Santa Cruz. The boardwalk was a prime destination for a kid. I remember the highlight was when I stepped up to a booth where the challenge was to throw a baseball as hard as you could and then guess your speed. I guessed mine exactly and won a plastic Chicago White Sox hat. Come on, in the nineties they had Bo Jackson and Frank Thomas! Bo knows . . . everything, by the way.

During that trip I woke up early in the morning with my grandpa and uncles to go deep sea fishing. I'm not an outdoorsy sort of guy. I'll take a hotel over a tent any day. Yet to my family's surprise, I ended up reeling in the most fish that day. I caught *nine,* which others on board conveniently took off my hooks so I never had to touch them.

I was on cloud nine until I stepped off the boat. With each step on dry land, my balance faltered. My orientation toward the world was distorted, not clearly as focused as it was when I boarded that morning. According to Wikipedia (the final authority on all things), I had something called sea legs, which is the "illusion of motion felt on dry land after spending time at sea."[1] When I stepped off the boat, my experience of normal life was disrupted. Wobbling from side to side, it was all I could do to keep my gaze focused forward. Fortunately this lasted for only about four hours.

Sometimes following Jesus feels like having sea legs, especially for those of us following him in the twenty-first century. Life is bumpy, and pacing behind Jesus as we seek to follow him is hard. Yet as we pursue Jesus, he pursues us even more. For Simon (Peter), Andrew, James, and John, their departure from the boats meant a total life disorientation. Jesus came to them while they were working on their fishing boats and said, "Follow me and I will make you fish for people" (verses 16–20, NRSV).

Having made it far enough in their childhood education in Galilee to realize they were going to continue the family trade, they knew fishing would provide humble stability into adulthood. They weren't the best of the best when it came to Jewish culture; they were the rest of the rest, and the rest aren't the best.

Imagine their surprise when Jesus took an interest in them. When he called them, he simultaneously affirmed their ability to *learn* from him and *become* like him. Without a doubt, they had spiritual sea legs when they dropped their nets and left their boats behind. Their moment had arrived. Normal fishermen, with the stench of fish guts rotting in the blazing afternoon sun, would follow the greatest rabbi the world would ever know.

Championing Disciples

These disciples were good at mending nets. They were likely average at best when it came to reading the Torah. Yet Jesus called them. A rabbinic teacher came to them and said, "You've got what it takes. You can do it. You can become like me." Jesus sees in us what we often cannot see in ourselves.

I know what it is like to be championed by someone in this way. Perhaps you do as well. Although my childhood memories are flooded with pain, they also have some wonderfully bright spots. People around me, although not always fully attuned to the severity of my home life, stepped up in a big way. They called things out of me I wouldn't have known otherwise. In a sense, these people fished for me by pulling me out of darkness and showing me God's love.

One of these people was my dad. After my parents divorced when I was a toddler, he was given custody every other weekend. Those weekends were bright spots in my young life. When I was with Dad, I was safe. I was loved unconditionally. I was encouraged.

Weekends, until I became a "big kid," involved Saturday morning walks through town, hoisted above everyone as I perched on the towering shoulders of his six-foot-eight frame. (I often napped with my hands and cheek on his head.) We'd transition to the car for a trip to Carl's Jr., where I'd get a kids' meal, always with my famous "cheeseburger plain." From there, we'd often find ourselves at the mall, which stood across the street, where my five-dollar allowance (or so) would land me my next Ninja Turtles action figure.

With Dad, I was free from the threat of verbal and physical violence. I was what every child should have the opportunity to be—fully loved and cared for. Nothing from my childhood shines brighter than those weekends with him. He represented what the love of God is like in real life. He still does. The image of resting on Dad's shoulders, being so content that I could fall asleep, gives me a picture of a heavenly Father who is safe enough, strong enough, and secure enough to walk with me through the highs and lows of life.

Eventually Dad remarried when I was in fourth grade, and he asked me to be his best man. I was his best friend, after all. Even as my weekend family expanded, Dad always took time for me. Through the years that followed, he championed my personal character development and gifted me his odd sense of humor. For the record, I always thought Dad was the combination of a comedian, sage, companion, cool old guy, and someone who was a tad quirky. And now I notice every day that I'm so much like him. I catch myself saying odd words like *thingamajiggy* to describe random household objects. I make up ridiculous words, phrases, and songs to communicate with my kiddos. I've even noticed that I inadvertently took on his home uniform: sweatpants (often really baggy or the type that narrow at the ankle) and a designated pair of house shoes. I am who I am today because Dad showed me how to be loved. Unconditionally. Joyfully.

He was *present*. There wasn't a baseball game where he wasn't in the bleachers cheering me on (even on the weekends when he didn't have custody). There wasn't a basketball game where he didn't offer me encouragement for my efforts. There wasn't a football game where he didn't flat out have a blast himself, since he, too, loves the game. Although he didn't coach my teams, Dad found ways to get involved, like the years he spent on the chain gang. My dad, the ultimate normal guy, isn't normal to me. Flaws and all, he's a hero.*

I've shared the story of my dad. But the list of those who championed me is long. The next names on my list are my grandparents Corny and Margaret. They made sure I had all my essential needs met, a safe place to go regularly outside the home, all the gear I needed to play sports, opportunities to learn to work and earn money, normal childhood fun, and so much more.

I didn't miss church or church camp because they committed themselves to making it happen. From them I learned that following Jesus means generosity and responsibility. I learned that I could be a Christian and still have flaws. I learned how to pray before bed, on my knees, offering all my trust to a loving God. Their home in the country near my hometown is still where I "go home to" to this day. They were and remain a light in the darkness, even though my grandpa is no longer with us. They were more than grandparents; they were a second set of parents. Grandma, you and Grandpa championed me. You still do. I love you. Of course, my list doesn't stop there. I could add my stepmom and uncles and aunts and keep going.†

Have you ever done something like this as a spiritual practice of gratitude? Who has championed you? You likely have your own list of people who saw something in you that needed to be drawn out. I'm guessing if you took the time, in a posture of prayerful reflection, you'd discover the grace and love of Jesus in the midst of it.

Jesus is the ultimate champion of people. He championed us by becoming one of us and showing us how to be the people God always had in mind. Starting with those first twelve disciples and spanning two millennia of other disciples who have followed him,

---

* Dad, since I know you will be reading this: thank you for calling something out of me that wouldn't be there without your love. You championed me.

† Actually, my list extends itself into the acknowledgments section at the end of the book.

Jesus hasn't stopped championing image bearers. The echoing hope of Jesus continues ringing in our ears as if to say, *I believe you've got what it takes to become like me.*

Normal Disciples

Just like they were for me after fishing in the Pacific as a fifth grader, when you get onto dry land, things may still seem as if they are rocking side to side. When those fishermen-turned-disciples of Jesus stepped off their boats, I doubt they shared my problems with equilibrium. However, they were disoriented in another way. This great teacher who decided to come to *them,* instead of finding the elite among Torah students, disrupted their existence in irresistible fashion. Their new teacher wasn't always clear about where they were going or what was coming next. Everything Jesus does challenges our categories of normal.

So, as followers, they did all they could to follow, often wobbling along in his trail of dust. We're the same way, aren't we? We can watch Jesus, but walking like him? Disorienting. It's like stepping onto solid land and suddenly realizing we've spent all our lives rocking unpredictably.

With Jesus, disorientation leads to transformation, which yields a fresh vocation for the sake of others.

Jesus, however, didn't leave them in their disorientation. Nor does he leave us in ours. We grow in him. We learn. We take up his invitation to follow, open ourselves up to becoming different kinds of people, and give ourselves to the work of championing others in a painful world (we "fish for people").[2] In championing his new disciples, Jesus was promising that they would grow in their capacity as humans and transform into the sort of people who make an impact beyond themselves. With Jesus, disorientation leads to transformation, which yields a fresh vocation for the sake of others. The disciples would become the kind of people who fish for others, who champion people and draw something out of them that changes everything.

Voices We Listen To

Personal transformation doesn't happen overnight. Often it takes risk and sacrifice. Change of this sort, although personal, isn't private. We don't change by ourselves. There is nothing private about following Jesus; he is always all up in our messes! His voice, if discerned wisely, gives us all the affirmation we need to move into the next phase of our journeys. However, we were designed for person-to-person community, so it is no wonder we are shaped by those around us.

Like Peter, Andrew, John, and James, we, too, are invited to follow Jesus as disciples. Transformation with Jesus draws us inward so we can discover what it is like to be more human, more *truly* human, like we were designed to be. A transformed life is grounded in our own identity as dearly beloved children of God, free of the voices of shame and free for the championing of others. It sounds nice, but much of the time, following Jesus's example and voice disorients. Like a person on a boat that is moving side to side, we stumble to and fro, seeking solid footing so we can take the next best step toward Jesus. In the process, our moment arrives!

We, like the disciples, are to become people with the capacity to fish well for others, just as Jesus fished for them that day. May we champion others with urgency because the moment to become more human like Jesus is right now.

This is hard, as hard as stepping on shore after a long day on the water. It also brings hope for living to our full potential as people made in God's image in this often painful world. Jesus doesn't leave us where we are when we give ourselves to his invitation to follow him. We have a lifetime of failure and success to grow into new kinds of people. He offers grace when we mess up and joy that is hard to express with words. And the beautiful thing is that with Jesus, we are championed to truly experience interior transformation so we can hold our pain as though hope echoes through the ages to meet us in this very moment. Jesus gives us hope that pain won't have the power to define us but can be used to refine us.

FORMATION EXERCISE

In life, many of us are blessed to know people who champion us, who remind us that we aren't alone. Jesus calls disciples and champions them. He sees something in them and invites them to step into the transformational journey. No matter the nature of our pain or struggles, we can step into the battles of life differently when others—including Jesus—come alongside us at critical points in our journeys.

Journal: Begin a list of people who championed you throughout the years. It might help to list them chronologically. After each name, write down one sentence describing how that person championed you.

Pray: Invite Jesus into a time of prayer over each name, in a posture of gratitude.

Share: Consider reaching out to the people on your list, either through a written note or a conversation, to tell them what they've meant to you.

Part Three

AN ECHOING HOPE FOR REAL LIFE

Real life isn't tidy. Often we can't easily make sense of our pain. Clarity about such things often eludes, so we only "see in a mirror, dimly" (1 Corinthians 13:12, NRSV). Sometimes it takes unforeseen disruptions to open our eyes to the depths of what is real.

Real life with Jesus requires owning the parts of our lives that we're tempted to ignore, neglect, or keep hidden so he can guide us to become more like him. This starts by inviting Jesus to transform our interior lives so that whatever comes our way, we can meet it with courage and grace.

CHAPTER 9

LOVE IN ADVANCE

*   *   *

*If Jesus is Lord, then Caesar is not, politics are not, power is not,
economics are not, religion is not, fame is not, fashion is not,
appearance is not, food is not, fitness is not, friends are not, and
family is not. . . . When we put everything else infinitely second
and come to Jesus as our everything, he sends us back into the
world as better versions of ourselves.*

—BRUXY CAVEY, *Reunion*

The church needs peacemakers who are growing in their capacity to respond to violence and insults with creative love
that is cultivated in the quiet spaces of their spiritual houses.
In the winter of 2014, I spent a couple of weeks in Israel/Palestine
with a great organization called the Global Immersion Project, led
by my friends Jon Huckins and Jer Swigart.* We had a dual purpose on this trip: learn about the ancient context of Jesus and
learn about the modern context in which conflict between Arabs
and Jews is intense. We spent several sessions learning from both
Israeli and Palestinian peacemakers.

Although I don't have time to offer a long history here, it's important to note that since 1948, Israel has occupied Palestine in
some form or another. Today, occupation looks like separation
walls, such as between Israel and the West Bank and between Is-

---

* You really should read their book, *Mending the Divides: Creative Love in a
Conflicted World* (Downers Grove, IL: InterVarsity, 2017). They frame the conflict in Israel/Palestine with wisdom and grace. They also are some of the most
helpful teachers of peacemaking I know.

rael and Gaza, and fresh-out-of-high-school soldiers with heavy machine guns—most of whom have never spoken to a Palestinian prior to being given such power. As you can imagine, the situation is tense on both sides, and most of the tension is driven by one thing: fear. Since choosing a side is folly in peacemaking, we chose to seek out stories on both sides of the walls, from both Palestinians and Israelis.

One of the peacemakers we got to know on our trip to Israel/ Palestine was Daoud Nassar, founder of Tent of Nations. His Palestinian Christian family has owned the same hill in the West Bank since 1916! In fact, this is the last Palestinian-owned hill—anywhere. They have the ownership papers to prove it, tracing back all the way to the Ottoman Empire. Nassar's family has been in court with Israel since 1991. Through seasons of persecution—military vehicles coming on the property and bearing a threatening presence, Israeli settlers coming with guns and acting out in violence, olive trees being torn down, the family being unable to get building permits and running water, and more—they have maintained this slogan: "We refuse to be enemies."

They are, in a beautiful sense, what Jesus was getting at when he talked about being "a city on top of a hill" (Matthew 5:14) by refusing hatred and instead choosing to "love [their] enemies" (verse 44). They encourage both cultivating an inward heart of love with Jesus and doing projects with him. Tent of Nations teaches about peacemaking, hosts creative camps for children, cultivates the land through eco-friendly means, and develops methods for harnessing power and water since the government refuses to give them access to such necessities.

On top of this, when they are persecuted, they choose to go through the legal system—tilted against them—to humbly expose injustice while loving their oppressors! Sounds a lot like the person who gives both shirt and cloak in the courtroom rather than retaliating (verse 40)! They model something Jesus clearly taught in the Sermon on the Mount: that love of enemies is central to the message of the kingdom of God. For Daoud and his family, how they react to persecution reflects the God they serve. The Sermon on the Mount feeds their imagination on how to represent Jesus in hostile circumstances.

The Sermon on the Mount (Matthew 5–7) is Jesus's manifesto for an upside-down world. Pair its teachings with the "greatest commandment" (22:36–40) and we can boil down everything Jesus taught into three instructions: *love God, love neighbors,* and *love enemies.* If we allow ourselves to be formed by Jesus, and if we thereby allow ourselves to be challenged by him, when we face our pain or the pain of others, we will have a surprising capacity for echoing hope in our world. Neglecting our heart and soul will give our hurts too much power over us. Neglecting the challenging words of Jesus will give our hurts too much power over others. To become like Jesus, we spend time with him and open ourselves up to being transformed into his likeness.

> *To become like Jesus, we spend time with him and open ourselves up to being transformed into his likeness.*

Our Interior Formation

If we want to hold pain and injustice like Jesus would, we need his wisdom and grace to transform the innermost parts of us. I need more of that. My guess is so do you. That sort of transformation is what makes it possible for us to refuse to be enemies or to live out any other teaching in the Sermon on the Mount. In Matthew 6, we have several examples of people who on the outside have it together but are disintegrated in the interior of their souls. The first verse of the chapter sets up what follows: "Beware of practicing your *piety* before others in order to be seen by them; for then you have no reward from your Father in heaven" (NRSV).

The ancient Greek word translated as "piety" here has a range of meanings, from "righteousness" to "justice" to "good deeds." It's a word about things being made right. (Sound familiar? I hear an echo of *shalom.*) Jesus was essentially saying, "Don't do good things to get the credit from others. Rather, do them as the outflow of the goodness of God in your life. Don't spend all your time focusing on the *exterior;* give yourself to the *interior* work of transformation." Why? Because outside behavior flows from what is in us.

And what is in us, in response to all sorts of pain, so often is *shame.*

UNDERSTANDING THE POWER OF SHAME

Let's get into the way worldviews shape people for a minute. In Western cultures, we tend to think of guilt versus innocence more naturally than Eastern cultures, who think in terms of shame versus honor.* Dallas Willard critiqued Western Christianity's application of these categories with the phrase "gospel of sin management."[1] Jesus certainly understood guilt and innocence, but he primarily taught about the way of the kingdom with a keen attention on shame and honor. Non-Eastern people certainly deal with honor-shame dynamics, but we will notice a key difference: individualism versus collectivism.

Okay. Stay with me. This is important for understanding basically everything we read about Jesus in the Bible. In most Eastern contexts, both ancient and modern, "Honor is essentially when other people think highly of you and want to be associated with you."[2] The opposite of honor in these settings can be described as shame, which "means other people think lowly of you and do not want to be with you."[3] To understand the Bible, these insights are invaluable! But then we need to try to build a bridge from the experience of those in the Bible to how many Westerners experience the world.

---

* Here, it is important to say that when discussing Eastern and Western worldviews, I do so as one fully conditioned by my Western lens. Where I describe this less than adequately, I ask for grace from my Eastern friends. Also, it needs to be said that although Western societies can be spoken of generally—as I do here—we need to acknowledge that numerous communities of Eastern origin exist within North America, and they likely do not so neatly fit a this-or-that approach to these worldviews.

The most helpful person for this is Brené Brown, who described shame as "the intensely painful feeling or experience of believing that we are flawed and therefore unworthy of love and belonging."[4] While the two worldviews likely overlap in people, Jayson Georges and Mark Baker bring some important clarity:

> Western shame is more *private* and *personal,* centered on the individual and his or her internal feelings. Eastern shame is *public* and *communal,* resulting from *others'* negative evaluation and community reputation. . . . The antonym of shame in Western societies tends to be *self-esteem*—"I think highly about myself." The opposite of Eastern shame is *honor*—"others respect me."[5]

Jesus's passion is to free us from shame of all sorts. Jesus will, over and over again, tell people who are of low status that the system has been upended. Slaves and free, men and women, rich and poor, sinners and saints—all are worthy of honor. Jesus, in fact, redefines honor altogether.

THE GREAT REVERSAL OF SHAME

Turning back to Matthew 6 with ancient Eastern spectacles, we can notice Jesus's teachings on doing good and pious deeds in private with an eye and ear for honor-shame dynamics. What do you do if you want to gain honor in a communal culture? You have to be visible doing honorable things. No wonder Jesus called this out by warning about displaying "piety" to be "seen by them," "praised by others," "seen by others," and to "show others" (verses 1–2, 5, 16, NRSV).

Taken together, these statements against pursuing public praise exemplify the desire for honor built into this culture. Jesus said there is no honor in seeking honor! In fact, the quest for exterior honor is the problem Jesus addressed here and throughout the whole Sermon on the Mount. It might not be clear in some sections, but the theme of seeking honor permeates Matthew 5–7 and beyond. For instance, defending one's honor might typically mean fighting back when you are hit. Jesus says don't be typical. Be a peacemaker by becoming the kind of person who loves and prays for enemies.

Jesus's desire for human flourishing requires that the system of honor-shame dynamics be inverted. No wonder he can say elsewhere that the last will be first and the first will be last (Matthew 19:30; also see Matthew 20:16; Mark 10:31; Luke 13:30). In Jesus, honor is redefined! In Jesus, the interior posture of our lives is the space from which we can live like him in the world. We love people; therefore, from where we stand, we become incapable of being enemies to them (regardless whether they treat us as enemies).

OUR TRANSFORMATIONAL AIM MAKES ALL THE DIFFERENCE

Jesus knows that the problem with shame and honor is where we place our transformational aim. That's why he flips the very definition of honor on its head. Honor in and of itself isn't the problem. It isn't as though Jesus wants the opposite—shame—for people.[6] Rather, when our aim is outward, the inward self grows tired (Have you ever been tired from doing too much?), cynical (Have you ever found yourself criticizing others who have it easier than you?), and in the worst cases, corrupted (like the leaders who fail in integrity). Then, of course, there's the need we think we have to manage things. All of which aim at the wrong transformational target.

- *Sin management* (what I can't do) manages to keep us locked in legalism while avoiding the pain that exists in the gray spaces of our lives.
- *Morality management* (what I must do) keeps checklists to mask the shame we'd rather not admit to.
- *Justice management* (what I must fix) serves our holy egos better than it serves the causes we'd take up. (Of course, doing justice matters for the sake of others, but how much more transformative would it be if we made it the outflow of who we are?)

The only thing that manages to free us from the shame of these unruly managers is an inward liberation that takes place over the course of a lifetime, with Jesus himself. Mystical as that may be, it's the core of Christian formation. Even in the midst of hurts, questions, and challenges of various sorts, this sort of inward virtue formation will give you the resolve to step into those situations with a profound sense of humanity that only Jesus can offer.

When we aim for inward transformation with Jesus, a development of Christlike character and a deep relationship to him, this allows the exterior of our lives to manifest good deeds as though it is second nature. In fact, if we want our lives to look like the exteriors in the Sermon on the Mount—if we want to be people characterized by peacemaking, loving even our enemies, treating our spouses with dignity, enduring hardships, serving the poor and advocating for the marginalized, living simply and free from worry, choosing love over judgment, mentoring others as models of Christian character and devotion, and worshipping God with fellow image bearers within our faith communities—then Jesus says go to your room.

> When you pray, go to your room, shut the door, and pray to your Father who is present in that secret place. Your Father who sees what you do in secret will reward you. (Matthew 6:6)

The transformation needed to become like Jesus takes place in the inner room of our spiritual home. It's not flashy. It doesn't draw attention to itself. This is about directing our aim inward so that our identity of honor comes directly from God's loving work within us.* Jesus says the interior of our spiritual house needs to be cleaned up and brought before him, and the outside will take care of itself. Reflecting on the Sermon on the Mount, Dallas Wil-

---

* I'm not saying that exterior things have no transformative power. They absolutely do! This is why the spiritual disciplines include both private meditation and communal worship and both giving to the poor in secret and serving the poor food and drink in public. However, the means through which God changes us corresponds directly to how we open up our interior to Jesus so that the work doesn't replace the formation of character.

lard wrote something that continues to free me from the unruly managers of shame:

> Jesus never expected us simply to turn the other cheek, go the second mile, bless those who persecute us, give unto them that ask, and so forth. These responses, generally and rightly understood to be characteristic of Christlikeness, were put forth by him as illustrative of what might be expected of a new kind of person. . . .
>
> Instead, Jesus did invite people to follow him into that sort of life from which behavior such as loving one's enemies will seem like the only sensible and happy thing to do. For a person living that life, the hard thing to do would be to hate the enemy, to turn the supplicant away, or to curse the curser. . . . True Christlikeness, true companionship with Christ, comes at the point where it is hard not to respond as he would.[7]

Jesus sets people up for human flourishing by teaching them that inward formation with God helps us respond to life the way Christ would himself! The invitation of the Sermon on the Mount is to redefine honor as that which comes from God alone. We can become "a new kind of person" who is identified as God's dearly beloved, deconstructing our shame labels and reconstructing our intrinsic value. Jesus is the great liberator from shame because he redefines it completely. Honor and shame have been flipped upside down!

Inward formation with God helps us respond to life the way Christ would himself!

Jesus's Challenging Words

We learn to respond like Jesus when we learn to both follow his example *and* live life with him in friendship on a personal level. It can't just be one or the other. As an example to explore, think about one of the most challenging commands in the Sermon on the Mount. In Matthew 5:44, Jesus invited his disciples into a countercultural teaching: "Love your enemies and pray for those who harass you."

Notice how love and prayer connect the internal and external parts of life. Love is something that is generated in the deepest places of our souls where God forms our character to look more like Jesus. And it doesn't stay in the abstract. When Jesus said that his disciples are to "turn the other cheek"—an external—it's the second-nature response that "comes at the point where it is hard not to respond as he would." Which begs the question, How would Jesus respond?

According to the apostle Peter, Jesus modeled his own advice to us. In fact, Peter directed this teaching to people in the harshest conditions imaginable: slaves. As Dennis Edwards said, "The slaves needed to be encouraged that even in their miserable place in society, God would honor their ability to follow the example of Jesus."[8] Instead of trying to preserve his honor by overpowering the Romans, Jesus *showed* what he had *told*. His inward disposition of trust in God shaped his response to his enemies:

> If you suffer for doing good and you endure it, this is commendable before God. To this you were called, because Christ suffered for you, leaving you an example, that you should follow in his steps. . . . When they hurled their insults at him, he did not retaliate; when he suffered, he made no threats. Instead, he entrusted himself to him who judges justly. (1 Peter 2:20–21, 23, NIV)

Jesus demonstrated a life so saturated in the love of God that even in the most shamed moment of his life, he didn't seek to avenge himself or reclaim his cultural honor. Jesus lived his teachings. In the end, he did this by allowing his shalom-shaped image-bearing identity to lead him to the cross. He *died* for his enemies and *never* retaliated. Violence never came from his hands or lips. He left us "an example" to "follow in his steps" of nonviolent love for enemies, driven by the trust we have in God. Jesus practiced love in advance so he could live out love on the spot. So, how do we do what he did?

PRACTICING LOVE IN ADVANCE

To practice love in advance is to practice peacemaking *before* conflicts surprise us. When Jesus grows our inward character, we are better prepared for life's battles—big and small. Honor is an identity as a beloved one of God, not something to prove by getting everything right.

The first-century Jewish situation differs from ours in so many ways. However, the practice of love in advance, even for enemies, has massive payoffs in regular life. I'm going to be blunt here: how we define *regular* is important. Nothing is regular, really. What is taken for granted by some, such as a general sense of personal safety, is a mere utopian dream for others. Even so, if Jesus, as a marginalized Palestinian Jew, could invite his first-century followers into this posture, I can imagine him inviting us all to receive this invitation in ways true to our contexts—and for the sake of others.

For some of us, resorting to physical violence is rarely a temptation. But let's be honest: Have you ever been angry at someone and said, "I'd like to punch that guy in the face!"? What about the person who tries to pass you on a dangerous road after tailgating you like a jerk? Do you feel the impulse to speed up and make the pass more dangerous? We have responded this way many times when our inward peace is tested by moments of outward chaos. Jesus teaches that we can cultivate love so we will respond with love.

I remember a couple of years ago when my kiddo was having a tantrum in Target. It was awful. After some loving words inviting her to understand that she couldn't have everything pink and sparkly from aisle 36, *she lost it.* On the ground. Arms and legs swinging. Yelling. Mom and Dad, apparently, were *the worst*. Our honor had left the building.

When I told her we needed to go back to the car, she refused. I had to pick her up and take her out of the store, still kicking and screaming. I worried people would think I had kidnapped her. Partway across the parking lot, my kiddo hit me in the face a few times, eventually causing my glasses to fall off. No doubt, my self-preservation instincts rose up within me momentarily, but they passed as God gave me the courage to tell her I loved her during it all.

I truly believe that one major reason I didn't respond with yelling or worse was that God had prepared me with love so I wouldn't retaliate. This clearly is a different sort of example, considering that my daughter isn't my enemy, but in intense emotional moments, humans have the propensity to lose sight of who's a friend and who's a foe. We naturally overemphasize the wrong done to us and minimize the impact of our retaliation. Things keep escalating.

This is hard. Really hard. Opening ourselves up to the peace of Christ isn't easy in a pain-filled world. An eye for an eye intuitively feels like justice when we've been wronged. But that sort of justice isn't restorative for you or the person who wronged you. It seeks to correct a wrong with the very sort of wrong that was already named clearly as *wrong*. Jesus shows us there is another way that doesn't involve us trying to restore our honor by violently shaming the other person.

REFUSING TO DEHUMANIZE

Matthew 5 is one of the places in the New Testament where peacemaking is explicitly taught.[9] For example, Jesus taught that we are not to return a backhand strike to the right side of our face but to offer the left side as well. This is an act of asserting one's humanity without resorting to dehumanizing violence. The person who just gave you a backhand as though you are an inferior now has to decide if he will hit you with a closed fist—a sign of fighting an equal foe. Jesus showed his first-century listeners (and us) that when we are shamed, we can assert our image-bearing honor! This is one of several examples Jesus gave for loving enemies and resisting them without using violence.

Love involves actions (I *do* things that are loving) and an inward posture (I *value* this image bearer of God). One without the other is less than Jesus's vision for each of us to become more fully human like him. You might not be convinced of nonviolence, as I am, but maybe you can agree with this: *Jesus teaches that all his followers are called to be peacemakers.* In hypothetical scenarios, where we might bring up Hitler or other abusers of innocent people, you and I might have differing ways to get in the way of evil. (And believe me, I have a lot of opinions about abusers and definitely do not promote passive acceptance of violence done by perpetrators.) I highly encourage you to think about the call to be peacemakers as existing on a continuum rather than the either/or choice of passivity versus warmongering.* The world is messy. Let's together do all we can to constantly invite the transformative peace of Jesus to shape and prepare us to love others—even those who seek to cause us pain. In this spirit, think about where you currently land on a few spectrums I've mapped out:†

---

* I believe that nonviolence is the teaching of Jesus and the early church for all Christians. However, I have many friends who disagree or agree in principle but modify what it means in practice. This is my attempt to build common ground so we can love the world like Jesus. As an example, one of my best friends (we were in each other's wedding parties) is a California highway patrol officer. I respect him as a man of integrity and faith. He also believes Jesus calls us to be peacemakers but finds himself in a slightly different place on this continuum. I question his theology (and he, mine) on this matter, but I'd never question his commitment to Jesus. We just happen to apply Jesus's teachings a little differently.

† These "continuums" are here to get us thinking and not to represent the options perfectly. My own perspective is held in holy tension with my John 17 conviction that before we are right on secondary issues we are called to be one. That said, my view is that "violent roles aren't a Christian option," "nonviolence as resistance" is the only justifiable option, and violence begins with "violent

When Is Violence Justified for Christians? (Roles)

├─ ┤

[violent roles aren't a Christian option]   [civilian violence as restraint   [local police officer]   [military]   [rogue militia]
in limited cases]

When Is Violence Justified for Christians? (Reasons)

├─ ┤

[nonviolence as resistance]   [force to restrain violent   [violence for local   [classic just war]   [violence for national   ["holy" war]
offenders]   safety as police]   interests]

What Counts as Violence?

├─ ┤

[anger expressed through actions: [physical restraint—   [violent force to deescalate—   [weapons and death]
"cleansing the Temple"]   holds, tackles, etc.]   fist fight, etc.]

By the way, *my bringing up peacemaking in this section is strategic.* I do believe it is central to Jesus's mission, message, and model. But to boil it all down, it simply makes sense. Paul called peace a fruit of the Spirit (Galatians 5:22–23). Develop peace in advance by getting to know Jesus. Then go express that inward virtue in visible ways to liberate others from pain and help you hold your pain in a different way. But that isn't the only area where this inward-outward, true honor works itself out against shameful forces. Think about these:

────────────

force to deescalate." On this last point, it seems clear to me that Jesus invites his followers to nonviolently resist oppressors in Matthew 5 in ways that assert their humanity. Anything that crosses the line into dehumanizing seems to be what Jesus might define as violence. Of course, this is a much bigger conversation that I invite you to explore using the resources I recommended.

PASSAGE	COMMON OUTWARD WISDOM (CULTURAL HONOR)	JESUS'S INWARD CHALLENGE (CHRISTLIKE HONOR)	FRUIT OF THE SPIRIT (GALATIANS 5:22–23)
Matthew 5:21–22	Don't murder	Keep your anger in check	Patience
Matthew 5:27–28	Don't cheat on your spouse	Deal with your lust	Self-Control
Matthew 5:31–32	Divorce is no big deal as long as you formalize it	Check your motives for divorce against your selfishness[10]	Gentleness/Love
Matthew 5:33–37	Keep your oaths	Don't make oaths; be known by your honesty	Goodness
Matthew 5:38–42	Get even	Stop the cycle of revenge by choosing peace	Peace
Matthew 5:43–47	Love people like you; hate enemies	Love enemies	Love
Matthew 6:1–4	Showy giving	Give quietly; be honored by God	Faithfulness
Matthew 6:5–8	Fancy prayers for the crowds	Spend time alone with God	Faithfulness
Matthew 6:16–18	Pious fasting to make a holy scene	Fasting to be alone with God	Faithfulness
Matthew 6:19–21	Hoarding wealth	A heart for kingdom treasure	Kindness
Matthew 6:25–34	Worry and fear	Trust God and seek the kingdom	Joy (contentment)

Matthew 7:1–5	Judge others to keep things in line	Give yourself to holy self-examination	Self-Control
Matthew 7:13–14	Take the popular path	Become someone capable of taking the unpopular path	Goodness/Self-Control
Matthew 7:15–27	Say and do things to keep up appearances	Put the example and teaching of Jesus first to persevere through the storms of life	Faithfulness

That list is my attempt to show that peacemaking as an inward character attribute adopted from Christ, which leads to nonretaliation, is one of many examples of how Jesus longs to form our character. You know, it might be a great list to pray through, one by one, as a way to connect with Jesus and become human like him. The echoing hope of the empty tomb looks like people fully alive as they grow to know (inward) and follow (outward) Jesus, free from shame and empowered by love. Then we will learn what it is to respond like Jesus and will respond that way as though it is second nature. When it comes to peacemaking, love leads us to honor people who dishonor us.

Refuse to Be Enemies

At the Tent of Nations, the last legally owned Palestinian hill in the West Bank, the Nassar family has endured numerous incidents of shaming by the authorities. Yet they continue to proclaim, "We refuse to be enemies." Cultivating inward love from God and expressing it in outward ways is a daily practice for them.

Palestinian people have had several responses to the Israeli occupation. One option is to embrace that the only hope left is violence. But, as I've heard Daoud say in person, "Violence only creates more violence." Inspired by Jesus and the early church, and secondarily by Dr. Martin Luther King Jr. and Gandhi, they are choosing a path that cuts through passivity and violence: nonviolent resistance. They've committed to turning the cheek to assert that they are image bearers by exposing the injustices of the legal system, going above and beyond (the "extra mile") to show that their oppressors can't determine the terms of engagement, giving generously, and demonstrating love to their enemies (Matthew 5:38–45). But how does anyone do that in an ongoing way? I'd be exhausted. Done. Give me a sword; I'm over this, Jesus.

As our group sat down and listened to Daoud's story, his numerous examples of persevering through hardship blew us away. After his casual presentation, we had a time for questions and responses. A question came up about how to deal with anger. Daoud's response was one of the most important things I learned on this trip: "For us, our therapy is that when we are frustrated, we start thinking about a new project. We channel this pain to be invested."

He went on to offer an example of this shift in energy. When they saw that Gaza was being bombed (which they could actually see from their hilltop property), they invested that anger into building a new cistern. Daoud explained, "By evening we are tired. There is no room to hate."

Some might wonder if this is simply a method for denying emotions. Rather, this is a chance to redirect anger in such a way as to put it to humanizing projects. This type of shift might actually be a way to prevent us from dehumanizing the other party, even if they are the oppressors in the situation. Daoud added, "We are not running away from our problems, but it is a way to keep the positive spirit. When we focus on our vision, we don't see our daily problems as huge problems. We see them as small obstacles."

Daoud's nugget of wisdom offers us a model for dealing with anger and shame, both in the small things and in the big. We can either allow injustice to lead us down the dark road of hatred and dehumanization or follow the path through our anger into creating good. Daoud invites us to put this approach to the test: What would it look like for you to partner with like-minded people to turn frustration into fruition? If we use Daoud's method, we may just find that glimpses of Jesus begin to emerge in some of the direst of situations. Although Daoud's family is shamed on a regular basis, they remain a beacon of God's honor, radiating love from a hill to the southwest of Jesus's birth town of Bethlehem.

I don't know what it would be like to daily remind myself, "We refuse to be enemies," in a situation like the Nassar family's. Their example of perseverance in the midst of pain and persecution inspires me to transform anger into the work of making peace. Processed anger and injustice exhaled with the love of Jesus gives birth to resilient creativity for peacemaking. When you know you are loved by God, refusing to fight with supposed enemies—as Jesus showed us—is part of the growth process of becoming more fully human. The interior, that space where we go to be with God, is where we are energized to live a life like Jesus. That space is where true honor is discovered.

FORMATION EXERCISE

Before anything else, Jesus desires to reshape the interior of our lives. We might call this virtue or character formation, but ultimately it involves getting to know Jesus personally so that responding to situations as he would becomes second nature.

Option one: Read the Sermon on the Mount (Matthew 5–7), which takes about fifteen minutes if you read out loud. Take note of every teaching that has an explicit or an implied internal application. For instance, "love your enemies" is about how we treat enemies but also about how we love them in advance. What qualities of the Jesus way might you want Jesus to cultivate within you? Name them in prayer and reflection.

Option two: Read Galatians 5:16–26 and then draw out a chart with each fruit of the Spirit (verses 22–23) listed in a vertical column on the left. To the right, ponder how you might cultivate each of these with Jesus. Take each fruit/virtue to Jesus in a time of prayer and meditation. How might Jesus invite you to grow in these areas? How might you practice each fruit/virtue in advance?

CHAPTER 10

TRAMPLING FEAR

* * *

Fear may be powerful if we give it energy through our thinking,
feeling, and choosing, but it is important to remember that love is
much more powerful and our brains were made to operate in love.

—DR. CAROLINE LEAF, *The Perfect You*

W hen I was a high school junior, my football team went
out to the wilderness for a short retreat. This was to
prepare us for a season of playing ball together. It really
was a powerful bonding experience. Team building exercises included rappelling, rock climbing, and rock jumping. For the record, these are three of my least favorite pastimes! Falling from
high things is the worst. I was already shaken up from rappelling
down a cliff, and then it was time for the grand finale: jumping
fifty feet off a cliff into the water.

Here's the thing: I've always had a love-hate relationship with
water. When I was in fourth grade, I was the one kid in class who
couldn't swim. I had ear issues when I was young, so spending time
in the water was rare. I was around world-class swimmers on a
regular basis. My late uncle, Dennis, was a record-breaking swim-
mer in our area. I had gone to swim meets since I was small to
cheer him on. Yet I couldn't swim. There I was at the end-of-the-
year pool party, ten years old, and a mom at the party brought out
bright and bold arm floaties. Embarrassed is an understatement.*

---

* I know that this mom was just trying to make sure I could participate. But . . .
Well, it makes for a funny story now.

Years later, I found myself at the edge of a cliff. One after another, my friends leaped off the ledge for pure joy. Of course, they were careful not to leap too far out and hit the cliff in front of them. They also understood that they had to jump out far enough to actually land in water. This didn't seem to be a big concern to anyone but me (oh yeah, and one other guy).

By the time the end of the line had come, everyone was in the water, cheering us on. It was terrifying and embarrassing all over again. But even though I felt that with each passing moment, my chaotic fear of the water below was overtaking my pride, I eventually mustered up the little courage within me and jumped. I survived for the sole purpose of writing this book.

Clearly, my relationship with water is a mixed bag. I like showers. I tend to drink about eight cups of water each day. But in certain situations, water has provoked fear. My experience isn't unlike that of the ancient Jewish people. As we will see, they associated water with fear in some ways as well.

Fear Is Real

As an adult, fear takes on different forms. For example, I have an irrational fear of wasps. When I pull into my driveway, I park far away from the tree the stinging insects love to hover around. I found out last summer that the talk of the neighborhood was why I parked at the front of our driveway by the street. *Well,* I wanted to shout up and down the street, *it's because I experience nearly pathological terror when I so much as see a yellow jacket!* Even innocent little honeybees (although less terrifying than their more aggressive cousins) have a similar effect when they are in my space. (Once, when I was on a relief trip with Mennonite Disaster Service in college, I was sitting in a parked van when a bee flew into the vehicle and up my baggy basketball shorts. Let's just say that the searing soprano I unleashed reached truly *operatic* vocal heights.)

So, yeah. Wasps. I wish my fear stopped there, but it doesn't. I sometimes fear conflict, and my instinct is to avoid hard conversations (why *yes*, that *is* thoroughly connected to my childhood). Sometimes I fear I'm failing as a father and husband. Other fears on the list? Hmm.

- finances
- failure
- almost reaching my potential but not quite
- not being liked enough by others
- losing my hair

I could go on. You probably would have quite a list too, if you were honest. In a world of brokenness, fear is natural and not something to be judged. Yet when we look at the teachings of Jesus, we find that fear is something that can be managed and, sometimes, overcome.

And don't we want that? Of course we do. Fear holds us back from our potential. I don't always love that pressure-inducing word, but potential and hope have lots in common. They both point toward what could be. Fear, put in its proper place, invites us to explore the possibilities beyond it.

The Gospels tell us stories about the calming of a storm in Mark 4:35–41 and Jesus and Peter walking on water in 6:45–52. Immediately after the storm is calmed, Mark records a story about a man who has multiple demons (5:1–20). We will look at that story in the next chapter.

The Sea Is Evil

In order to understand the intensity of these two stories involving traveling on the Sea of Galilee by boat, we need to jump into the worldview of first-century Jewish people. I'd sum up their sentiment as, "When you are out at sea, bad things can happen to you." So much so that the sea becomes, in multiple places in the Bible, a metaphor for danger and horror. The sea was considered practically demonic to ancient Jews—the domain of monsters.[*]

If you've ever been out at sea, you know the power of a wave and the untamed depths of the ocean. The risk of sailing in the ancient world was exponentially greater than today. I've seen both the Sea of Galilee and the Mediterranean. They are glorious. But with bad weather conditions and a first-century boat, I think I'd be scared out of my wits. Even in Genesis 1, the creation liturgy says that the Spirit of God was hovering over the deep chaotic waters (verse 2). These waters had to be tamed by God in the creation process so that land had a separate space to thrive. Throughout the Scriptures we see examples of God pushing against evil as depicted by the waters of the sea. Here's a sampling:[1]

- Psalm 104:7: "At your rebuke they [the waters] ran away." This is not talking about low tide at the beach. Without God raising a hand, the waters scampered away and were defeated.
- Psalm 89:9–10: God rules "over the surging sea" and "crushed Rahab [a sea monster]."
- Psalm 74:13: God "split the sea with . . . power. . . . [God] shattered the heads of the sea monsters."

Have you ever wondered why it was so important that the Hebrew people cross through the sea at God's initiative? Well, in parting the waters, God was seen as pushing back evil! In other places, such as Daniel 7, the beasts that emerge from the sea represent the spiritual forces that give power to evil empires. The sea is where demonic monsters and chaos are found.

---

[*] That's why at the end of the Bible, the writer of Revelation made a point about God's renewed creation: "There was no longer any sea" (21:1, NIV). When God is "all in all" (1 Corinthians 15:28), the sea will no longer exist. (Remember that this is a metaphor for demonic evil. I imagine that the restored world will have beautiful beaches.)

JESUS AND THE STORM

The sea as a place of evil is the background for an important story in the life of Jesus. He got on a boat with the disciples on the Sea of Galilee. A storm hit and the disciples were terrified. But Jesus had gone missing. He wasn't there, so where was he? He was "sleeping on a pillow." Exactly where you want God in the flesh to be: napping. So, in their horror, "they woke him up and said, 'Teacher, don't you care that we're drowning?'" (Mark 4:38).

The first thought you should have is, *How could Jesus sleep through that?* I can barely sleep when my kids come into our bed in the middle of the night, let alone at sea in a storm! Now, if you don't have problems staying asleep, maybe you are on your way to becoming more like Jesus than you might have thought. Good for you. After this, Jesus ordered the storm and lake, "Silence! Be still!" (verse 39).

Notice that Jesus wanted his disciples to have full trust in him. His response, after things calmed down, was, "Why are you frightened? Don't you have faith yet?" (verse 40). *Faith* in ancient Greek doesn't refer only to cognitive beliefs about God but is a relational word that means trust or fidelity or allegiance.[2] Jesus wanted them to grow in their trust so that even tossing waves and blowing winds would not shake them to the point of fear. Of course, fear is a natural response and isn't something Jesus would want to weaponize in order to shame anyone. Rather, he wants to help all of us notice our fear and bring it into conversation with our God, who can be trusted. The disciples' transformation at this point in the life of Jesus was important because this wasn't the only storm they would face. They would confront fear again.

JESUS, ARE YOU ASLEEP?

Have you ever had a situation that truly terrified you? As an adult, these are hard to admit. But let's be real for a moment. If you have ever wondered how you were going to make ends meet, you've been afraid. If you have ever loved someone who was suffering or dying, you know what fear is. Fear is real. Even as a kid, you likely faced fearful circumstances. In our journey together through this book, I've shared some of my hardest childhood moments of pain. If we were in a coffee shop, sipping espresso, I'm sure you'd have your own tales to tell. You have unique stories of pain and fear, without a doubt.

When I was a child, fear was a dominant emotion. Those years of domestic violence kept fear front and center when the abusive boyfriend was around. At one point, he moved in with us. This kept fear almost constant. I believe I was between five and six. The exact timeline is a bit blurry, but the fear I experienced remains clear. Our live-in abuser had times when things seemed to level out. His promises to drink less, hit less, and try harder embedded him further into our lives. Worry was constant. How I survived with a basic sense of self is a miracle in and of itself. Good people plus a loving God: honestly, that is all I can credit.

At one point, his coercive ego manipulated Mom into putting my bed in the corner of the living/dining room area (near where a table might go in some home layouts). For what must have been months, I slept outside my room, separated from that part of the house by a pocket door each night. My room, if memory serves correctly, ended up being a place for his workout equipment and personal items.

It was made clear that I was not under any circumstances to open the door to the hallway during the night. Disturbing him was not an option. I was instructed that once I was in bed, I was to stay there. Having been physically abused by him already on various occasions and having witnessed him beating my mom, I wasn't moving. I was so afraid. Looking back at situations like this, I'm tempted to ask, *Jesus, were you asleep? Were you aloof to the painful storms that raged inside my home?*[*]

---

[*] My Lydia is six as I record this story. One thing my wife and I have tried to do is create a household ethos where fear doesn't exist—at least relationally. I wish I could will away the bad dreams and anxious thoughts that come to her, but I cannot. However, she knows that she is safe with us and unconditionally loved. I imagine that Chloe, just over one year old, will share a similar sense of safety.

Fear overtook me to the point where I had a dilemma one evening. As I recall, it must have been around dawn. No one would be up for a couple of hours, and I had to go to the bathroom. My instructions were clear: "Do not get up and come through that door for any reason until after we are all awake." I followed directions, not knowing whether the choice I was making was the right one.

When I could hold it no longer, I defecated on myself on that mattress in the dining room. I still remember the thin light-colored blanket covered in dry streaks of human feces as Mom got me out of bed and cleaned up the mess. She wasn't angry at me. She offered nothing but love. She, as I recall, was furious at her boyfriend and ashamed that I was afraid to get up. In a moment of strength, Mom made sure the live-in abuser personally came to me and reformed the policy. Oddly, it is one of the more sensible moments I remember with him as he clarified the rule with a kinder demeanor.

No child should live in fear. I'm not alone. Perhaps you have stories that are the source of pain, shame, or other negative feelings. I'm sorry. It isn't right. Know above all else that you are loved—all of you, even with those painful memories. God saw everything and wept. Jesus still weeps over the suffering in this world. He isn't asleep and ignoring our struggles. He's with us in them.

JESUS AND PETER ON THE SEA

Our second story out at sea takes place two chapters later in Mark's gospel. Remembering that the sea is a place of chaos and evil, we shouldn't be surprised by the fear put on display. I mean, the disciples were once again on a boat, and a storm was blowing in all over again! Yeah, I know what you're thinking: *No worries. If I were a disciple on the boat, I'd know that Jesus was going to kick this demonic sea storm's butt!* Except for this detail: "Evening came and the boat was in the middle of the lake, but he was alone on the land" (6:47). Jesus was not on the boat! This was not good. Jesus "saw his disciples struggling," so "he came to them, walking on the

---

My compassion for my childhood self has exponentially increased as I parent a kiddo who is the age of that little boy.

lake" (verse 48)—as one does. Upon seeing him, the disciples "thought he was a ghost and they screamed" (verse 49). It's no wonder they were afraid; they thought they'd seen some sort of evil spirit. The sea is demonic—they'd expect that sort of thing!

Clearly, "seeing him was terrifying," so he calmed them down by saying, "Be encouraged! It's me" (verse 50). All good. No need to fear; Jesus is here. Mark's version of the story ends with Jesus getting in the boat, which was enough to settle down the winds and waves. Matthew's telling, however, gives us a bit more. Peter, to verify that it actually was Jesus and not an apparition, said, "Lord, if it's you, order me to come to you on the water" (14:28). Jesus then summoned him out of the boat and onto the water.

This story is wild. Jesus walked on the flippin' water! Seriously. Then Peter joined him! Naturally, we're inclined to focus on Jesus's divine power when we read this mind-bending story. But make no mistake about it: Jesus walked on the water as a human being. Yes, we could explore the ways in which this story also clues us in to the fact that Jesus is God, but his full humanity is on display here!

We've neglected the human half of the story line for so long that we can't imagine this passage being about anything other than what we *can't* do. *Of course Jesus did it—he's God in a bod!* That works in theory, except for one problem: Peter. If this is only about divinity being put on display, then why did Peter get to walk on water? I used to imagine Jesus using some sort of mutant power straight out of *X-Men* to help Peter's body levitate at sea level. But that isn't in the story anywhere. Peter leaves us with another option that is consistent with the gospel accounts, over and over again: *Jesus was showing Peter who he could become, not who he couldn't be.*

Peter faced a challenge: Can I be human in a new kind of way, just *like* Jesus?

Sure, you aren't going to jump out of a boat to prove how human you are. That's not the point at all. But there's no way Peter stepped out of that boat without confronting fear. Fear, although natural, can be trampled under our feet as we seek to follow Jesus wherever he may take us.

When Peter began to sink, it was only then that he cried out for

Jesus to come near. Jesus grabbed his dear friend with his soon-to-be nail-pierced hand, pulled him up, and said, "You man of weak faith! Why did you begin to have doubts?" (verse 31). This begs a question: What exactly did Peter doubt? The story makes it pretty clear. Peter doubted that he could be the kind of human Jesus was, that he could trample over the evils of the sea like Jesus had.* Our potential to overcome these fears is how we can resist evil in our world with Jesus. He shared his full humanity (what it looks like when God is human) with Peter to show this young disciple that he had more courage than he realized. People who realize their potential to be like Jesus help others do the same.

Conquered Fear, Unlocked Potential

Jesus stepped into the chaos to pull Peter out of it. The fears of the evil sea would not consume his disciple and friend. I don't imagine Jesus's words about lacking faith being said out of anger or disappointment but rather as an affirmation of the person he saw in Peter. *You don't have to doubt who you were created to be; you are a human, which means you were made to trample the sea.* He must have been overjoyed by the fact that Peter joined him on the sea at all! What human does that? Well, trampling the sea is the destiny of anyone who steps into her image-bearing potential.

Fear is present throughout the world today. I finished writing this book in 2020 during the COVID-19 pandemic. The total deaths go beyond anything we would have dreamed up in 2019. Schools closed down here in Seattle during the second week of March. We ended the academic year from home. Social distancing and masks have become part of everyday conversations, and social media rages on, politicizing the issue in ways that aren't helpful. We've also had a wave of protests following the murders of Ahmaud Arbery, George Floyd, and Breonna Taylor, which exposed the fear that Black Americans face each day. Justified anger

---

* I first heard a similar point made by Ray Vander Laan: Peter doubted that he could become like his teacher.

about these injustices translated to people taking to the streets in protest.³ Fear and anger abound. Sometimes anger is rooted in the pain caused by the disruption of shalom. This sort of righteous indignation can be a holy plea for justice and peace.

I'll admit it: I deal with anger and fear at times.

For me, these emotions come up in many ways. Black, Indigenous, and People of Color (BIPOC) continue to live to suffer at the margins of our society. COVID-19 is claiming the lives of too many people throughout the world. These two issues are framed as left versus right rather than an invitation to embody humility, to be honest about the problems, and to work together to bring true shalom to these situations. We need to be willing to look at the web of sin, the 273 trillion choices and our own 35,000 that contribute to the suffering and fear in our world today. What will I do differently as I step off the boat and into the disruption of shalom right in front of me? Anger and fear, however justified, don't have to be the end in and of themselves. We can steward these emotions toward a holy end. Truthfully, this isn't usually an easy task.

It seems things aren't going to get better anytime soon. I fear that many more people throughout the world are going to die before an effective vaccine is created. I'm afraid that more BIPOC folks are going to be subjected to injustice and death. Much of the time I feel more like the disciples trying to wake Jesus up than like someone who has internalized Jesus's call to not be afraid.

Sometimes I wonder, *Even if I shake Jesus hard enough, is he still willing to wake up and calm the storms of life?* The perpetual storms and struggles, the constant onslaught of pain and devastation, the many almost-but-not-quite glimpses of hope overwhelm me and make it difficult to navigate the already tumultuous waters of life. Even when I was a kid, fearing violence in my soiled bed, God saw me with compassion and opened me up to an early trust in Jesus. And he is worthy of that trust. Just look at Peter, who walked with him out on the sea. Peter's brief trot on the surface of the deep influenced his ongoing personal development for the rest of his life.

Well, my friend, what are *you* afraid of? Jumping off the cliff into the water below terrified me. I get it. Fear keeps us looking out over the deep instead of experiencing the pure rush of joy that could be ours if we'd take a leap of faith.

How might fear be holding you back from your potential? Name it. This is sometimes a hard step. But if we can become people who name our fear, rather than shoving it deeper into the ignored spaces of our bodies, hearts, and minds, then we can begin discovering what might exist on the other side of it. If you can name it, then maybe you can imagine yourself carrying it in a knapsack that you bring out to sea with you each time you sail. It's likely heavy. If you can carry it, then imagine stepping to the edge of the boat. You look up and see Jesus standing on the surface of the water. Letting go of the sack, you take your first step. Then another. And a few more. Now you are both in stride.

> *How might fear be holding you back from your potential? Name it.*

From the surface of the water, having released fear to the hellish deep—where it ultimately belongs—you start to imagine life without that knapsack holding you down. Your lungs fill, expanding with each inhale beyond a capacity you thought possible, no longer constricted by a slouched posture caused by being weighed down. You can stand up tall. You can breathe. You can walk in such a way that your previous potential is now your present posture toward life. You have trampled the sea—just like Jesus.

FORMATION EXERCISE

Fear is natural and is nothing to be ashamed of. Neither should it be a limitation to becoming more like Jesus. Fear, a major contributor to pain for many, doesn't need to have such a power over us that we never take risks to step into our God-given potential. We become human like Jesus when we take the risk of radical trust and obedience, even when it disrupts our sense of equilibrium.

Scripture: Read or listen to Matthew 14:22–33. It helps to listen to stories like this.*

Imagine: With all five senses, imagine you are part of the story. What does it look, feel, sound, smell, and taste like? In your mind, compose the place. (It helps to close your eyes.)

Do you identify with a character in the story as you listen and imagine? Are you a disciple? Peter? Someone watching from the shore? Jesus? Another?

What do you sense Jesus might be saying to you through this story?

Now reread the final two paragraphs from chapter 10 in this book. How might you imagine yourself releasing your knapsack of fear in light of what you experienced from the imaginative reading of Matthew 14? What potential does Jesus see in you? In prayerful conversation, talk to God about it all.

Journal: Journal if it helps you process the exercise.

---

* I currently use an app called Dwell. David (NIV), Kylie (NIV), and Ryan (MSG) are my preferred reader voices at this point (until they add other translations of the Bible, such as the CEB or NRSV). I also love the audio Bible *Inspired by . . . the Bible Experience* (Zondervan, 2008).

CHAPTER 11

THE PROCESS OF PRESENCE

*   *   *

I learned that my life—my average, ordinary, routine, everyday
life—has infinite depth and dimension and meaning and significance.
I learned that the present moment, with all its pressure and
heartbreak and work and struggle and tension and questions and
concerns, is way more interesting and compelling and mysterious
and even enjoyable than I had ever imagined.

—ROB BELL, *How to Be Here*

Our identity shapes how we step into the world. Even when we know we are loved, the deserts of life test us. As I sat on the sofa in my living room, my body felt frozen. It wasn't cold to the touch, but I was inwardly frigid nonetheless. I couldn't move. Yet my mind was screaming at me, *Get off the couch and play with her. She's right in front of you. She's amazing. Play with her. Be present.* I still couldn't move. My daughter was there, but I was somewhere else. I was emotionally spent and was losing my capacity for being present to the moment.

Less than two years prior, we had moved. We relocated about a thousand miles to the north, from central California to Seattle, to fulfill my dream of starting a new kind of church. After a series of unfortunate church events, it was finally time to lean into the gifts that so many people told me they saw in me. Apparently, I'd been molded for this moment. The truth is that my confidence quickly faded.

I told myself I was ready. Everything that had happened in my church leadership career had prepared me for this moment. It was time to plant the church of my dreams. But fewer than two years into the process, I was sitting on the couch, unable to move. The anxiety of it all overwhelmed me.

Movement is one of those things that reminds us we are actually human. If you've ever been to a wax museum, you know the sculptures look real except for one thing: they can't move. Animation is the sign that life is present. My life was starting to feel more like a wax pose, and if something didn't change quickly, this molded-for-this-moment pressure was going to melt me under its emotional heat.

What I desired was a new sense of equilibrium. I longed to know that what I was doing mattered. But I felt lost and hopeless. The crisis I faced was rooted in my longing for a truer sense of self. When I showed up in Seattle with a three-month-old, two crazy pups, and a wife removed from all her other significant relationships, I thought, *This will all be worth it.* But there we were, the two-year mark impending, and we had nothing that looked like a church. Several people I thought were in it for the long haul had the church-breakup talk with me.* I was tired and felt like a failure. This led me to a therapist, spiritual direction, and an ongoing process of transformation.

What I didn't know at the time was that this moment of crisis was rooted in something good. Deep inside my bones I wanted to become more human like Jesus, who endures the worst of hurts and gives birth to hope.

Disengaged and Dehumanized

Jesus claims that his offer to us is a life of restful presence (Matthew 11:28–30). Anytime he could remind people of their truest selves, their humanness, Jesus would. One example immediately comes to mind from the gospel of Mark. In chapter 5, Jesus found himself before a man who had lost touch with his humanity.

---

* By the way, I don't hold this against anyone, and I own my part in it. People left for a variety of reasons. It was definitely hard during those early years.

In the twenty-first century, stories of demon possession may seem far-fetched or like archaic ways to explain mental illness.* Rather than analyze whether demons are real—Jesus surely believes they are—let's focus on the man involved. His demonization left him howling, cutting himself with rocks, and breaking chains designed to keep himself and others safe. He was in a state of unrest, disassociated from reality (verses 3–5).

What is demonic possession in the New Testament ultimately about? There are despairing forces at work in the world, seen and unseen, personal and systemic, that seek to dehumanize God's good image bearers. They perpetuate the disruption of shalom.

This man was no longer living in a community, partially for his safety and mostly for the safety of others. He was living and acting like a beast to be feared rather than a person to be loved. I wonder if deep within him his true humanity was in tension with his outward actions. Like being frozen when you long to be present, part of him (even perhaps in the subconscious) had to have longed to be at home in his body again. His physical disengagement from society is a picture of the distance he'd traveled from his image-bearing personhood due to these evil forces.

A HOLY INTERRUPTION ON A SUNDAY MORNING

I was at church one Sunday, preaching a message on Jesus and politics.† Specifically, the message looked at how Jesus's kingdom is concerned with reconciliation and restorative justice, especially with regard to those on the margins of society. We looked at how Jesus spent much of his time with social outcasts and economically disadvantaged people. Our culture, specifically in the United States, often favors retribution over restoration, and the socioeco-

---

* Although I'd guess that if you asked folks on other continents if they've encountered something that transcends modern medical explanation, you'd hear numerous stories that would blow your mind.

† Even though this may make you wonder about my political affiliation, as a follower of Christ, I find common labels unhelpful. Jesus's politics are about people, not partisan allegiances. I'm constantly trying to learn what the ethics of Jesus might look like in the world today.

nomic forces of this system affect the poor and disenfranchised the most. Black, Indigenous, and People of Color find themselves more likely to be marginalized in our current state of affairs, so when we discuss these issues, we also must confront racial biases.

I grew up believing that everyone who makes good choices has an equal opportunity to make something of himself or herself. The idea was that no matter where we start out in life, all we have to do to be successful is work hard, develop character, and increase our grit. While there is some general wisdom to personal responsibility and growth, many people are underresourced. This is especially true for economically disadvantaged persons and many persons of color.*

There are forces at work throughout our society that leave some folks at the bottom of the socioeconomic ladder. That might be you or someone you love. And perhaps the system was somehow rigged against the demon-possessed man in our story. The systemic web of sin is like a tsunami about to hit land. Those with assets, like a helicopter, can get out of its way. However, many are caught in the wake and have to respond to its full wrath. Those without the resources to flee quickly have a predetermined disadvantage that has little to do with personal choice.

The Sunday that I spoke about the challenges many people face in a system of privilege and retribution, be they driven by socioeconomics or race, a woman burst through the back doors of our small church building. Many of her words were hard to understand, but it was clear that mental illness, and possibly self-

---

* We could add several other communities to this list. I'm not an authority on the topic of justice, but I continue to learn from those who are. Dominique DuBois Gilliard's *Rethinking Incarceration: Advocating for Justice That Restores* (InterVarsity, 2018) and Bryan Stevenson's *Just Mercy: A Story of Justice and Redemption* (Spiegel & Grau, 2014) are great starting points. I will also say that I do not see myself as an authority on the topic of racial justice. I look to the work and experiences of others: the earlier thinkers and practitioners, such as Martin Luther King Jr., Howard Thurman, James Cone, and John Perkins; and the newer generations of thinkers and practitioners, such as Dr. Bernice King, Osheta Moore, Latasha Morrison, Brenda Salter McNeil, Austin Channing Brown, Drew Hart, and so many others.

medicating, had led her to a dehumanized state of mind. Her arms were covered in what appeared to be a combination of scars and ballpoint pen scribbles. Her hair was unkempt. Mascara dripped down her cheeks. Scabs covered her neck.

At first, she meticulously stacked Bibles in the back of the room, disrupting our coffee area. This was loud in and of itself. Her mannerisms evidenced that she hadn't been fully present or in a state of rest for a long time. In the middle of the sermon, I looked up and asked, "Is she okay?" as an intern attempted to help her. But when she began yelling and crying inconsolably, the gravity of her situation broke the hearts of everyone in the room. As she yelled in what can only be described as nonsensical desperation (and I mean this without assigning any judgment to this dear child of God), she was helped out of the room as people from our church sought to discern whether there was anything that could immediately be done to help her. Even if she didn't fully understand, we wanted her to know she was safe and loved. Then we prayed as an act of solidarity with her and in resistance to the demonic forces of pain at work in our world.

Then I lost it.

I wept in front of everyone.

Although I consider myself a fairly vulnerable person and communicator, I don't cry very often during a sermon. But in this moment the emotion overwhelmed me. Without knowing her backstory, I can say that this was a woman who was clearly a personal victim of an entangled web of sin. The 273 trillion choices that create systems of oppression, which we each contribute to for good or ill, kept her bound. Any ounce of complicity she had with these forces was likely out of desperation. For whatever reason, this precious daughter of God became a walking, talking example of the very thing I was speaking about. Jesus weeps with her even more than I did that morning.[*]

---

[*] To be clear, I am not claiming this woman was demon possessed. She does, however, show us how systems of disrupted shalom alienate the most insecure among us. That fact hasn't changed since Jesus liberated the demonized man two thousand years ago.

JESUS'S KINGDOM IS PRESENT IN PAIN

We don't know what initially led to the demon-possessed man's situation. But as the story continues, we get more clues about the forces that rob individuals and communities of their innate image-bearing vocation. Jesus commanded the "unclean spirit" to leave this man (Mark 5:8). We find out that it wasn't only one demon but a "Legion" (verse 9). A Roman military legion—ten cohorts of soldiers—is about five thousand men! If Roman soldiers come to town in this formation, violence and destruction will swiftly follow. Why would the author of this gospel decide to tell us this bit of detail? Because for the writers of the New Testament, the forces of evil corrupt God's good world at two levels: the *personal* and the *systemic*.[1]

Mark highlights that this man is not only personally demonized but also a victim to the dehumanizing forces of an oppressive empire. Rome oppressed those at the bottom with a system that favored the rich and powerful. These demons were the manifestation of the far ends of suffering and dehumanization that empires impose. The demonic and the systems work in tandem, even when we don't recognize it.

How did Jesus take action? He sent those demons, those spiritual henchmen of the Roman conquering machine, into a herd of pigs (verses 11–13). As someone who spent six years of my life as a vegetarian for animal welfare reasons, this story is hard for me. But in that world, where the gentiles*—Rome—were represented by unclean animals like pigs (according to Jewish law), Jesus sent a powerful message. His kingdom, his way of redeeming people's pain, was in direct confrontation to the forces of evil that empowered the Roman Empire. They may have had the power of war horses and chariots, but Jesus came with the power of God.

Jesus's kingdom expanded, unlike Rome's, by humanizing oth-

---

* The word *gentiles* really means "nations" in ancient Greek. If you want to understand the context of Jesus and the early church, the word *gentile* in the singular doesn't exist in the New Testament. I did a podcast episode on this called " 'Gentile' Isn't in the Bible . . . and Why It Matters" (*Theology Curator* podcast).

ers. Jesus marched armed with peace as his weaponry, love as his banner, and an innermost sense of self as his body armor. Where Rome's expansion required legions to pillage new lands, Jesus's nonviolent kingdom requires the will to discover one's full humanity in relationship to the Creator, in the context of community, for the sake of all creation. This was Jesus's desire for the demon-possessed man and for the dear child of God who caused a holy interruption that Sunday morning.

Jesus Is Fully Present to Us

The story concludes with a dehumanized man rediscovering that he was human after all. The demonization that led to his distancing and dehumanization was remedied. He no longer had to live in the hills outside town. He could go home. He could return to his family, healed of his shame!

His gratitude led him to want to return the favor to Jesus by following him on his journey as a disciple. Perhaps there was some work he could do for Jesus on the road? Maybe he could be a spokesman who got up at Jesus's speaking events and shared his story about how he used to be a man possessed but now is a man obsessed with the gospel? Any good show or product needs a testimonial, of course. But Jesus wouldn't have it. He said no.[2]

Why not? That is my first reaction each time this story is read. In so many other places, Jesus invited people to drop everything and follow him. Maybe Jesus had a bias against previously possessed persons (to henceforth be referred to by the abbreviation PPP), but that isn't consistent with what we know about Jesus's life. The answer comes at the end of the story. Jesus told him to "go home to your own people . . . and tell them what the Lord has done for you" (verse 19). He wanted him to go home and be fully present to the people he had been distant from all this time.

Here we see a key human quality of Jesus: presence. He was a master of leaning into the moment rather than dividing his attention. Jesus practiced presence, and he valued it for others. He was attuned throughout the Gospels—and certainly in this story—to the person in front of him. It takes a solid sense of self to pull this off on such a consistent basis. Thus, Jesus helped a man who had lost himself begin finding himself again.

> *Jesus was a master of leaning into the moment rather than dividing his attention.*

I can imagine the haunting echoes of the man howling outwardly, while inwardly a part of him was crying out to simply be present again. His body was doing one thing while his image-bearing humanity called for something better. Perhaps all of us have a true human self that calls out from deep within us when our bodies feel trapped by our circumstances. Our bodies can be in the room, but we may fight to be there with them.

We Can Become Present Like Jesus

Not all stories are as dramatic as a first-century exorcism. Not all people will need to be freed from such obvious oppression and distancing from a fuller human self and a loving community. The dark forces in this world attack us all differently. If we aren't careful, we make the sensational stories the only "real" stories of transformation and give ourselves an excuse to stay stagnant. But the fact is that many of us have a more gradual and sometimes less obvious journey to embark on.

The road before me is long when it comes to discovering a life of presence. That crisis of being frozen on the couch a few years back catalyzed what I hope is a lifelong process of growth. It's what led me to a therapist and a spiritual director. It woke me up to my need for a renewed experience of Jesus. And what I'm beginning to discover is that the more attuned to the moment I become, the more gratitude I have in my life. I don't have to disassociate from the simplicity of what is right in front of me to find contentment. I don't need my church to grow by the thousands to find joy. And I don't have to stay on the couch.

The other night I was up in Lydia's room after putting her to bed. At the time of writing this chapter,* she is nearing four and a half. She is hilarious, compassionate, imaginative, and smart. I'm learning what it means to be a dad who is more fully present to her, more human to her. And it has made me full of gratitude in the little moments. Even situations like the other night when I was up in her room for the billionth time.

She isn't good at going to sleep, staying asleep, or letting us get our beauty sleep. Since becoming parents, we haven't really slept. Perhaps this is why parents start college funds: with the hope that this investment in their children's future will be an investment in the recovery of eighteen years of sleep debt. When I was upstairs (after Lauren and I grew weary of calling out to her, "Go to bed!"), I stepped into the room with more than a little irritation. But as I prepared to lecture her about the rules of bedtime, gratitude washed over me and presence invited me to change my emotional posture.

I looked at her, my eyes full of empathy, and said, "Lydia, I just want you to know that you are an amazing little girl. I love you so much." She stared back into my eyes with one of those looks that don't come often. Her eyes were full of what seemed like a mirror of empathy and gratitude. We gazed at each other in a daddy-daughter moment of deepest connection. I knew that her response would melt me, in the best possible way. Then she leaned toward me and gently and sincerely uttered these words: "Daddy, I just did a quiet toot under the blankey."

This was nothing short of a reminder that being present to real life isn't about capturing a bunch of perfectly delivered lines by channeling my inner Danny Tanner whilst expounding my fatherly wisdom to D.J. or whichever Olsen twin happens to be playing Michelle in that particular scene.† It's not only about the

---

* This is a friendly reminder that my stories are chronologically out of order because of the nature of this book's flow and the fact that several sections came together over the course of a couple of years.

† For those of you born after 1995, this is a reference to *Full House*. Netflix, as it often does, rebooted the show as *Fuller House* in recent years. Writing this footnote makes me feel old.

dramatic stories of transformation catalyzed by exorcism-like experiences either. To be present like Jesus is to embrace the imperfections of life while committing ourselves to being an echoing hope of resurrection.

We can find joy in perfectly imperfect times. Jesus has something to show us about real human life, a life that embraces both the deep moments and all the toots a four-year-old can muster. We can move forward each day, no longer feeling stuck in our heads but able to be present to the moments right in front of us. Being present is Jesus's posture; it can be our posture too. Pause for a moment and take that in. Take a deep breath and say,

"I,"

and exhale saying,

"am here."

Feel the weight of your body against the earth. Breathe deeply as your lungs expand and contract with the present moment. This is the life Jesus modeled for us and invites us to enter each and every second of the day. Painful circumstances, whether ours or that of others, will always be present in our lives. With Jesus's help, may we be present to all of life: the mess and the beauty, the pain and the hope.

FORMATION EXERCISE

One of the hardest things to do in a culture fixated on distraction is to stay present to the moment. We're tempted to dwell on the past or to dream up an imagined future. To stay present with God and others truly takes practice. Embrace this slightly longer exercise to focus your attention, right here and right now.

So, then, just as you received King Jesus the Lord, you must continue your journey in him. You must put down healthy roots in him, being built up brick by brick in him, and established strongly in the faith, just as you were taught, with overflowing thankfulness. (Colossians 2:6–7, NTE)

Pray and meditate: Take a moment and close your eyes. To center yourself in your body, take a few minutes and breathe. Inhale through your nose and count to five. Feel your lungs fill up with air. Exhale through your mouth for five seconds until the oxygen has left your chest. In through your nose, out through your mouth.

Invite Jesus into the rhythm of your breaths. As you inhale, say in your mind, *"Come to me . . ."* As you exhale, say, *"And I will give you rest"* (Matthew 11:28). If you feel led, personalize as it feels natural.

Sense the flow of your body as you release tension in the peaceful presence of Jesus. Feel the aches you often don't slow down enough to notice. Be fully present with a God who is fully present to you.

After about five minutes, restfully transition into the next exercise.

Scripture: Read Colossians 2:6–7 slowly.

Reflect: Invite Jesus to bring his reign and friendship into your shared experience of this passage:

"Just as you received King Jesus the Lord" (verse 6, NTE).

To call Jesus "Lord" is to proclaim him as your sole allegiance. How does Jesus experience your allegiance to him as you go about your life? Ask him to show you. Listen. If that is hard, imagine what you think he would show you, based on what you know of him. (Hint: Avoid false narratives about God and yourself.)

"Continue your journey in him" (verse 6, NTE).

Life in the kingdom is a life in process. Just as all relationships are a journey, so also is your life in God. What characterizes your present leg of your journey with Jesus? Where is Jesus on the trail, and how is he actively present on the path with you?

"Put down healthy roots" (verse 7, NTE).

Rootedness is one expression of presence. Consider if you can find contentment in the present moment. The past is behind you. The future is paces ahead of you. Can you be present and content where you are in this season of life? Ask Jesus what healthy rootedness might mean for you.

"Being built up . . . in him" (verse 7, NTE).

Something is being built up with every choice you make. If your roots are indeed healthy (to switch metaphors for a moment), then what is built up will be strong. What spiritual bricks have you and Jesus stacked up together that bring you joy?

"Being . . . established strongly in the faith[fulness]" (verse 7, NTE).

Faith (the Greek word usually has the idea of fidelity or allegiance in mind, thus "faithfulness") establishes us. In other words, it is an anchoring point of life in the kingdom. Faithfulness requires two parties. So, how has Jesus been faithful in bringing the kingdom in your life? If this is a hard question to come up with concrete responses for, ask Jesus about why that might be. Don't judge your own process but allow it to build and establish you afresh.

"With overflowing thankfulness" (verse 7, NTE).

If it's the true expression of your soul, consider thanking Jesus for the journey thus far. Perhaps write a list of things that come to mind. Allow this time of thanksgiving to give you an opportunity to remember how God has revealed the kingdom to you in the past, while at the same time being present to your whole experience of God in this moment: body, mind, and spirit.

Pray that Jesus would root you in the now.

CHAPTER 12

RELEASING THE STONES

*   *   *

*We can embrace our humanness, which means embracing our
broken natures and the compassion that remains our best hope for
healing. Or we can deny our brokenness, deny compassion, and, as
a result, deny our own humanity.*

—BRYAN STEVENSON, *Just Mercy (Adapted for Young Adults)*

You've been wronged. Now what? (Okay, I'm jumping right in, aren't I?) But here's the thing: you *will* be hurt by someone. Certainly there are different degrees of wrongs. A bad attitude from a loved own is quite different from betrayal or abuse. For each type of conflict we face, a different pace and strategy are needed to discover whether reconciliation is possible on the other side.

An argument with a parent, spouse, or friend might take a week or two to resolve. We may need to cool down, gain some perspective, and then engage in ways that are safe and healthy. But eventually, if the relationship is healthy, these conflicts end in forgiveness and reconciliation. This isn't so easy with conflicts involving trauma.

As I've said, my childhood was hard. Alongside the pain, I also experienced joy as a child. Mom was compassionate and fun, especially when she had the space to breathe. My grandparents, uncles and aunts, church, and dad gave me opportunities to know love. Understandably, I kept these people in the dark about the abuse because if such things came to light, I feared that my mom would get in trouble. I believed I was protecting her. Some of these people knew there were "isolated incidents" here and there.* They didn't know how hellish it truly was at home, though.

Often I'd daydream about when I wouldn't have to fear my abuser any longer. I was done with random acts of violence and verbal abuse. I never knew when the next abusive incident would come. I couldn't brace myself—or perhaps I constantly braced myself. Violence would hit home without any notice. The older I got, the more I knew that I shouldn't have to take crap like that. A time would come when I'd be strong enough, brave enough, and big enough to fight back. If this man, my greatest enemy, continued to make life horrific, a day of vengeance would come when I'd defend my mom. I wouldn't be too small forever.

Seventy-Seven Times

Conflicts often lead to situations where vengeance or forgiveness become two paths forward. One day Jesus was approached by Peter, who asked, "Lord, how many times should I forgive my brother or sister who sins against me? Should I forgive as many as seven times?" (Matthew 18:21). Listen to Jesus's rabbinic response: "Not just seven times, but rather as many as seventy-seven times" (verse 22).

This story has some fascinating ancient context that hugely deepens how we think about forgiveness. In Genesis, immediately after Cain killed Abel, God had mercy on the murderer and made known to all people that "anyone who kills Cain will suffer vengeance seven times over" (Genesis 4:15, NIV). After this, a character named Lamech entered the story and admitted to having committed murder. He claimed for himself what God had said

---

* Although my dad knew that life wasn't easy with my mom, he didn't know the extent at all. Based on the little information he had, he left an open invitation for me to move in with him full time. I almost took him up on the offer at one point in fourth or fifth grade but feared losing my friends in the process. Eventually, he, my stepmom, and my stepsiblings all moved to a neighboring town. Since I was in private school by then, I moved in with them in the middle of seventh grade.

about Cain: "If Cain is avenged seven times, then Lamech seventy-seven times" (verse 24, NIV). Notice that this was a warning to the enemies of Lamech. Anyone who killed or tried to harm Lamech would receive vengeance seventy-seven times worse.

Can you imagine how revolutionary Jesus's words would have sounded to a first-century Jew? I mean, Lamech's story was part of their heritage! After hearing this, their little internal voice would be saying, *Wait . . . in the same way that the story of Lamech claimed vengeance toward enemies, Jesus says that this is how often we ought to forgive our enemies?*

Yeah. No thanks, Jesus. To be a good forgiver would mean giving up our fight for Israel.

This wasn't the first time Jesus said something like this. The Sermon on the Mount says that the listeners used to be taught to love neighbors and hate enemies (Lamech's preference), but Jesus's new yoke was to "love your enemies and pray for those who harass you" (Matthew 5:43–44). Jesus's way is never about vengeance but always about forgiveness and, when possible, reconciliation. His words from the cross are some of the hardest to echo in our lives: "Father, forgive them, for they don't know what they're doing" (Luke 23:34).

Jesus knows conflicts will happen.* Forgiveness is always a desired outcome. We are called to offer forgiveness and seek reconciliation whenever it is possible. There are times when reconciliation would result in a lack of safety. This isn't what Jesus was getting at. Sometimes the faithful thing to do is to offer forgiveness but remain apart.

Forgiveness is the opportunity to release our bitterness and to truly desire that the offending image bearer find healing and transformation—even apart from our direct involvement. If we think about Jesus for a moment, this becomes clear. The people who executed Jesus were not the people he ate fish with on the

---

*This is only an introduction to themes relating to conflict and forgiveness. There are several good books on these topics. I'm a big fan of those written by Miroslav Volf, for instance.

shores of the Sea of Galilee after his resurrection (John 21). He had forgiven them. That was enough.

Forgiveness is the opportunity to release our bitterness.

Jesus's Approach to Conflict

Jesus enacted wisdom in a story preserved for us in John 8.[1] In this story, a woman who had been accused of adultery, which was a transgression against the Jewish law, was apprehended. According to the text, this woman had been dragged out of "the act of committing adultery" (verse 4) and brought in front of the temple. Of course, we know that mob justice is never justice at all, even if it is written into the laws of the land. It is always driven by a certain impulse to control the world.[2]

Flexing muscle is what men have done throughout much of history. Whether it be coordinating a sex trade ring or snatching up a woman to put Jesus in a philosophical trap, men have a track record of using and abusing women. Patriarchy is alive throughout history—even today. In fact, the word itself comes from ancient Greek and Roman cultures. In Greek, the word *patriárkhēs* (πατριάρχης), means "father or chief of a race." We can break down this compound word into its parts: *patri-* comes from the Latin word for "fatherland" and the Greek word for "lineage" (which comes from root word for "father"), and *-archy* comes from the Greek word for "ruler" or "authority." One way to think about patriarchy is "fatherly-rule." When power is consolidated in such a way that men have greater access, this is patriarchy.[3]

There are several lenses we could use to approach this story; however, I want to focus on the theme of how Jesus used wisdom when he approached unjust conflict. Here he played the role of mediator and advocate. But in another sense, he was in the mix of the conflict since the religious leaders were attempting to trap him.

The legal experts and Pharisees brought a woman caught in adultery. Placing her in the center of the group, they said to Jesus, "Teacher, this woman was caught in the act of committing adultery. In the Law, Moses commanded us to stone women like this. What do you say?" They said this to test him, because they wanted a reason to bring an accusation against him. (verses 3–6)

Jesus was in the middle of a tricky situation: Does he affirm what the scribes and Pharisees who are present (not all of them collectively, as we sometimes imagine) claim about the law? Does he affirm the Torah by condemning this woman? If you know the story, you know the punch line. Jesus said, "Whoever hasn't sinned should throw the first stone" (verse 7).

As the story continues, the men stood, confounded, as Jesus casually drew in the sand. In a moment when they would have expected him to explain to the woman that she must die—forcing Jesus to affirm a sentence his audience clearly believed was inconsistent with his nonviolent teachings—Jesus, of course, used his wisdom to reverse the trap. In the end, the men dropped the stones.

UNDERSTAND BOTH SIDES

The first observation we can make from Jesus's wisdom is that in the midst of conflict, it helps to *understand both perspectives.* This doesn't mean we agree with both, especially in situations where injustice is present. However, the fact that Jesus knew where both parties were coming from allowed him to engage in a different way. He had the ability to create a space for an actual conversation. These men were ultimately using this image-bearing woman as a trap, believing this was part of the path to purifying Israel. Jesus knew that the liberation of God's people, which was a good motive, was behind their ungodly actions. Jesus showed them that this sort of holy freedom cannot come at the judgmental captivity of vulnerable people in their midst.

This woman found herself in a compromised situation, without a doubt, but it was likely due to her own brokenness and desperation. She is the clear victim in the story. The man she was involved with wasn't even brought out to be punished with her. There is no doubt she was a prop in a patriarchal game.

EXPOSE DEHUMANIZING BEHAVIOR

The second example of wisdom from Jesus comes as he *exposes dehumanizing behavior*. These men turned an image bearer into an object. Sadly, this shouldn't surprise us. Women have been treated terribly throughout history and even are today. The first-century world of Jesus was horrendous when it came to the treatment of women, especially those who were not elite Roman citizens. When we read the Bible but forget about the massive injustices women faced at that time, we lose sight of the intensity of Jesus's actions on behalf of women and other marginalized persons.

This applies even to Jesus healing people. Often, these outsiders were victims of a larger system of Roman oppression and religiosity. Jesus basically was saying, "Here's one thing I can do: I can make you well and liberate you from the hellish circumstances you are already facing simply because of your ethnic origins." Similarly, when Jesus fed people, he wasn't simply doing it because they were hungry that day from walking too far. He was feeding people who probably didn't have a lot of food. All these things, of course, were exponentially worse for a woman in these circumstances.

Years ago, at a National Youth Workers Convention, I heard Mike Pilavachi give a powerful sermon based on this story in John 8. His reframe of the narrative has never left me. Rather than see this story as we often label it, "The Woman Caught in Adultery," it's time to relabel it: "The Men Caught with Stones in Their Hands." This is the thrust of the story. Jesus exposed hypocrisy and invited them to consider that grace is the better story line in this conflict.

When the men left empty-handed, Jesus told the woman, "Neither do I condemn you. Go, and from now on, don't sin anymore" (verse 11). In other words, "Go have a life without all the baggage you carry as a result of your choices." This was not a judgment but an invitation to lean into the best possible life with God and others. Jesus wanted her to thrive as she grew in her capacity for a shalom-shaped life.

DISCERN THE THIRD OPTION

The third thing we can learn from Jesus's wisdom in conflict is to *see the third option*. Jesus knew he couldn't merely say, "It's all good." We would find a huge discrepancy from his character up to that point if Jesus said, "Okay, go ahead and kill her." Instead, he pointed toward something that no one saw coming. He told the men with the stones in their hands, "Whoever hasn't sinned should throw the first stone" (verse 7). What these men didn't know was that they weren't setting the trap for Jesus; they were setting their own trap! And the outcome was that they were disarmed from further sin and the woman was freed from their violent aims.

CHOOSE LOVE

Finally, it's important to notice that in conflict, Jesus teaches us to *choose love, not winning*. Jesus didn't defend himself in a game of rhetorical one-upmanship. He used wisdom to bring about love as the ultimate outcome. Jesus paused the argument, got quiet, and wrote in the sand, which was likely his attempt to center on love rather than debate for the sake of debating. This is something I've struggled with in my adult life. I'm defensive by nature. I want to win the argument. This is not a good quality to bring to a marriage. Love over winning is key when we are in conflict, including a willingness to forgive at least seventy-seven times.

Forgiveness After Conflict

For years, I regularly entered conflict with Lauren by crafting "logical" arguments and using fancy oration skills. I could talk my way into being "right." This all came to a head during a time of preparation for a spiritual retreat. It was sometime during the first five years of married life. I was reading a book by Dallas Willard, and he started talking about a word I didn't know the definition of: *guile*.* In one of his books, he wrote, "The importance scriptural teaching places on guilelessness is very great."[4] I looked up the term and learned that it has to do with using words cunningly to deceive or attain a goal. Willard highlighted how guile can be a form of manipulation and sin.

Sometime after reading that book and attending the retreat, Lauren and I were in a heated argument. I'm good with words, and I was letting her know how good I was by arguing my point. It was intense. My opinion was the "logical" one, of course, and hers was "ridiculous."† I spent several minutes intensely telling her why my ideas were right and trying to convince her that she needed to look at it objectively. I don't remember why we were in conflict mode, but I'm certain it would probably be laughable to us now.

Then, midsentence after several minutes of defending my idea, I heard a still, small voice—the voice of the Spirit—say one word. You guessed it: *guile*. I stopped talking. I interrupted the argument. I started to weep. This caught Lauren off guard. I was feeling convicted to the point that I had to explain why my entire disposition had changed. I said something like, "Can we pause for a second? This is going to sound weird right now, but I need to ask for your forgiveness. I need to tell you about the word *guile*." I wept. She held me.

I'd like to say I never had this problem again, but that isn't completely true. It's truer today than it was yesterday. This moment of interruption taught me so much about the nature of seeking forgiveness, which at times can be hard because we have to admit we are wrong. Choosing love over winning is always the Jesus way.

I also think of my "Lamech" moments, where I want vengeance.

---

* The only context for this word I'd had up until that point was a character from *Street Fighter II* named Guile.

† I hope you recognize that these air quotes indicate sarcasm.

My childhood pain is something I wanted to eventually give back to my abuser in full measure. But when I look at Jesus, I see a different response to conflict, especially when we are the wronged party. What Jesus did in response to enemies was so unorthodox. We are taught to fight back harder; Jesus forgave harder. We are taught to respond in kind; Jesus responded with kindness. Paul's letter to the Romans says that "while we were God's enemies, we were reconciled to him through the death of his Son" (5:10, NIV). Although humans rebel against the shalom of our Creator, God has responded to us through Jesus by absorbing the worst of human and demonic violence on the cross.

Jesus not only taught forgiveness in the midst of conflict but also took the initiative on God's behalf to reconcile us back to God, one another, and all of creation! Jesus could have fought back. He was strong enough, brave enough, and big enough. But instead of the road of retaliation, he chose to walk the road to the cross. And when he saw unjust conflict against a woman, Jesus exposed her accusers' hypocrisy, causing them to lose the grip they had on the stones of judgment.

The Road to Forgiveness

When I was in high school, the time came to forgive my enemy. At this point he had been out of my life (via a restraining order) for several years. So, I never did speak to him about this, but in my heart and disposition toward him, I released my bitterness and anger to God. Have I done this fully? Most of the time I think I have. Am I still angry at the injustice of abuse? Yes. Am I free of the burden of carrying the heavy load of bitterness toward my abuser? *Absolutely.*

Forgiveness is a choice we make and a road we take. We need to know what we are choosing when we say "I forgive you." To forgive is to release the impulse to avenge and to desire that the offending image bearer find a new path that doesn't dehumanize the self and others. It is often an emotional journey that doesn't come to its destination overnight. It is also an act of truth telling. As

Miroslav Volf said, "Every act of forgiveness enthrones justice; [forgiveness] draws attention to [justice's] violation precisely by offering to forego its claims."[5]

Forgiveness is a choice we make and a road we take.

To respond to a wrong, we can forgive or we can retaliate. The way of Jesus is to enthrone justice by means of peacemaking and forgiveness. We can stop the cycle of vengeance. We may want to fight back seventy-seven times, but in the act of forgiving, we are acknowledging that we were, in fact, wronged. With strength we choose to "forego [justice's] claims," releasing bitterness and its power over our lives. Even when we feel justified to have stones in our hands, there is nothing more powerful than releasing them.

Whom do you hate? Maybe that's too strong a word. Whom are you mad at? Anyone come to mind? Maybe someone who is a direct source of deep hurts comes to your attention. Maybe you are entitled to metaphorically throw rocks at someone who has caused you deep sorrow.

Foregoing the claims of justice names the injustice that caused you harm. It frees you of the burden of bitterness. Forgiving as Jesus did redeems pain by destroying its power over our lives. Each time we forgive, we embody the echoing hope of resurrection.

FORMATION EXERCISE

Forgiveness is a choice we make and a road we take. Conflict, whether big or small, brings with it the potential for pain. Stepping into conflict is a powerful act when we do it with Jesus's wisdom. Forgiveness after conflict redeems pain by helping us release bitterness and offers a way for us to identify with Jesus's gift of forgiveness in a fresh way.

Scripture: Read or listen to John 8:2–11 multiple times. Attempt to compose the place in your mind as you identify with each of the following characters:

- someone in the crowd observing
- Jesus, stepping into the conflict with your full human self
- the woman
- one of the men carrying a judgmental stone

After each time through the story, write down a one-sentence summary of what you experienced from each perspective.

Imagine: In a posture of prayer, imagine that you have rocks in your hands, at your disposal to use in a conflict. You now have three clear options in the midst of conflict:

1. You can throw the stones at the other person in complete disgust. Seems like Jesus isn't a fan of this approach.
2. You can use the stones to build a wall between yourself and the other person to reinforce the "wall of hostility" (Ephesians 2:14, NIV) that Jesus came to tear down.
3. You can do everything within your power to build a bridge toward the other person: to seek to understand the other perspective, to expose dehumanizing behavior, to discern a third way forward, and to choose love, not winning.

Reflect: Can you think of a conflict you have faced in the past? How did you manage your pain in that situation? What did you do with your metaphorical rocks?

Is there a current situation where you sense the need to either release the rocks or use them to build a bridge toward the other person or party?

Pray and journal: Give yourself a few minutes to pray and journal about anything that came up during this time with Jesus.

Part Four

AN ECHOING, RISKY LOVE

In this section, we start in the darkness and move toward the light.

The journey with Jesus, in the echoes of hope and in the midst of uncertainty and pain, invites us to embrace his humanity as our own. This is especially true in hard situations. Just as he stepped into Jerusalem with courage and trust in God the Father, we can step into pain with empathy, bravery, and trust. We can accept the invitation to find resurrected life in the middle of what feels like death.

CHAPTER 13

WHEN GOD WEEPS

* * *

God is like Jesus. God has always been like Jesus. There has never been a time when God was not like Jesus; we haven't always known this, but now we do.

—BRIAN ZAHND, *Sinners in the Hands of a Loving God*

The Kingdom of God is without coercion, persuading by love, witness, Spirit, reason, rhetoric, and if need be, by martyrdom, but never by force—[but] to resist the Kingdom of God always leads to a self-inflicted Gehenna . . . the consequential hell of going against the grain of love.

—BRIAN ZAHND, *"Vive la Révolution!"*

Twice Jesus cried in the Gospels. God, turned human, wept. We imagine the God of the universe as "bigger" than crying. But in Jesus, we meet a God of *profound* empathy. For some of the men I grew up around, crying was seen as a sign of weakness. Jesus is proof that the opposite is true. Jesus shows us that God is emotive and experiences pain, sadness, and frustration.

As we've discussed many times in this book already, Jesus is human. And in a broken world like ours, what is more human than tears? Luke 19:41–44 tells of one of these moments:

As Jesus came to the city and observed it, he wept over it. He said, "If only you knew on this of all days the things that lead to peace. But now they are hidden from your eyes. The time will come when your enemies will build fortifications around you, encircle you, and attack you from all sides. They will crush you completely, you and the people within you. They won't leave one stone on top of another within you, because you didn't recognize the time of your gracious visit from God."

Can you imagine the scene? Jesus was tearfully sobbing out these words of lament over his beloved Jerusalem. Like a cathartic moment when you can finally cry it out, Jesus released his emotional dam even as he prophesied that the walls of the city were damned. Jesus wept over judgment. He mourned over destruction. When he warned of the fires of hell, he grieved.

Let's be honest. Sometimes we need the tears of God to wash our broken souls. When Lazarus died, Jesus took time to weep over him and all who mourned rather than instantly fixing the situation by resuscitating him well beyond his burial. When we lose a loved one, whether through the finality of death or the smaller losses of relational distance brought on by poor choices, we don't need a God who makes us feel jolly. We need a God willing to hurt with us so that this same God can show us how to heal. God's tears seen in the human face of Jesus might be the greatest gift God offers us beyond salvation and the hope of resurrection. Sadly, in Jesus's day—and in ours as well—many would not heed his warnings. He knew this. It tore him up.

> *Sometimes we need the tears of God to wash our broken souls.*

Okay. Now I'm going to take a bit of an author's gamble. If it doesn't work, I might lose your attention. You might put this book down, bored, and walk away. But if it does, if we can pull off these next pages together, then you and I are going to have a front-row seat to one of the most shocking moments in the life of Jesus. One that we totally take for granted until we stop and think about it. One that has the capacity to completely change how we think about suffering and real redemption of our pain. These tears show us more than we may have realized!

What the Gehenna?!

Throughout his public ministry, Jesus warned people of a coming destruction and invited them to repent and follow him. This warning had ramifications for how people sought to live for God, including the choices they made and the authenticity of their worship. It also had a looming historical ramification, as I've hinted at a few times in this book. Jesus knew that Jerusalem would be destroyed by the Romans within the generation of his first-century disciples.

One way he described this coming national tragedy was with a single Greek word, *Gehenna,* which most modern Bibles translate as "hell." The term is a transliteration of a phrase that comes out of the Hebrew Scriptures: "the Valley of Hinnom."[1] This location is referenced throughout the Hebrew Scriptures and is a valley just outside Jerusalem.* It was a place of bloodshed (sometimes child sacrifice; see 2 Kings 23:10) that eventually was used to destroy dead bodies.

The prophets said it's where fires devoured corpses and flames seemed to burn nonstop. In this valley, the worms didn't die (they had plenty to eat) and corpses were utterly destroyed (Isaiah 30:33; 66:24). It was where Babylonian attackers would place the slain corpses of vanquished Jewish fighters (Jeremiah 7:30–32; 19:6–9). Many believe that during the time of Jesus, this place below the city became a trash heap of burning fire.[2] We also know histori-

---

* Today, you can drive through this small valley, which is surrounded by modern life, even parks, just beyond the borders of Jerusalem in the West Bank. It borders the historic city of Jerusalem on the south and west and connects to the Kidron Valley close to the southeast section of the city.

cally that when the Romans seized Jerusalem in 70 CE, dead bodies were placed in this valley (and the connected Kidron Valley). My point? Gehenna was a literal place, its storied history full of repeated death and decay.*

By taking up the warning language of Jewish prophets who had come before him, Jesus placed himself in continuity to their message and ministry. Appealing to Gehenna, he evoked a literal place, not in the underworld but outside Jerusalem. Most of the time Jesus used *hell* in an image-saturated way. *Hell*—in first-century Jewish culture—helped listeners understand the danger in this life of not joining up with God's kingdom purposes.

When we are curious about why Jesus wept over Jerusalem, we should keep in view his "hell" warnings, which were directly connected to his words about Jerusalem's coming doom. *Gehenna* is used a dozen times in the Greek manuscripts from which we derive our English New Testament.[3] Here are a few examples:

- Matthew 23:33, 36: "How will you be able to escape the judgment of [Gehenna]? . . . All these things will come upon this generation."
- Mark 9:47–48: "It's better for you to enter God's kingdom with one eye than to be thrown into [Gehenna] with two. That's a place where worms don't die and the fire never goes out."
- Luke 12:5: "Fear the one who, after you have been killed, has the authority to throw you into [Gehenna]."†

The Gehenna passages are just the tip of the iceberg when it comes to Jesus's prediction about a coming crisis for the people of

---

* Bible nerd alert: Although it is true that some rabbinical sources and intertestamental Jewish literature use Gehenna (a literal place) as an image of postmortem judgment for evil people, Jesus seemed to have the Old Testament usage mostly in view.

† Now, don't accuse me of taking "hell" out of the Bible. I simply replaced an English word with a Greek word that comes from a Hebrew phrase. I blame Jesus for this one.

Israel.* Here's what should shake us up in the best way: *Jesus's warnings of judgment led him to weep.* His empathy, not vindictiveness, moved Jesus to do all he could to teach and model a new way of being God's beloved ones. As his disciple, Peter said years later, "The Lord . . . is patient with you, not wanting any to perish, but all to come to repentance" (2 Peter 3:9, NRSV). Let's keep these ideas within reach, but now let's ask some important questions.

Jesus's Empathy and Invitation

What do we need to notice so far? Jesus cried over the fact that many of his people would perish at the hands of the Romans in 70 CE. What does that have to do with your life? Quite a bit, actually. Jesus doesn't want you to perish under the weight of your hurts. In fact, the way we handle a crisis matters greatly. We learned this all too well during the early days of the COVID-19 pandemic. When we mess up, Jesus says, *I'm still here.* When we hurt, Jesus *shows* us that he feels pain with us. When we face hell on earth, Jesus's echoing hope reminds us that he conquered all forms of hell, death, and evil.

> *When we mess up, Jesus says,* I'm still here. *When we hurt, Jesus shows us that he feels pain with us.*

Jesus offered people the path of peace, and they chose revolt instead. They couldn't wrap their minds around a messiah like him, so he was rejected and legally murdered. When we hear his words "It will be more bearable for Sodom and Gomorrah on the day of judgment" (Matthew 10:15, NIV) or "for Tyre and Sidon"

---

* At this point, it is important to say that I don't plan to make any major claims about how these passages apply to the afterlife. Although I find it difficult to hold to a view that claims eternal conscious torment based partially on what I present here, I'm sure it's possible. In light of evidence from the rest of the New Testament about death and perishing, I find approaches that emphasize conditional immortality the most helpful. I'm not a Universalist.

(11:22, NIV), we've got to hear them through his tearful love for people on a dangerous path. The towns where Jesus grew up (Nazareth) and lived as an adult (Capernaum) are examples of places that rejected his way of peace. Each warning communicated the same thing: nationalistic zeal (which perpetuated poverty and violence) was a misstep from God's heart.[4] Jesus was not condemning these people but pleading with them to course correct so they wouldn't contribute to systems that lead to death.

God's heart is offered to all who experience hurts. That means everyone, including you. We shouldn't be surprised by ancient people who took a violent posture in God's name. (Sadly, Christians have done this throughout history, usually not from the position of true oppression.) When people have been abused; when their land, possessions, and dignity have been stolen; and when crimes against their humanity are built into law, what else do we expect but a violent eruption of anger? The line between collective pain and violence is quite narrow.

Knowing this, Jesus was unlike false messiahs; he was a radical reformer within Judaism. By inhaling peace, Jesus's followers would learn to exhale reconciliation rather than hatred. This was an alternative then. It still is.[5]

Your hurts don't have to fester. Your pain doesn't have to perpetuate the cycles of pain in your community. There's a reason that many who were abused go on to abuse others: they were conditioned for it.[6] There's a reason that when we've been chewed out by our boss at work, we're tempted to metaphorically turn "the tongue [which] is set on fire by the flames of [Gehenna]" (James 3:6) toward our family. Pain, left to its own devices, takes on a destructive life of its own. Jesus gives us a revolutionary solution to this problem: holding our pain with him.

JESUS PREDICTED THE DESTRUCTION OF JUDEA

After hearing Jesus's cryptic prediction about Jerusalem being destroyed in Luke 19, the disciples got a chance to ask him to clarify what to expect, and Jesus offered his friends practical advice on how to respond to the coming calamity (Matthew 24; Mark 13; Luke 21).

Jesus told his listeners, "Not even one stone will be left upon another. All will be demolished" (Mark 13:2). Jesus also gave a general expectation about when this would happen: "I assure you that this generation won't pass away until all these things happen" (verse 30).

Check this out. Jesus was being quite practical. In a sense, he's giving them wise advice. The rulers in Rome were going to flatten everything, so he said, in my paraphrase, "Run to the mountains" (Matthew 24:16; Mark 13:14; Luke 21:21); "Don't fight. Get out of Dodge! And you'll know when it's time. Armies will surround the city" (Luke 21:20); "An act of desecration will happen at the hands of the Romans in the temple" (Matthew 24:15–16; Mark 13:14); "If you don't leave soon enough, when the invading armies come in from Rome, they will take some to have their way with and will leave others behind to die." This is why Jesus said of men in a field and women at a mill that "one will be taken and the other left" (Matthew 24:40–41).* Conventional wisdom of the time was to get ready for a fight. Jesus offered different advice.

Jesus was right. The devastation proved to be one of the worst examples of rape and pillage imaginable.[7] Those who took heed of Jesus's words were more likely to survive.

JESUS GAVE WISE ADVICE TO HIS FRIENDS

When I was fifteen, I made some poor choices and did a bit of partying. I had resisted getting intoxicated up to that point, but some friends urged me to give it a try. So I did. And then again. And a couple of times after that.

The first time I smoked pot was with some friends from youth group. I stayed over at one of their houses one night, and they finally convinced me to give it a try. A lemon-lime Gatorade bottle, somehow creating a chamber for the smoke, was the pipe of choice. Besides the act of smoking, the other memory I have of that first time was that we somehow ended up at church, high as kites. I re-

---

* You might be thinking, *Isn't this about end times?* Well, maybe. But what if it's actually part of how Jesus describes the impending destruction of Jerusalem in 70 CE? For end times stuff, I'd start with Romans 8 and Revelation 21–22.

member talking to a couple of the youth leaders while stoned. It was a conflicting, exciting, and fearful moment. They didn't figure it out. This skater with bleached hair and his buddies with blue and purple dyed hair always acted goofy. We pulled it off.

The next day, thinking that this fun experience wasn't a big deal but also feeling like I needed to fess up to one of my best high school friends, I went to my summer job at the fruit-packing house with an odd grin. No, I wasn't still high, but I was definitely acting strange when I saw him.

When I told him I had smoked weed for the first time, he was immediately concerned.* Not in a pompous or tattletale sort of way but genuinely worried. He kept a cool head about it but spoke truth into my life. He saw more potential in me than that path would lead me down. He didn't judge me but truly spoke with wisdom and concern. It took a while for his words to make a full impact, but eventually, in partnership with God's gracious Spirit, he convinced me and modeled for me that there is a better way to live. By the end of that summer, I made the choice to stop and had only one slipup the following autumn. Had Peter not spoken the truth with love, I honestly believe I would have followed a destructive alternate path.

Loving warnings change people's lives.† Jesus gave several loving yet truthful warnings throughout his ministry (and in this particular teaching session on the Mount of Olives). By doing this, he was offering advice for how to lean into the good life God offers rather than devastation. He went on to describe what ignoring his prophetic advice would be like: "The sun will become dark, and the moon won't give its light. The stars will fall from the sky, and the planets and other heavenly bodies will be shaken" (Mark 13:24–25). Jesus predicted a soon-to-come earth-shattering event

---

* Look, I realize there are situations that, for some, could justify the use of marijuana in moderation, such as possible medicinal uses. However, substances are *definitely* not something a teenager should be dabbling with.

† Peter, thanks for your friendship during those critical years.

that would dramatically change the first-century world.[8] Just as we might say that 9/11 or COVID-19 was earth-shattering without meaning that either of these was caused by a literal earthquake, the same applies to Jesus's intentional use of hyperbole: something big was going to happen. It would be earthshaking.

At some point in your lifetime, your world will be shaken. Jesus knew this about the people in his own time, so he warned them and empowered them with good advice for when things would go bad. One thing that can be challenging for many people is figuring out which voices to listen to. Some of us, when we are hurting, look for voices that affirm what we think we want to hear.

If your pain, for instance, drives you to seek a divorce from your spouse,* you are more likely to favor the advice of those who think divorce isn't a big deal. They'll likely tell you things like, "Do whatever makes you happy." The same is true if you are about to make a shady business deal when your profits are down. Situations that affect our livelihood are painful. You'll likely have friends who say, "It's the only way to make it in this business." Jesus's wisdom is hardly conventional and never sacrifices integrity. He told his disciples to choose peace and run if needed. Jesus likely also has wisdom for us today, as we hold our pain with him.

Jesus's tearful warnings about Gehenna came to pass. Josephus claimed that over one million Jewish people were killed during the war.[9] While we can't know for sure whether that number is accurate, the death toll was massive. During the war, so many dead bodies had to be disposed of that they were tossed into the valleys below: Gehenna and the connected Kidron.[10] This was the hell Jesus warned of and wept about.

---

* Abuse is a form of unfaithfulness. If you are abused, you do not have to stay to honor God. Nor should you ever see abuse as a just punishment to make you submit to your partner (this is typically an attitude of men toward women). Get out. Get help. Don't listen to voices telling you to live with an abusive person. That advice belongs in Gehenna. A great book on this is David Instone-Brewer, *Divorce and Remarriage in the Church: Biblical Solutions for Pastoral Realities* (Downers Grove, IL: InterVarsity, 2003).

Jesus's Tears for All Our Hells

Let's pull this all together. Pay attention to what Jesus's tears tell us about both being human *and* the character and posture of God. If we get these wrong, our grid for walking through the hurts in our lives and the lives of those we love will be distorted. Jesus sobs over any hell we go through, whether self-inflicted by poor choices or due to the circumstances of living in a broken world. Although many of us may never face anything remotely like the Jews (including messianic) in Judea in the first century, we will still face deep pain and loss more than once in our lives. And as much as we will want God to wave a magic wand and clean up all of life's crap, it usually doesn't work that easily. So, what can we learn about how Jesus holds the pain of others and holds our pain with us?

First, notice that *Jesus weeps most for those who would not accept his message.* Let that sink in. He wept *even* for people who yelled out "Crucify him!" just a while later (Luke 23:21). This shows us that Jesus's empathy, and therefore God's empathy, is for everyone. Enemies? *Jesus weeps for them.* Family and friends who don't get it? *Jesus laments with tears for their safety.* Jesus's sobs later turned into pleas to his disciples to "watch out that you aren't deceived" (21:8) so they would have the best chance of making it out with their lives and their ongoing witness to the world. Jesus's tears remind us that his posture, and therefore the postures of the Father and Spirit, toward the whole universe is love. This love encompasses even those who, by executing Jesus and taking up arms against the Romans, directly rejected Jesus's invitation to join the peaceable kingdom of God. Jesus weeps when people suffer, no matter who is at fault.

Second, notice that *Jesus will have no part in coercing people into obedience.* He seeks to influence and persuade but always refuses to manipulate us. Warnings of coming judgment are given by Jesus as an act of love, not as a way of forcing people to choose the way of the kingdom of God against their wills. Jesus assured the disciples that they were not alone in their call to offer the love and peace of God's kingdom. He promised them that in moments of challenge, they wouldn't need to worry about what to say as a defense "because what you can say will be given to you at that moment . . . [by] the Spirit of my Father" (Matthew 10:19–20). The early followers of Jesus, in their pains of proclaiming the Lord and Messiah, could rest assured that God's Spirit would influence their very words! God's influence and empathy for us is so much greater than God's manipulation of us could ever be.

Next, we need to notice how *Jesus models empathy and never looks like our false narratives about him.* This is the sort of human empathy each of us can emulate. It is also the empathy that is a direct revelation of God's posture and heart toward all human-kind, including you. Why do we allow false narratives of a God who loves us when we have it all together but inflicts pain when we don't? Too often, the narrative of a vindictive and judgmental God enters our hearts and minds when we confront pain. But if God truly looks like Jesus and if Jesus truly looks like the human beings we each are invited to become, then why do we ever convince ourselves that God is distant or that God is punishing us or that God is causing suffering to teach us a lesson? We have to get that narrative far from our minds and allow the life-giving Holy Spirit of Christ to transform our inner beings. Then we can discover the incomprehensible empathic belovedness our Creator has for us as image bearers.

As a pastor, I've met so many people who have had *horrendous* things happen to them. Horrendous. Does this mean that God doesn't love them? By no means! Yet in a pain-filled world like ours currently is, where shalom is scarce, our perception of God's posture toward the universe easily comes into question when we've faced trauma and injustice. Some versions of Christian theology tell us that God is just waiting for the chance to push us into Gehenna, and if we mess up, that's what will happen.

But nothing could be further from the truth. Jesus is the one crying over the "Gehennas" that we face.

Jesus Weeps over Our Pain

Somewhere between my third- and fourth-grade years, the abusive boyfriend took us out on his boat. If you are already thinking, *That's the place where chaotic and evil things happen,* you are right. The boat was small and rusty but still had a motor that worked. I don't know what compelled us to get in a vessel on water with a man so unstable. But he had a way about him. He regularly operated somewhere between intimidation and flattery, making us want to believe he was changing into a good guy. He wasn't. Although he likely framed the day as a fun day for us all, nothing could be further from the truth.

Sure, it started out fun. What kid doesn't want to be on the lake? Pine Flat was popular for fishing and water skiing, so spending a hot day out on the water started with lots of excitement. I remember putting my hand in the water. The cool resistance against my arm as we cruised along kept me content for quite some time.

Then he asked, "Kurtis, is it true that you still can't swim?" Without a moment of hesitation, he pushed me off the side of the boat into the lake. My mom screamed and helped me grab the sidewall. She was horrified. She was also on the lake with a drunken maniac. By this time, he'd consumed several beers. He said, "You are going to learn to swim right now." For what must have been thirty minutes, he had me hold on to the side of the boat with one arm and kick my feet and stroke with the other arm—as if this were how to teach someone to survive in the water. I had no escape. I simply had to endure his cruel, manipulative tactics.

I tell this story as a picture of what some people imagine the God of Christianity to be like. Many of us have been taught that if God is displeased with someone who isn't "measuring up," then God will snap at some point—now or after death—pushing us into the chaotic deep end of the "lake of fire," fully knowing we can't swim (Revelation 20:10). Many Christians (and *former* Christians) believe that Jesus somehow is *excited* about hellfire and brimstone and an impending tribulation and judgment. He's not. He weeps over every child of God who takes a path that leads to unnecessary suffering, just as he weeps for those caught in the horrendous wake of evil that takes innocent victims down with it.

This is why Jesus gave wise advice to his friends about the upcoming hell on earth of 70 CE. He did all he could to persuade them. He never manipulated or coerced them. He wept for all of them. The God that Jesus reveals in his vocation as the perfect image bearer, the fully human one, wants to rescue as many people as possible from suffering without revoking the freedom of choice in this world.

I have no idea if you are reading this book in the hope of finding a remedy for your deep pain. That's a tall order that I won't be able to fully deliver on. But it's entirely possible that your pain can be held a different way. It starts with believing that the God that Jesus reveals is in no way committed to causing pain. Jesus isn't inflicting direct vindictive punishment when we have hurts. Jesus does all he can to leverage pain to a greater good, but that is second best to what he will do when he returns to bring ultimate healing and shalom to this world. For now, his tears are the source of pain's redemption, for in them we discover that even God suffers with us.

FORMATION EXERCISE

Even if we have a picture of God in our minds, an intellectual category for how we think and talk about God, getting that to saturate the inmost pain points of our souls is often challenging. I invite you to think about how, when you authentically sit with your hurts, your experienced narrative of God differs from the picture we have of Jesus weeping.

Scripture: Read the stories of Jesus weeping over Jerusalem in Luke 19:41–44 and raising Lazarus in John 11:1–46.

Pray: Imagine Jesus standing on the hillside weeping over Jerusalem. Imagine that instead of the destruction of the city, Jesus is gazing over the pain you are holding, making your pain his own.*

Sit in the quiet, inviting Jesus to be present to you. Perhaps he has holy advice to offer you or wants to give you a sense of peace. (This might not be as direct, but pay attention to nudges, impressions, pictures, and other ways the Spirit may speak to you.)

Journal: Reflect and put your thoughts and prayers to paper. Be curious about your reactions without judging yourself for having them.

Take Action: Bring in friends, counselors, family, or any other trusted party. Vulnerably tell them what you are discovering about Jesus and your pain.

Then continue bringing your pain and joys before the One who echoes hope into the most painful places of our souls. Our hells will be overcome by a love so heavenly that it took God's becoming earthly and weeping for us to truly imagine the power of divine empathy.

---

* Please don't do anything that makes you relive trauma in ways that will cause more harm than good. If you have traumatic memories, process them under the supervision of a mental health professional. In all these exercises, please use discernment!

CHAPTER 14

THE CUP AND THE COPELESS

*   *   *

*Like most of us, when I walked through my own valleys of darkness
and suffering and loss, God was often revealed to me in the
darkness rather than in the light. The valleys were where I became
intimate with God, far more than the mountaintops.*

—SARAH BESSEY, *Miracles and Other Reasonable Things*

I t hasn't been long since my precious dog Sadie died.[*] Let me be
vulnerable about the impact of her death: after typing that first
sentence, my face fell into my hands, my chest sank, and I am on
the brink of tears. The words "It just isn't fair" came out in this
moment. I'm still grieving, and the pain surfaces in surprising
moments.

Perhaps you know loss like this. A pet, especially a dog or cat,
has personality and spends hours a day with you. I work from
home, so the lack of Sadie's presence is felt exponentially. I realize
that some readers have different relationships with animals (which
is valid), but many of us find deep love and companionship from
our pets.

After I'd been married to Lauren for six months, she started
asking whether I'd be open to getting a puppy. I didn't want a dog.
Lauren insisted I did. When I was a kid, we had a dog for about a
week, but we ended up giving it away. The idea of a pet seemed
like a lot of work. Yet each day Lauren would show me pictures of

---

[*] Sadie passed away on August 18, 2019, after nearly a week of fighting. We miss
her so much.

puppies on Petfinder with a glow in her eyes and an "Aaawww-www." Eventually, she made it clear that I needed to get on board with being a family with a dog.

Why the hesitation? Because I didn't want the responsibility of caring for an animal. Chores like giving a bath or cleaning up puppy poo didn't sound like a good way to use my time. Add to this my personal allergy issues and the financial burden of vet bills and dog food, and the cost of caring felt like a big deal.

After getting Sadie, I found that my suspicions were partly true. She'd leave "surprises" on the carpet. Eat stuff. Teethe . . . on the furniture. Yelp for hours if left alone. Taking care of Sadie was hard work. But work that would prove worth it.

The little pup grew on me so much that I eventually pushed to get a second dog. We named her Mylee (she misses her sister). Mylee remains a companion to me; in fact, she is sitting next to me as I type.* Not only did the idea of having indoor dogs grow on me, but I also found joy in caring for both of my pups.

Over the eleven years we had with Sadie, there were multiple scares. The summer of 2011 we discovered she had a heart murmur and a small liver. We thought she was going to die. I remember weeping outside the Los Angeles Cathedral as I heard the news. Only a few years in, I was smitten with her. She could look me in the eyes and I'd know what she needed. She could give me a playful nibble-lick to the nose and I knew her love. And since that scare, part of me held fear about the day I'd have to eventually say goodbye. It seemed like it would be unbearable. I wasn't wrong.

Jesus and Anxiety

On the night Jesus would be betrayed by Judas and handed over to be crucified, he went out of his way to pray. He knew that love now asked him to suffer. Jesus held the pain of the world in his body as

---

* Really, she's like, *Okay, bro. I get it. You have a book to finish or whatever. But can we please go for a walk so I can poop over and over until you run out of bags for the last one and have to use a large leaf to pick it up? That is my favorite. Also sniffing. I like that.*

he pleaded with God the Father in the Garden of Gethsemane, just outside the main part of the city. He took a few of his closest friends with him to pray and keep watch. Jesus prayed that "he might be spared the time of suffering" (Mark 14:35), asking Abba Father to "take this cup of suffering away from me" (verse 36). Ultimately, he gave himself to the will of the Father.

Luke's telling of this story adds a grim detail: "He was in anguish and prayed even more earnestly. His sweat became like drops of blood falling on the ground" (22:44). Jesus experienced anxiety. Some believe this was hematidrosis, where blood exits the body through the sweat glands, possibly due to extreme stress.* Jesus's anxiety over his impending suffering and death offers us grace for our own anxious moments. When we are anxious, Jesus gets it.

John 13 says that before heading out to the garden, "Jesus knew that his time had come to leave this world and go to the Father. Having loved his own who were in the world, he loved them fully" (verse 1). It highlights another important detail: "The devil had already provoked Judas, Simon Iscariot's son, to betray Jesus" (verse 2). At this point, Jesus "began to wash the disciples' feet" (verse 5).

We are told that Judas had already been influenced by the devil to carry out a betrayal. Did you catch that? Not only did Jesus wash Judas's feet, but the storyteller (whom we presume is the apostle John) framed the narrative with this fact in mind! After a dialogue between Jesus and a reluctant young Peter, the storyteller gives us another piece of inside information: "He knew who would betray him" (verse 11).

Jesus had learned of Judas's plot against him. Yet Jesus waited until after he had the chance to wash his feet to expose Judas and dismiss him from their gathering. Jesus willingly took a risk to love Judas, even though he'd eventually suffer as a result.

---

* From what I could find, it seems there is debate in the medical community about whether this is a legitimate condition. It is at least considered quite rare. Either way, it seemed worth mentioning as a possibility.

Judas gets a bad rap. No, I am not minimizing his actions against Jesus. However, his own struggles likely brought him to the point of choosing to collude with evil. Luke's version of the story says that at some point "Satan entered Judas" (22:3), which means that he opened himself up to the influence of darkness. I imagine that Judas genuinely loved the other disciples and Jesus, yet something took root within him, leading to a horrible choice. It was a choice he regretted in the end, which sadly led to suicide (Matthew 27:1–5).

The question I continue to ask myself is, Is love worth the pain it causes? For Jesus, the answer is *yes*. He loved his friends through his horrible execution and beyond his resurrection. Love is risky, even when it isn't tainted by betrayal. This is something that has been hard for me to grasp. Coming from a childhood of trauma, I believed for most of my life that love would lead to happiness. I thought pain had been left in the past since I now had a deep relationship with Jesus. Part of me imagined a life where things had finally come together and pain was rare. Of course, that is a fantasy. There is no love without pain. Love is patient and kind; it is also painful. When we truly love, we take the risk that it will cause us pain somewhere down the road. Love is vulnerable.

> *The question I continue to ask myself is, Is love worth the pain it causes? For Jesus, the answer is yes.*

An Obscure Night

Jesus found himself bearing what he called a "cup." The spiritual writer James Bryan Smith said, "A 'cup' is anything that we struggle with accepting as our lot in life. And our cup is usually the thing that makes it difficult to believe God is good."[1] Jesus had to decide whether love was worth the pain that would follow. Would Jesus choose love even if it meant the cross? Would he choose love, even though his love had already been betrayed by someone he had "loved . . . fully"? This wasn't an easy decision for the human Jesus to make. From what the story tells us, Jesus even asked for the cup of suffering to be removed as he wrestled with whether or not he could endure a drink from it. I'm eternally grateful that he chose the harder path. By stepping courageously into the injustice of that night, Jesus shows us that we can fully trust God, even in suffering and death. Love was worth it for Jesus.

Jesus was experiencing, in some ways, what has been called the dark night of the soul. This phrase is based on a poem written by Saint John of the Cross, who was a sixteenth-century Spanish mystic. The poem is eight stanzas, each having five lines of text. Among many things, the poem reflects on God's desire to purge us of all our attachments so that what is left is the endless love of God.*

One thing that helps us understand Saint John of the Cross's intention is to consider the phrase *noche oscura,* which we typically translate "dark night." The phrase *dark night of the soul* doesn't occur in the poem itself, but what is more interesting is when we consider the word *oscura.* Gerald May, psychiatrist turned spiritual director, pointed out that for John (and his teacher, Saint Teresa of Avila),

> It simply means "obscure." In the same way that things are difficult to see at night, the deepest relationship between God and person is hidden from our conscious awareness. . . .
>
> John is addressing something mysterious and unknown, but by no means sinister or evil. . . . It is the secret way in which God not only liberates us from our attachments and idolatries, but also brings us to the realization of our true nature. . . .
>
> This is not to say that all darkness is good. Teresa and John use another word, *tinieblas,* to describe the more sinis-

---

* Of course, Jesus didn't have sin in his life that needed purging, but he did need to trust God as he stepped into the ultimate test of his truest human nature: suffering for the sake of all creation.

ter kind of darkness. . . . In *oscuras* things are hidden; in *ti-nieblas* one is blind. In fact, it is the very blindness of *tinieblas,* our slavery to attachment and delusion, that the dark night of the soul is working to heal.[2]

Dark nights of the soul, from this perspective, aren't for our detriment but for our good. They can be part of God's work for liberation in our lives, where God leverages challenging circumstances to bring us into newness. In a world free from sin, these nights would be obsolete, but in a world where attachments distract us from our full image-bearing vocation, spiritual obscurity takes us deeper into the depths of our formation into Christlikeness.

Jesus was confronted with whether he was going to step into his destiny as the ultimate example of being human in a broken world: self-giving love.* Pain—stepping into the obscurity with a cup God is inviting you to bear—comes only as the result of loving too much.

The Risk of Love and the Reality of Loss

As is true for anyone I've met, loss and suffering are real. This applies not only to the massive, life-altering shifts life brings us but also to regular life. For instance, have you ever lived somewhere for only a short time, and because you knew that a move was impending, you decided that building authentic friendships wasn't worth it? Why invite someone in if you are going to pack your bags in six months? Or have you ever had a job where you had friends at work but never took the step to develop those friend-

---

* I understand this phrase might affect readers differently, particularly some who are of marginalized identities. What I want to make clear is that this situation was driven by Jesus never losing sight of his identity and never being forced to give this sort of love away. He did so as a bearer of a particular cup. Jesus doesn't, however, call people in suffering situations to give their autonomy away to oppressors. For Jesus, this was a powerful and courageous moment, not a moment of defeat. This should inform how we think about the idea of Jesus modeling self-sacrificial love.

ships outside of work because it might make things complicated at work if the relationship went south? Being vulnerable is risky. It opens us to anxiety. Ultimately, it makes us confront our own mortality and the mortality of others.

To love is to risk loss; rather, to love is to commit to the inevitability of painful loss. Anxiety over death, subconscious as it often is, creates the greatest barrier to a joyful life with others because it hinders us from the depths of vulnerable love. When we know that we will one day lose someone, preparing for the worst—coping in advance—can become a force almost as powerful as the love we so desperately desire. I've come to believe that love is worth the risk. Enduring pain is worth the love gained. I wouldn't have truly come to this realization if it weren't for my dog Sadie. God brought her into my life, through my wife's persistence, and I will never be the same as a result. As Richard Rohr said, "None would go freely, if we knew ahead of time what love is going to ask of us."[3] Love risks pain. I finally believe that pain is love's cost and that the payment is worth the sacrifice and is the evidence of love's authenticity.

Three significant stories of love and loss come to mind as I reflect on my own obscure nights. These include my uncle, my grandpa, and Sadie. I'm going to share all three with one ultimate point: the discovery about the risk of love that I made when Sadie died opened up a space within me to grieve my uncle and grandpa in a new way. It was painful. It was sacred. It shows just how complex pain and grief really are.

MY UNCLE

During my sophomore year of college, I got a haunting call from my brother: "Kurt, I'm sorry, but we have one less uncle in the world." My uncle Dennis passed away in a car accident on a January evening in 2004 on his way home from a meeting. This was the kind of death that just happens. One day you take for granted that a loved one is accessible, and the next, you almost believe that person is only a phone call away.

My uncle left behind an amazing young wife (my aunt Andi is

still amazing), three children under the age of twelve, and a large community of family and friends. His impact on my life will remain for as long as I live. As I said when reading a short reflection at the funeral, with 1,200 in attendance (to give you a picture of the many lives he touched), "I am the man that I am today because my uncle Dennis chose to invest in a young life. I am grateful for the twenty years that I got to have him in my life and am jealous because he is able to look God in the face in glory. I will miss my uncle Dennis for the rest of my days."

I miss him regularly, even now, more than fifteen years later. Early in my marriage, I actually had a couple of dreams where Lauren met my uncle Dennis and he told me how happy he was for me. These I count as gifts and true to a world where he is still in it. The injustice of losing someone all of a sudden hurts in a unique way, but I'm grateful for how he invested in my life—especially when I walked through so many years of trauma as a child.

MY GRANDPA

In the summer of 2010, my grandpa Corny Penner passed away from bladder cancer. He was in his early seventies, still leading the church volleyball nights and active in work. Around the previous Thanksgiving, my grandpa was diagnosed with cancer, which led to some surgeries. Throughout this process, there was a part of me that thought Grandpa was going to beat this cancer. The surgeon was confident that when the bladder was removed, so were all the tumors.

During the months following surgery, my grandpa was recovering from this invasive procedure. He was up and moving around like he had not been in several months. We had a couple of family nights and even did a weekend trip to Pismo Beach. That spring, we all believed he had become cancer-free, but then new symptoms crept in during June. He passed away in July.

My grandpa had assumed the role of a second father in a true sense. As a child, I was mostly with my single mom, so Grandpa assumed a more active role in my upbringing than in most families. In fact, there were two times in my life when I lived with my grandparents in some capacity. The first of these was after a final climactic incident of abuse in fifth grade. The second was when I was a senior in high school and was working for my grandparents part time (I bounced between them and my dad). He was more than a typical grandpa. I also inherited the faith of my grandpa (well, I hope to attain some level of it). Grandpa was known as a generous man who was in love with Jesus.

After learning about Grandpa's cancer around Thanksgiving, I went to his home to spend time with my grandparents during Christmas break. We walked around a field and enjoyed a piece of fruit. In order for me to process all that was happening, I wanted to hear how he was handling it. I asked him, "Grandpa, how are you doing emotionally with all that is going on?"

I didn't want the simple answer about how God was in control but was looking for the raw essence of my grandpa's emotional posture. His answer, although spiritual, was as raw as it could have been. He answered in a way that I will never forget: "Well, Kurt, I have a lot of goals and things that I would like to accomplish for the Lord. But if he thinks that I have finished everything that he has for me to do, then I have perfect peace."

In awe, all I could say was, "Wow, Grandpa."*

Grandpa was ready to bear whatever cup was before him. Jesus had a similar posture. Hebrews reflects on this by saying that Jesus "endured the cross, ignoring the shame, for the sake of the joy that was laid out in front of him" (12:2). Like Jesus, my grandpa had a profound sense of joy in the face of death.

I don't believe with any ounce of my being that my grandpa's death was God's plan or that God wanted this to merely bring about something good. Just as Jesus wept over Jerusalem when she was headed down hell's path, he sobs over death. Just as Jesus wept at the tomb of Lazarus, his dear friend who died too soon, he wails at the thought of any of God's children suffering and dying.

---

* I speak for all his kids and grandkids in saying that he was truly a man of God.

What inspires me, however, is that my grandpa had become so like Jesus that even when anxiety was likely present, it was over-shadowed by a profound peace from God. This was my grandpa's obscure night. It didn't end well, in one sense. But in another, it ended with a man who, being freed of his attachments, was ready to see the face of God. He had truly finished everything—likely more than he, in his humility, ever realized.

MY PUP SADIE . . . AND SO MUCH MORE

I knew that I didn't have many years left with our puppy-girl Sadie. The same is true of our Mylee. I wasn't prepared for Sadie's sudden sickness and death, both the experience of loss and the obscurity it would impose. At the beginning of the summer, I took her to the vet for a persistent reverse sneeze. We believed it was likely allergies and agreed to monitor her. Over the course of the next few weeks, her symptoms subsided. With our whole family in tow—Lauren, Lydia, baby Chloe, Sadie, Mylee, and me—we took a road trip from Seattle to Crescent City, California, to visit my dad and stepmom. With an overnight stay in Eugene, Oregon, in both directions, this trip was an adventure for us all. We had so much fun!

Then we returned home to Seattle and spent a couple of weeks there. A few days prior to our next big summer trip, I noticed Sadie was a bit more hoarse than usual (she's always had loud breathing patterns, but this was slightly worse). I wasn't worried and figured her allergies were bothering her again, but I asked the house sitter to keep an eye on her. And although there were a few questionable moments while we were away, our house sitter did a great job updating me on suspicious coughs. We had no idea what would happen upon our return.[*]

Sadie saw us, as did Mylee, and jumped for joy! After a week away, this was a normal welcome-home party for us. The problem was that as the kids went down for bed and Lauren and I stayed up

---

[*] We got back to Seattle from Fresno on a Sunday. We already had a vet appointment lined up for Monday.

late to situate ourselves, we noticed that Sadie's breathing didn't slow. It was fast. She was panting in a way that could easily be mistaken for excitement, but her little twenty-two-pound body was laboring for oxygen. So at 2:00 a.m. I took her to the emergency vet hospital down the street. I was given grim news: without major interventions, Sadie would die. X-rays confirmed that she had pneumonia, but we didn't know the cause. She stayed there in an oxygen incubation tank overnight as we prayed and discerned. Money was definitely an obstacle.

The next day, we talked to the vet about our options (by the way, we were treated with so much kindness at the animal hospital that it was truly a gift). We came up with the only plan we could afford (well, *afford* is relative, since we are still paying for it today): we would take Sadie home with an oxygen tank and see if this form of therapy could give her enough time for her lungs to heal. She came home on Monday night and passed away on Saturday morning. That week was one of the greatest gifts and the greatest pains of my life up to this point.

We had moments when we thought she'd pull through. People supported us through prayer and encouragement and even asked to contribute financially. We fought for Sadie's life with all we had. On a couple of occasions, when we thought it was time to say goodbye, she fought just enough to give us another day with her. Finally, on Saturday, it was clear that she couldn't fight any longer. She held out for us long enough to give us the time we needed to say goodbye. I even got one last nibble-lick to the nose the evening before she passed. It was a week of deep sobbing and telling her how much she had taught me about who I have become and about love in general.

With my puppy-girl, I was entrusted with the nurture of a creature for the first time. Because I knew fear and helplessness as a child, I promised myself that I would end the cycle and be a safe presence when I grew up. Sadie was my first pet and thus my first opportunity to "parent" in a way that was the opposite of the worst of my experiences as a kid. In the eleven years of looking after her, God opened me up to seeing ways that my pain is redeemable. I nurtured her both as a way of caring for that scared little boy (who will always be part of me) and as preparation for when my own children would be born. In my taking care of her, she took care of me. As I type, I'm sobbing heavily (which is rarer as time passes but is a sign that there is still much grief and holy appreciation for her). Thank you, Sadie, for all the gifts you gave us. We love you.

Love Gets the Final Word

I share these three stories about death to draw out what I'm learning: *love is worth the sobs.* I spent most of Sadie's life worried about the day when something would go wrong. I feared having to face her death. I feared that I wouldn't have what it would take to get through it. And yet I sit here knowing that nothing can brace me for the sting of death to my soul. All the tears, all the moments when my body shakes and the sobs come from the deepest parts of my chest not only are me weeping for a loss but also are a sign of risky love.

This risky love for a pup opened me up to the other loves I've lost. As I grieved Sadie, I simultaneously grieved my uncle Dennis and my grandpa Corny in a new way. The pain that emerged in the process of losing Sadie brought up some grief stored somewhere in my subconscious, somewhere within my body, that God invited me to truly feel. When grief causes anxiety for me, allowing it to wash over my body, fueled by tears of love, brings a sense of hope and an invitation to risk it all on love.

Bracing ourselves or finding ways to cope are natural as we prepare for or deal with loss. Grieving in advance is normal. Coping with grief is wise for a season in many cases, especially if a person struggles with depression or certain forms of mental illness.* However, I've come to see the gift of experiencing the weight of loss as well. Not everyone is in a place where this is safe or

---

* Mental illness is not to be stigmatized here. I don't want to suggest that people abandon coping mechanisms that might be needed due to their health history and healing journey. I'm not suggesting a one-size-fits-all method but am rather sharing something meaningful in my own journey.

healthy—and I likely have deeper layers to explore as well—but what I have been learning is that coping both before and after a loss can minimize the love I've experienced. Gerald May reflected on this:

> In my psychiatric practice how many times did I help patients cope with their feelings, tame the power of their emotions? I no longer believe that was helpful. . . .
>
> I have come to hate that word, because to cope with something you have to separate yourself from it. You make it your antagonist, your enemy. . . . Wild, untamed emotions are full of life-spirit, vibrant with the energy of being. They don't have to be acted out, but neither do they need to be tamed. They are part of our inner wilderness; they can be just what they are. God save me from my coping. God help me join, not separate. Help me be with and in, not apart from. Show me the way to savoring, not controlling. Dear God, hear my prayer: make me forever copeless.[4]

I don't know whether I can handle a copeless life yet, but I want to love like that. Jesus, instead of coping, drank the cup set before him. Like him, we will find ourselves in an obscure garden at some point in our journeys. We will mourn the love lost when the Judases in our lives let us down. We, like my grandpa, will face an obscure night when we have to come to grips with our mortality. We may have a cup that seems impossible to bear, like the one Jesus had to accept. But know this: love is worth the pain and heartache that it risks. To truly love, we must embrace what is real: love will lead us to pain. This pain is worth it. And love, not pain, will get the final word.

FORMATION EXERCISE

At the end of his earthly ministry, Jesus prayed in the Garden of Gethsemane, "Take this cup of suffering away from me" (Mark 14:36). "Cup" refers to the suffering he was about to endure. All of us have, or will have, cups to bear. In fact, anytime we step into relationships, we risk bearing a cup of pain. Love not only risks pain but also leads to it. In the end, Jesus shows us that risky love is worth it and is the cost of becoming human like him.

Scripture: Read or listen to Mark 14:32–42. As before, it helps to listen to stories like this.

Imagine: With all five senses, imagine you are part of the story. What does it look, feel, sound, smell, and taste like? In your mind, compose the place. (It helps to close your eyes.)

Do you identify with a character in the story as you listen and imagine? Are you in anguish like Jesus? A sleeping disciple? What do you notice about the scenery? How does Jesus's prayer sit with you?

Now, having immersed yourself in the story, think about your own obscure night or cup. How might Jesus help you step into that situation with risky love? Don't just think about it; talk with him about it. Pray and journal to capture some of what you are noticing.

CHAPTER 15

THE GOODNESS OF FRIDAY

* * *

The revelation of God's true character on Calvary was the explosion of light that in principle expelled all darkness and the explosion of love that in principle destroyed all hate. . . . But we will only benefit from this revelation if we hold fast to the conviction that the perfect, self-sacrificial love manifested on the cross defines God to the core of his being.

—GREG BOYD, *Benefit of the Doubt*

At my first retreat for training as a spiritual director,[1] I brought heavy burdens. It was the beginning of a season of questioning several things about my life and ministry. I had stepped into the in-between, that place of overlap between what is now and what is not yet. Fortunately, I had a space to sit with God and others as I sought clarity.

Truth be told, I didn't get clarity during that week. Only a reaffirmation of the echoing hope. Don't you love that about following Jesus? When we want answers, he usually lets us linger in the questions a bit longer.

As we've seen, affirmations of God's love prepare and propel us into whatever life may bring us next. That's the gift I experienced at this retreat. For example, during a formation exercise, I was handed a block of modeling clay. We were invited to use it as a tool for prayer and discernment. *The artistic folks, for sure, have an edge here,* I thought. *Here goes nothing.*

Nothing.

That's the best way to describe my art-prayer. Those of you who got bad grades in penmanship as a kid or avoided taking art as a high school elective know exactly what I'm talking about. Art = prayer? *Does not compute.*

Directionless, I rolled a clay ball. At this point I had no idea what would come next. A blue heart-shaped bowl I made for my mom when I was a child came to mind. It wasn't beautiful, but she loved it because it came from me. Aren't most moms awesome like that? As far as I remember, that lost childhood relic might be the last object I made from clay and was put to fire to solidify.

Then I remembered another lost childhood artifact from even earlier in my life: a clay print of my small hand that had hung on our wall for a short time. Not quite sure of these connections, I decided to press my adult-sized hand into the center of the bowl. It took a lot of work to get the handprint to show since the clay was quite stiff. With enough pressure, my hand made an impression, and my childlike prayer solidified as well.

In one way, my hand represented my whole life and current circumstances before God. The fog that kept me visionless kept the Lord unintimidated. I wanted answers; Jesus gave me a reminder, as though echoing back from lessons learned with him in other seasons.

When a leader announced that we needed to have at least one clay item that could hold water, I quickly recalled that first bowl I'd made as a child and worked the clay edges upward so that my flat hand became a saucer, ready to receive. My handprint was now a carved-out space to give myself over to the will of God with my hands open: a hand mounted on the Father's wall of love.

Jesus had to do the same thing. He opened his hands to nails, which left imprints of pain. His hands healed but forever displayed scars. His handprint features impressions of his fidelity to God the Father, even in the fog of humiliation, torture, and death.

So Much for Good Friday

In order to experience the joy of Easter morning, we have to endure the pain of Good Friday. *Good* Friday? What an odd thing to name it. What part is *good* about the torturous execution this day commemorates? It's bad marketing! It's like calling Folgers coffee, when it should be called "Folgers . . . falsely advertised ash beverage." (Forgive me. Having spent some years living in Seattle, I've become a bit of a coffee snob.)

When it comes to this day, how we frame it informs what Christianity teaches about what good actually is in reality. Some impressions we've sent into the world make God the Father seem like the kind of God who abandons and possibly even abuses the Son. That simply can't be true.

The nature of a book is that it is a one-way conversation. I get to say things directly to you. However, if we were sitting over a cup of specialty coffee, I'd want to hear all about what you imagine God to be like. I'd be equally curious about whether you've ever felt abandoned by God, a family member, or someone else. Of course, we will come to see that Jesus understands these feelings. Just think about Peter denying Jesus three times (John 18:15–27)! Peter, arguably the closest friend Jesus had, forsook that commitment in Jesus's greatest moment of agony. Abandonment, the utter sense that you are alone, is like being a lost wanderer when the only echo you hear is the repeated chorus of your own voice. Isolation disrupts God's desire for us. Intentional solitude as a spiritual practice is not loneliness; it's intimacy between us and our Creator. Abandonment, by contrast, is the violence done at the revocation of intimacy. The idea that God could ever forsake someone in such a way should be counterintuitive. We are designed for relationships with God and one another. This pattern of shalom creates the conditions we as image bearers need to carry out our purpose: to reflect God's stewardly love to the world.

When we feel abandoned, when our pain features more in our picture of God than Christ's love does, we risk allowing distorted pictures of God to rule over us. James Bryan Smith highlighted this:

> We are shaped by our stories. In fact, our stories, once in place, determine much of our behavior without regard to their accuracy or helpfulness. Once these stories are stored

in our minds, they stay there largely unchallenged until we die. And here is the main point: these narratives are running (and often ruining) our lives. That is why it is crucial to get the right narratives.[2]

The stories we tell ourselves about God matter. Whether we are in a season of pain, unclarity about the future, or questions about our purpose in life, when we encounter Jesus's compassionate humanity afresh in the midst of our curiosities, we step into the pain, unclarity, and questions in a completely different way.

How we see God in these moments of doubt gives us the framework we need to avoid distorting two images: our image of our self-worth and our image of God's perfect love toward us. The execution story of Jesus calls these two images into question for many people, especially during seasons of hurt or doubt.

IS GOD GOOD ON GOOD FRIDAY?

Good Friday is why, as Christians, we believe we can be saved from the powers of sin and death. A fancy word for the theory of how this works itself out is *atonement*. While I don't want to get too far into the weeds about this theological concept, it has clear ramifications for us as we think about God's posture toward God's children (including the Son of God!) and the story we tell ourselves about our intrinsic worth.

Whenever I wonder about the story Jesus is telling us about God's posture toward suffering humans, one thing that makes an instant impact on me is that Jesus died the most shameful death imaginable. He died as an outcast, executed with an excruciating method reserved for slaves, rebels, and vanquished enemies.

Jesus identifies with suffering humanity, first with the marginalized of the world and then with all others who struggle with hurts. Why, we wonder, would the King of the universe suffer and die like this? It speaks volumes about how God sees every image bearer. God gives us Jesus so we can become like him in our suffering. For those of us who have easier lives than Jesus, a poor first-century Palestinian Jew, one way we can participate "in his sufferings" is by "being conformed to his death" (Philippians 3:10). When my position in life isn't in the margins of culture, it's harder to experience the depths of Jesus in some ways—I can't quite relate to him. But suffering is an experience in which disciples are invited to "say no to themselves, take up their cross daily, and follow [Jesus]" (Luke 9:23). When we suffer, when we feel abandoned, beat up, humiliated, thirsty, and exposed, this is an opportunity for pain to do its purifying work as we identify with our suffering friend and Lord.

Of course, Jesus experienced unimaginable pain during his final hours of life—to the point of feeling utterly abandoned. In Matthew 27:46 and Mark 15:34, Jesus said, "My God, my God, why have you forsaken me?" (NRSV).

These words have been the source of many discussions throughout the centuries about the relationship of God the Father to God the Son. In some circles, the wrath of the Father against the Son is emphasized. Some have countered and said that if we aren't careful, the story of how the Trinity relates becomes something like cosmic child abuse. I've heard many firsthand accounts from people who have that picture and struggle to relate to God. Some have even walked away from faith. A God who is an angry Father hits too close to home. I get it. I've asked God similar questions as Jesus did, hundreds of times. It's probably what you've asked too: *God, where are you? Why did you leave me here? Why? Why? Why?*

I've heard some people say that in Jesus's final moments, God the Father turned away from God the Son in disgust of the sin that was placed upon Jesus. God withdrew presence while simultaneously pouring out wrath against the Son. No wonder, when some folks come to God with curiosity and hear this story, they are left wondering if we must "conclude that Jesus came to save us from God."[3] If you believe we need to be saved from God, then how does that inform your pain? Can you really trust a God like that with your hurts? Perhaps. But I wonder if the story is so . . . much . . . better.

A beautiful thing about the cross is that it reveals to us both the fullest picture of who God is and what God is like and the greatest human expression of love that we are called to imitate: self-giving love. The way we hold our pain and come alongside others who hurt is an opportunity to emulate the love put on display at the cross of Calvary. If the God of Good Friday is truly good, then the story of God the Father is nothing like abandoning a child or, worse, the sort of abandonment that involves emotional distance and physical abuse. Something more is going on here.

Let's temporarily jump into the deep end for a moment. It makes my whole point. When Jesus asked why God had forsaken him, he was quoting the first line of Psalm 22.[4] The whole verse is "My God, my God, why have you forsaken me? Why are you so far from helping me, from the words of my groaning?" (verse 1, NRSV). The psalmist felt abandoned, as if God had walked away in a most desperate time of need. The word *groaning*, of course, brings up images of the Hebrews in Egypt, groaning in their slavery, awaiting the day when God would hear their cry for help (similar to the groaning of creation, humankind, and the Spirit in Romans 8). The desperation in the psalm is clear. Notice also what happens when we compare Mark 15 to Psalm 22:

MARK 15	PSALM 22
garments (verse 24)	garments (verse 18)
two thieves bracket Jesus (verse 27)	bulls, lions, dogs encircle the psalmist (verses 12–13, 16)
wag their heads (verse 29)	wag their heads (verse 7)
cannot save himself (verse 31)	let God save him (verse 8)
reviled (verse 32)	scorned (verse 6)
great cry (verse 34)	great cry (verse 1)
centurion's cry; universal salvation (verse 39)	universal salvation (verses 27–31)

The chart comes from Timothy J. Geddert, *Mark,* Believers Church Bible Commentary (Scottdale, PA: Herald, 2001), 385. Also, to be clear, the label *universal salvation* doesn't imply Universalism as a theological system.

This comparison shows us that Mark certainly had the whole psalm in mind. He wanted us to notice these similarities so we would see that these things would have been on Jesus's mind as well. The other reality is that in ancient Jewish culture, it was common to quote one line of Scripture in order to bring up its entire context. So when Jesus quoted the first line of this psalm, he evoked every line. What does this mean? *That in his reference to total abandonment, Jesus was looking toward perfect redemption.*

Think of that image! The very cry of horror from the cross becomes the *definition* of echoing hope. Now we get to the question of God's character and God's posture toward image bearers. What can happen is to have in mind that God utterly abandoned Jesus to death. God pulled light-years away from him and was no longer in fidelity with the Son. And if we twist it further than what is logical, we can end up with the impression that God laid on Jesus a punishment for sin to satisfy an arbitrary set of rules. We have either a God who gets in the mess with image bearers or a God who demands appeasement through retribution.

> *The very cry of horror from the cross becomes the definition of echoing hope.*

Psalm 22 is about God identifying with us when we *feel* abandoned but actually are not!

Sit with that a bit more. We *feel* abandoned. We actually aren't. It reminds me of those moments when I was a kid, wondering whether God would save me from the abuse. It brings up moments of anxiety, fear, inadequacy, and hopelessness. *Where's Jesus?* moments come up for me. Yet if Jesus and the writer of Psalm 22 are correct, we are *never* alone. Never. What feels like divine social distancing is more like God crowding in on your six feet of space.* The problem is that pain blocks our perception, not

---

* Yes, this is a COVID-19 reference. If you read this book after the pandemic and those lines don't make sense, that's likely a good sign.

God's pursuit. God the Father, the Son, and the Spirit are always moving toward us—toward this world—to bring about as much good as possible in a given situation.

If we assume that Jesus has in mind only the first line of the psalm, we inevitably lose the echoes of hope resounding from his cry on the cross. In the darkest hour of his human life, God the Father didn't go missing. God is present even when we can't feel him. God doesn't pull away from us. God doesn't take wrath directed at us and throw it at Jesus instead. God doesn't need to be appeased to bring salvation. As Jesus died, the Father—just as at Jesus's baptism and again at the transfiguration (Mark 9:2–8)—had only love and affirmation toward the Son. Jesus knew this. He also knew that his pain felt like forsakenness.

What if forsakenness was the *experience* of the psalmist but not the *reality*? How does Psalm 22 end? It ends with the affirmation that what felt impossible to overcome has been accomplished by God on behalf of the sufferers! "[God] has done it" (Psalm 22:31, NRSV) means that God's empathy for image bearers compels God to experience the weight of suffering with us, with an ultimate end in mind, which the Bible often calls salvation—being rescued from circumstances that we could never deal with all alone.

When it comes to Jesus on the cross, this includes rescuing all of creation from slavery to sin, death, and the powers of evil by perfectly standing in for humankind and showing us what love in a broken world looks like at its core: self-giving love. In the moment when Jesus felt the most alone, he also experienced a Father of solidarity through his suffering, an empathic Father who remains close to all who feel abandoned, especially the left out, ignored, and oppressed. José Cárdenas Pallares reflected brilliantly,

> In placing Psalm 22 on Jesus' lips, the first Christians are seeing Jesus as truly abandoned—just as abandoned as the oppressed and crushed people of the psalm. His grief, like theirs, is indescribable and scandalous. It is the pain of the poor, whose cry mounts to God, and to whom God cannot remain insensitive.[5]

The grief of Jesus was shared by his Father. Grief won't get the final word, but it did get a powerful one as Jesus took his last breath.

WE ARE NOT ABANDONED

God the Father had no wrath to pour out on Jesus, only a plan to restore him after his darkest hour. While the feeling of abandonment was valid in one sense for Jesus, the truest experience Jesus had on the cross was that he *wasn't* alone. Thus, Luke's telling of the story shows us that even to his last breath, Jesus's Father communed with him: "Father, into your hands I commend my spirit" (Luke 23:46, NRSV). This is why, as Jesus quoted the one line of the psalm, and thus evoked every line of it, he brought to mind the comfort of the psalmist:

> Because he didn't despise or detest
>   the suffering of the one who suffered—
> he didn't hide his face from me.
> No, he listened when I cried out to him for help.
>   (Psalm 22:24)

As I said a bit ago, you probably know what it is like to feel abandoned. Likely, there were moments when the feeling mirrored your reality. Abandonment is one of the worst human experiences, a great injustice to God's dream for shalom. We were never meant to be alone (to which all of you extroverts yell out, "Amen!"). We are made for one another. Loneliness is a symptom of a world enslaved to evil. Jesus conquered such powers of darkness through his cross and resurrection, but the final enactment of that victory will not be fully realized until he returns to judge, purge, heal, resurrect, and restore the cosmos.

We are made for one another. Loneliness is a symptom of a world enslaved to evil.

So in these times of "already but not yet," when we feel abandoned, we know it's a symptom of something that's wrong and is not caused by the direct action of God. Perhaps you have even experienced moments when in crying out to God, you were touched by the One who never forsakes us (Hebrews 13:5). You are never alone—just as Jesus was never alone. God the Father was with him. The Trinity is with us. One of those persons of God also models what the fullness of human love looks like. Jesus shows us how to love and how to receive the love of the Father, even in our darkest hours of life.

A Father Who Holds a Son

In Luke 15, we get one of the clearest images of what God the Father is like. Jesus told the story of a son who forsook his father. After squandering his early inheritance, this prodigal chose to go home. The son was starving. He had hit rock bottom. With a speech prepared and rehearsed (you know you've had to do this sort of thing before . . . we all mess up!), he planned to ask his father if he could become a hired hand so that he wouldn't have to starve. Of course, the story ends with the father wrapping his arms around his son, which serves as an illustration of what God the Father is like: when God's children go their own way, God welcomes these exiles back with a firm and holy embrace.

Jesus differs from the prodigal son in one specific way: he never rebelled against and never was exiled from the Father. But, since we know how the Father embraces sinful exiles, why would we not expect the Father to have this same sort of affection toward the Son? When Jesus suffered for the sin of all creation, the Father was with him and so was the Spirit. I have a cross* that visually displays this unfathomable love of the Father:

---

* I bought this cross on Amazon. It is called "Holy Trinity Wall Cross." Here's a link: https://amzn.to/31wuG3g.

The powerful thing about this cross is that it helps us imagine the way God the Father, along with the Spirit, was present to Jesus during this moment when he absorbed the evil of the world on our behalf. The Father is holding Jesus. Do you need to experience such a kindness from God? I know I do. Jesus's main task was to model self-giving love, to endure suffering and death as our substitute who could defeat the powers of darkness on our behalf, conquering them through a love so powerful that we still hear its echoes two thousand years later. The Father held Jesus as they, together with the Spirit, "reconciled all things to himself" (Colossians 1:20) through this ultimate act of love.

How do you picture God? Can you imagine God holding your pain, embracing you as you bear your burdensome cross, even when it feels like you are alone? The triune God's posture toward the universe is love. God's attitude toward pain is compassion. God's remedy for our hurts is allowing the hurt of this world to do its worst to Jesus. We can be held by that God who "will never leave you or forsake you" (Hebrews 13:5, NRSV).

FORMATION EXERCISE

Our narratives about God shape our experience of and response to pain. If we believe God is capable of abandoning us, then we will feel alone in our worst moments. The truth is that although we will feel forsaken, God is always pursuing us. Love is the posture from which God holds our pain, just as the Father held the Son as he died for the sin of all creation on the cross.

Spend some time looking at the cross in this book. It represents something profound: God is with us in our most painful moments, just as God the Father was with God the Son during the crucifixion.

Reflect: What does this metaphorical picture of the Trinity during the death of Jesus narrate to you about God?

Pray: Sit in silence with the picture in front of you and invite Jesus into your pain, questions, challenges, and fears. Talk to Jesus through prayer and/or journaling.

Close with a simple prayer. Inhale slowly, saying, *You'll never leave me,* and exhale, saying, *or forsake me.* (Do this with your eyes closed and picturing the Trinity cross for a few minutes.)

CHAPTER 16

GARDEN OF HOPE

* * *

God knows and understands the grief of death. In our trinitarian
understanding of God, we believe that God the Father suffered in
the death of his only begotten Son. This means that we do not
seek a God who does not know loss. Rather, we seek a God who
knows the deepest kind of loss and has determined to end death
once and for all.

—VALERIE REMPEL,
Why Do We Suffer and Where Is God When We Do?

One of my favorite things, ever, is a game I play with my fifteen-month-old. For several months she's been able to say "Dada." When she started to connect the idea that these two syllables create my name, I was overjoyed. I have early memories of getting her out of bed to change her diaper and her looking up at me and saying "Dada" with joy. Over time she started saying it with adorable and hilarious baby inflection. "Dada! Da . . . daaaaa. DADA!" So I started responding to her with her name in the same tone: "Chloe! Chlo . . . eeee. CHLOE!"*

There is nothing like hearing someone you love say your name. Even today, as I was working on another chapter, Chloe, encouraged by her older sister, Lydia (who, for the record, is an amazing big sister), started again: "Da . . . daaaaaa." Lydia, echoing her sis-

---

* Hey, Chloe. If you ever get to an age where an old book from your Dada interests you, I hope you read this story and know just how loved you are. You are young right now, but I know God will guide you through the ups and downs of life. You and Lydia are truly gifts that Mommy and I are grateful to God for!

ter, shouted similarly. Here's the thing: I was in the zone. But eventually I couldn't take any more of the cuteness. I snuck around the corner and said their names as they sat at the kitchen table. Chloe couldn't stop laughing, and Lydia was glad I finally acknowledged their silly fun. Hearing those girls shout my name isn't simply about being reminded of a title I bear as a result of shared DNA. When they say Dada, Da-aaaaaa, or Daddy, I feel known by them and experience a gratitude beyond what I knew was possible. When they call me by name, I know I am loved.

Jesus has the same quality to him. He calls people out, by name, inviting them to experience the life they were created for. We'll take notice of a couple of examples of this sort of naming as we come to the close of our journey. My hope is that you are coming to see yourself as Jesus sees you. I desire that you would find yourself named as God's beloved image bearer. That you would discover that the shalom-shaped life Jesus modeled is, in fact, a life you can adopt yourself. I hope that you find the echoing hope of the first Easter morning, one that calls you out by name into a life where pain is redeemable as we become human like Jesus.

If this is the sort of life you long for, come with me to where our journey began: a garden with an echoey empty tomb.

Spending Time with the Gardener

In the previous two chapters, we moved from a garden of obscurity to a moment of self-giving love unlike the world had ever seen before or will ever see again. Now, in the garden where Jesus was laid to rest, we find Mary Magdalene in John's telling of the story. The Sunday morning after Jesus was crucified, Mary showed up at the graveside to mourn and found that the tombstone had been rolled away. On this "first day of the week" (John 20:1, 19), she discovered that not only had Jesus gone missing from her life, but now his body was missing too! This was a lot to hold.

In that moment of anguished hopelessness, she looked up and suddenly saw two angelic beings inside the cave-like tomb (verse 12). They asked her what might be the rudest question you could ever ask at a cemetery: "Why are you crying?" (verse 13). Can you imagine asking someone who is sitting at a graveside, "Why are you weeping?" Isn't this the epitome of insensitivity? After this offensive question, Mary turned around and saw a gardener.

This "gardener" then asked the same question: "Why are you crying?" (verse 15). (Good one, Captain Obvious.) Thanks to the narrator, we already know that this was a case of mistaken identity. This was the resurrected Jesus (verse 14)! Mary, who didn't have a clue at this point, answered by asking whether this person knew the whereabouts of Jesus's body. In her despair, she couldn't see that Jesus was standing right there in front of her—until that dramatic moment of shock that created a whole new world of possibilities for her (as if seeing two angels hadn't been unnerving enough). Jesus said one word that changed her world forever: "Mary" (verse 16).

Jesus said her name.

Something interesting happens here that requires us to know the rest of the gospel of John. In chapter 10 Jesus identified himself as the good shepherd who knows his sheep by name. Sheep respond when they hear his voice (verse 14–16).[1] What was happening in this scene with Mary? Jesus demonstrated his intimate shepherding approach to his loved ones by essentially saying, "I know you, Mary. Not only do I know you by name, but as soon as you start to understand how intimately I know you, you're going to recognize me for who I Am." At this moment of shock, she cried, "Rabbouni," which means "teacher" (20:16). Upon hearing Jesus say her name, Mary couldn't help but echo a name back to him!

The impossible had happened, and now her imagination for seeing a life full of purpose was unlocked! At this realization, Mary tried to cling to Jesus. Wouldn't you? If he died and his body got lost after that, she'd better not lose him a second time.

To this, Jesus responded, "Don't hold on to me, for I haven't yet gone up to my Father" (verse 17). In other words, "Don't get used to this, because I'm not going to be around for long. For my mission to be complete, I must leave to reign at the right hand of God, as we set up something fresh and new." The question is, What is this new thing that was kick-started by the resurrection and ascension of Jesus, the one enthroned as the world's true Lord? To answer this question, we ought to look a bit closer at John's gospel as a whole.

JESUS'S NEW THING

The gospel of John begins with a strong emphasis on creation. It clearly has Genesis 1, the creation story at the beginning of the Bible, in mind:

> In the beginning was the Word
>   and the Word was with God
>   and the Word was God.
> The Word was with God in the beginning.
> Everything came into being through the Word,
>   and without the Word
>   nothing came into being. (1:1–3)

This "Word" is a reference to Jesus without debate. It is the Word that is identified as God, the one through whom the cosmos came into being. By verse 14 of this chapter, it becomes clear that this Creator/Word/God "became flesh." The human Creator has now been formed in the womb of a human mother.

In John, Jesus died on the sixth day of the week, rested in the womb of the earth on the seventh, and was reborn through the echoing hope of resurrection on the eighth. But we all know that weeks have only seven days. God rested, so people rest (Genesis 2:2), just as Jesus rested after the intense week he'd endured. Now, on the eighth day, or "the first day of the week" (John 20:1, 19),[2] a renewed creation week has begun. Jesus is the beginning of a renewed human family.

If we add to our curiosities about John's creation theology an observation of his use of seven signs, reminding us of the seven days of creation, this gets even more interesting. The signs are as follows:

1. Water to wine (2:1–11)
2. Healing an official's son (4:46–54)
3. Healing a man by a pool (5:1–9)
4. Feeding five thousand (6:1–15)
5. Walking on water (6:16–21)
6. Healing a blind man (9:1–7)
7. Raising Lazarus (11:1–44)

These signs all point in the same direction: a new sign would signal a new set of seven—a new creation week. N. T. Wright helps us here, noting, "The Word through whom all things were made is now the Word through whom all things are remade. . . . Jesus's resurrection is to be seen as the beginning of the new world, the first day of the new week, the unveiling of the prototype of what God is now going to accomplish in the rest of the world."[3] If Jesus is the prototype of what humans are destined for, in his resurrection he unleashed the destiny of the whole cosmos. If that sounds like a big deal, it's because it is.

> *If Jesus is the prototype of what humans are destined for, in his resurrection he unleashed the destiny of the whole cosmos.*

RENAMING CREATION

When Mary Magdalene stood outside the tomb weeping and she thought the gardener showed up, she was mistaken on one level and profoundly correct on another. Jesus, the new Adam, the image bearer of God, was reclaiming the role of humanity in himself. He was inviting his "brothers and sisters" (20:17) to join him in becoming the stewards of God's world that we were meant to be from the very beginning. Jesus not only taught his followers to be people of shalom but now embodied it with the hope that all humans would join his movement of resurrection!

The end of the Bible, Revelation 21–22,[4] describes in imagery what the return of Jesus will bring to our world. We read of a heavenly New Jerusalem coming down to *this* earth. Eternity in God's restored earth will be the completion of creation, the beautiful union of heaven and earth. "Death will be no more. There will be no mourning, crying, or pain anymore, for the former things have passed away" (21:4).

Although the word *new* gives us English readers the sense that the "new heaven" and "new earth" (verse 1) will be brand-new, the Greek word *kainos* (καινός) literally means that something is new in nature or quality. We might think of it as something that is fresh.[5] Romans 8, another key passage about the Christian hope for this world, says that "the creation itself will be set free from slavery to decay and brought into the glorious freedom of God's children" (verse 21). The new week of creation that began with Jesus's resurrection and ascension will culminate in renewed heavens and a renewed earth.

Sound utopian? Sure does. But the point isn't that this is going to happen out there, sometime in the future. Rather, it's about living as though that future world has already started. When we take our pain, empowered by Jesus, into the world as energy for compassion, we model, like Jesus did, what God intends this world to be like. At Jesus's second coming, all poverty, pain, sickness, injustice, violence, and death will cease. Pain and loss will be healed, and those who do not persist in unbelief will hear Jesus call their names (Revelation 2:17; 3:5). A lamenting disciple experienced a foretaste of this when the resurrected Jesus simply said, "Mary."

NAMED BY JESUS

There's power in being named by Jesus and in partnering with him in naming others. A book that models this, *God in a Brothel,* tells the story of how Daniel Walker goes into sex trafficking situations to gather intel and coordinate raids with local authorities in various places throughout the world. He witnesses girls as young as five being exploited for sex. Walker, who writes under a pseudonym to protect his ongoing work identity, sensed a call to not ignore this dehumanizing perversion but to get involved with radical peacemaking work.

In the subtitles of each chapter, a different girl is named: "Her Name Is Mahal" or "Her Name Is Emily." They have faces and names. They aren't abstract ideas. They are named by God and named by the author. Sadly, mission after mission, Walker noticed a pattern as girls lost their sense of self-identity. After a few years of this sexual slavery, the girls would lose the life from their eyes. This state of dejection "murders the person but leaves their bodies alive."[6]

One of the names Walker highlights in his account is "Melissa." She was forced to work in a bar and would soon be sold to the highest bidder, but in the last moments, a coordinated raid saved her life. Three years later Melissa was full of life once again. When Daniel Walker saw her again, she informed him that her goal is to become a lawyer to advocate for girls who are in bondage. She later sent him a postcard to thank him for saving her:

> I wish that you will never be tired of helping such many children like me. . . . Thank you for all the help and support that you have given and showed me. I promise I will try my best to achieve all my goals in life, I'll reach for them. . . . I will never forget you, never.[7]

Melissa, a girl whom corrupt men wrote off as an object for their perversion, was "named." She was liberated into her true identity. Her rescue from the pit of evil opened a whole new world of possibilities for her. Jesus desires that we step into the world's pain, echoing hope to the hurting as we wait for him to bring creation to an eternal state of shalom.

Melissa wasn't only called out by name. In finding freedom from the darkness, she was empowered to leverage her pain for the sake of others. It's true in many cases, as the old saying goes, that "hurt people hurt people." But when hurt people are named, when their identities are given room to image God to the world to their full potential, then "hurt people heal people."

Can you imagine being called out by name by Jesus? You aren't likely in a circumstance like Melissa. None of us were in the garden with Mary when Jesus spoke her name. But Jesus still calls people out of darkness and suffering of all sorts. Jesus still speaks words of life, healing, and possibility. Jesus still calls your name.

Life with the Resurrected Jesus

Mary didn't recognize Jesus until he said her name, but in naming her, Jesus names all of us who listen for the echoing hope that redeems our pain. As in Jesus's parable of the prodigal son, he shows us that even after our rejection, the Father is pursuing us with open arms (Luke 15:11–32). Jesus shows us that in the new week of creation, all are welcome to the party to experience the embrace of God.

We all need hope, but the fact that hope exists at all is a reminder that things aren't right. When all is made right, hope will be a mere memory, actualized by an unfathomable love. Dennis Edwards said, "Hope gives people who appear powerless the wherewithal to survive, and in many cases, to thrive."[8] Hope is born out of loss, inequities, struggle, and pain to point us toward a day when we will all be free from such burdens. This is why Paul the apostle said that becoming like Jesus is like looking at him with unveiled faces, in all vulnerability, and in the process of life moving from "one degree of glory to the next degree of glory" (2 Corinthians 3:18). Following the resurrected Jesus is a process of growth, not a one and done.

Even Peter denied being associated with Jesus three times. Jesus, in John 21, welcomed him back with arms open. He affirmed Peter as many times as Peter repudiated him: three times (verses 15–17). Jesus told Peter that *love* was the defining characteristic of their relationship. Peter moved from painful shame to powerful redemption because Jesus . . . is . . . alive!

Echoing hope isn't only the power of resurrection motivating you to persevere. *Echoing hope is now your vocation:* you are the echoes of Easter that this world needs. Let your pain energize your empathy. Let the holy embrace of a loving God move you to embrace others.

> *Echoing hope isn't only the power of resurrection motivating you to persevere. Echoing hope is now your vocation.*

Where Is Jesus?

As I've shared throughout this book, my childhood was full of trauma. You'll recall that at the beginning of our journey together, I shared about a traumatic memory that my therapist invited me to use in a spiritual practice. I was to imagine that memory and ask, *Where was Jesus in the room?* This risked a great disappointment. I composed the place and came up completely empty. Jesus was nowhere to be found.

As I sat at my kitchen table, pleading with Jesus to show up in the room with my fourth-grade self, I yielded defeat. I wondered whether composing the place of such a painful memory had been merely to reopen a wound. I struggled to find a positive spin for this exercise that I could report back to my therapist.

Where was Jesus in the room? Nowhere to be found.

Maybe you have stories in which you struggle to see how Jesus could be in the room with you. We all have bad memories that remind us that God can't always intervene how God wants to. Some people have stories that are more severe than mine. Others have experienced different kinds of grief. But we have one thing in common: sometimes when life is difficult, Jesus is hard to find.

I remember that as I prayed through this memory, I wanted nothing more than to find Jesus without forcing a pseudospiritual experience. As my doubts compounded, all at once something shifted. I had the sudden sense that Jesus was in the room! Jesus showed up—but not where I would have guessed. I expected he might be in the corner of the room as a gentle observer. Or perhaps trying to get in the way of the abuser. But Jesus wasn't anywhere that I expected.

He was next to me.

Jesus was holding me.

As the words "You were holding me" fell from my lips, I lost it. My body shook. Tears flowed. It was perhaps the most cathartic experience I've ever had. Each time I uttered "You were holding me," a rush of emotional healing poured out over my body. Jesus was there. He was holding me, both as a fourth grader and even now.

Jesus, in that moment of prayerful remembering, offered his empathic humanity. That memory was rewired in my brain, opening up new ways of experiencing life with God and others. My past cannot be erased. It cannot be overcome by willpower. But it can come into contact with the echoing hope of the resurrected Jesus. Jesus was in the room, and I was unaware.

He was holding me. My guess is that he holds us more often than we realize, as he holds our sorrow as his own. The wounded hands of Jesus hold us in our pain, preparing us for our ultimate healing on the day when heaven's hope will heal earth's sorrow.

May you come to know that you are held by the loving arms of Jesus, even when all hope seems lost. May you find comfort in the mysterious embrace of the fully human one, God in the flesh, who knows your pain more intimately than you could ever comprehend. Hear Jesus say your name as you cling to him for dear life.

The Father's arms are open, ready for the day when we start running toward a divine embrace. Jesus is ready to meet us, just as he met Peter on the shore and restored him three times, no matter the pain or shame we hold at this point of life's journey. Pain happens. Love makes us vulnerable. But in all of it, Jesus holds us with his tender humanity. So, may we hear an echoing hope from an empty tomb, proclaiming the word that the Father professed over the Son: you are loved, you are loved, yes—*you* are loved.

So, what do we do with that sort of unconditional love? When others hurt, we offer it as indiscriminately as Jesus does. When we hurt, we allow it to empower us to move through suffering in a new way. Love isn't the remedy to pain—at least in this life. Just as Jesus didn't neglect his own pain but went to the cross and laid down his life for friends and enemies alike, so we embrace pain and invite it into companionship with God's love. The echoing hope of the first Easter invites us to hold our pain with Jesus and to watch as he redeems our hurts by healing our humanity one day, one tear, one love at a time.

FORMATION EXERCISE

Jesus's pain was redeemed in resurrection. This is the ultimate fulfillment of hope for all who follow him. Resurrection for us, on that final day, will be the moment we become fully human forever, just like Jesus. The ultimate redemption of our pain is coming, and in many ways, because Jesus stepped out of a tomb that first Easter morning, our pain is redeemable even now.

Scripture: Read or listen to John 20:1–18. As a reminder, it helps to listen to stories like this.

Imagine: With all five senses, imagine you are part of the story. What does it look, feel, sound, smell, and taste like? In your mind, compose the place. (It helps to close your eyes.)

Whom do you identify with in this story? Which character could you play in a reenactment? Jesus? Mary? The angels? Peter and John? An onlooker?

What do you sense Jesus might be saying to you through this story so far?

Now read or listen to the story one more time. When Jesus says "Mary," imagine it is your name being said. Spend time meditating on the impact of Jesus's naming you in this moment. How does it open you up to a new way of holding your hurts? How does it reframe how you live your life each day? Jesus says your name. He must truly love you.

Journal: Journal if it helps you process the exercise.

EPILOGUE

*   *   *

The tomb is empty. A hope unleashed two thousand years ago echoes with God's love for this world. *Hope*—that even though so much here is wrong, there is a God who will move heaven and earth to make things right.

Jesus is what it looks like when God shows us how to be human. Immunity to pain is something that cannot be claimed of God since in Jesus we have a God who experienced excruciating suffering. In Jesus, God suffers with us all.

> *In Jesus, God suffers with us all. And because of his presence, suffering doesn't get the final word. Love does.*

And because of his presence, suffering doesn't get the final word. Love does. If I've learned anything in my journey with pain, it is that the love of Jesus helps me step into my pain differently. I don't have to ignore it to make it through the day. I don't have to let it define me either. Rather, what defines me is God's declaration of love and my own quest to become more fully human like Jesus.

This can be abstract for me at times. However, I continue to find that the classical spiritual exercises, such as prayer, Bible study, solitude, silence, worship, and so on, open the windows of my interior just enough to let God's healing light in—however dim it may seem at times. Then there are those moments when in my own way, Jesus and I have "conversations." We spend time together. And these don't always occur during the formal devotional times I carve out. I'm learning to work with Jesus. Play with Jesus. Drive with Jesus. Parent with Jesus. Hang with my friends with Jesus. And hopefully I'm becoming more *like* Jesus in the process. Spending time with Jesus, I've found, begins with an intentional awareness that he is *always* in the room—even if it isn't obvious at first.

One of the things I continue to learn is that although wounds heal, scars don't easily disappear. I'm increasingly okay with that. As an adult, I've returned to my scars to discover that in them I bear the marks of healing, though I'll never be able to make them fully fade away. Jesus's scars didn't disappear either, so I guess I'm in good company. The fact that I still have them is an invitation to explore how else God might redeem my pain to bring more shalom to my soul and to send me out to echo hope for the flourishing of others.

In Jesus, I'm learning the rhythms of redemption as I become more fully human *like* and *with* him. May you step into your next moment with an overwhelming awareness that Jesus is *for* you, *with* you, and *in* you. May you discover a holy courage to face challenges, pain, and loss with Godlike empathy for yourself and others.

And may the echoing hope of an empty grave empower you to bring the humanity of Jesus with you wherever you go.

Now and forever.

—Kurt

AFTERWORD

*   *   *

"Does God hurt with us?" This is a deeply personal question that cuts to the root of our theology and lives. Since early in the history of Christian theology, certain versions of the doctrine of "divine impassibility" (which argues that God remains untouched by suffering) suggested that the answer to that question is no.

But then came the twentieth century. Advancements in technology tragically increased human suffering, and increased the stakes of the ancient question. At the same time as our species was making significant advancements in medical science that lessened the suffering from disease, we also learned how to mechanize war and subject entire regions to totalitarian control. From the Gatling gun to the hydrogen bomb, from the Third Reich to Pol Pot, the capacity to inflict suffering became exponential—and cast the ancient question in a new light. The crematoriums of Auschwitz and the killing fields of Cambodia haunt our memories and torture our imaginations. In the ghastly light of the Holocaust, the language of divine impassibility became untenable. From a cell in the Flossenbürg concentration camp, shortly before his execution at the hands of the Nazis, Dietrich Bonhoeffer penned these words: "Only the suffering God can help."[1]

The triune God not only knows the sufferings of Christ but also knows the sufferings of each and every one of us. But this truth does not stop with abstract theology. It can become part of our lives. For that to happen, we must find better ways of talking about God and our suffering. This is what Bonhoeffer—as a theologian, a pastor, and a sufferer—understood.

The God revealed in Jesus Christ is all-loving, all-knowing, and all-powerful. Yet the world we live in is full of unjust suffering. We confess that the living God is love, yet babies get brain cancer and brides die on their wedding days. How do we reconcile this? We can't ignore the problem of pain.

Kurt Willems understands that without authentic freedom, we do not actually exist as authentic beings. We are more than just a movie playing in God's head. We have will. We have freedom. We have choice—and all the possibility and pain that choice contains. To be something other than a figment of God's imagination, we must have some degree of real freedom. But that freedom seems to come at a high price.

But here is the good news—God does not stand aloof from us. God participates in our suffering. Through Christ, the "Man of Sorrows," human suffering mysteriously entered the fellowship of the Trinity. This is not merely the comfort of divine solidarity with human suffering (though it's that too); rather, Christian hope asserts that *suffering is not the end.*

The apostle Peter echoed Isaiah when he said, "by his wounds you were healed" (1 Peter 2:24; Isaiah 53:5). What *Echoing Hope* has shown us is that when we bring our wounds to the wounds of Christ, it does not multiply woundedness but begins the healing process. Yet Christian hope for healing in Christ is even more bold, for we confess that in the end death itself will be fully undone. This undoing began on the first Easter and now, amid our woundedness, we await the day when death is destroyed "so that God may be all in all" (1 Corinthians 15:28).

It is not human pain, but divine love, that will have the final say.

This is our echoing hope.

—*Brian Zahnd, lead pastor of Word of Life Church*

ACKNOWLEDGMENTS

*   *   *

This book is a dream come true. Many people shared in its fruition. I have to say a huge thank you to my agent, Rachelle Gardner, who from the beginning believed in me and what would become this book. The same is true of my editor, Paul Pastor (along with the whole team at WaterBrook). Paul, you are truly the creative partner who brought this project to life.

Many other thank-yous are in order, some of which won't fit here. Thanks to my "beta" readers who gave me valuable feedback on early versions of this book (T. C. Moore, Stephanie Zimmerman, Kyle Warkentin, and others named below). And to all my friends and family members who have supported me through the years—I'm grateful.

I think of my early years at Dinuba Mennonite Brethren Church. I'm grateful for my first church and for the ways many of you stepped in at strategic points in my life (more than I can name here!). Thank you . . . Glen and Peggy Zimmerman—for love, safety, fun, and early memories. You are amazing. Brent and Teresa Cummings—for guiding a misguided kid toward the love of Jesus and ministry to the local church. Also, you showed me that church could be cool. Pastors Bob and Grayson—you showed me Jesus and encouraged my path during crucial years.

Without the support of the community at Immanuel Junior High and High School, I don't know where I'd be in my walk with Christ. Thank you . . . friends and teachers—for creating space for me to discover more of Jesus during my teens after such a challenging childhood. Also, thanks to several families, including the Thomases, Souza/Yockeys, Alvarados, and so many others.

I've had some amazing mentors in recent years. Thank you . . . Steve Reimer, Jeff Wright, Perry Engle, Chris Lewis, and Todd Spencer—for guiding me closer to Jesus and profound wholeness. Mark Baker, Valerie Rempel (especially Spiritual Memoirs!), Tim Geddert, Lynn Jost, and others at Fresno Pacific—for shaping me as a person, pastor, and communicator. Michael Williams, Jim Wellman, and others at the University of Washington—for empowering me to explore scholarship and teaching while calling out my gifts. And Stewards of the Mystery (a spiritual direction training cohort), particularly Steve Reimer, Kathy McFaul, and Tara Owens, along with other staff, program mentors, and cohort members—for cultivating space to encounter God in one another. This book is in many ways the outflow of our two years together.

I have too many friends who contributed to this book directly or indirectly to name them all. Thank you . . . Jeff Zimmerman, Jason Ekk, and Brad Bowman (and your wives and kids)—for this: We ride together. We die together. You each deserve a page of acknowledgments, but you'll have to settle for a round of drinks and nachos. Your influence on my journey goes beyond words. Forrest Jenan—for our thousands of conversations and hundreds of memories that continue to shape my life. You are a great friend. Anthony Alvarado—for being a brother and for amazing memories. Zach Penner—for being able to laugh together and for being a friend/cousin I can count on. Juanita "Shelly" Carter—for being a cousin and friend who continues to inspire me to follow Jesus. Peter Thomas—for significant memories of seeking Jesus together as teens . . . and football. Daragh Hoey—for making Seattle feel like home, for great memories with our families, and for a friendship that will last a lifetime. Derrick Miller—for memories dating back to Pop Warner football, through youth group and college, and into these years of friendship and support. Matt Craft—for the amazing times with you, as couples, or with the kiddos. Your family is a gift to us.

Hank Johnson, Josh Crain, Justin Douglas, Ryan Showalter,

David Flowers, Keith Miller, Jeff Miller, Jacob Evers, Drew Strayer, Jon Hand, Alan Claasen Thrush, Luke Embree, Devin Thomas, and *so many other friends* I've made through the BIC—for solidarity, friendship, and holy sarcasm. Cohort friends from Paseo, some who include Gavin Linderman, Lance Linderman, Jason Phelps, Paul Bartel, and Austin Livingston—for our years of transformation together, which have shaped this book and my life in so many ways. Also, Jan Johnson and Keith Matthews—for the fresh wind of God you helped create space for in that group. David Castro—for the long talks about life, writing, and "solving the world's problems." Nathan McCorkindale—for great conversations, seminary memories, and ongoing friendship. The Bests and Smiths—for being our friends and giving us space to lean into the kingdom.

Jenn and Andrew Shaffer—for your partnership in ministry and life. Brett Thatcher—for taking the risk of moving to Seattle and for your loyal friendship. All my church family members at Pangea Church, past and present (too many to name here!)—for times of laughter, tears, hope, joy, and everything in between. You are a *gift*. And the list goes on: my brothers-in-law, Bryan and Paul Suhovy; my friends Guy Graham, Ryan Morey, Benjamin Corey (and the Undiluted Group), Tony Scarcello, Orlando Ramirez, Brian Henderer (and others from California Christian College), Jay Kim, Adam Souza, Nick Chandler, Riley Endicott, Nick Larsen, Rev. Canon Britt Olson, and Tim Gleghorn; and all my other friends who will have to go unnamed here, know that I am grateful.

The many people who support my work as a writer and podcaster—for every email, share, and conversation that you allowed my work to help facilitate ... wow ... thank you! Some early supporters of this particular book need to be named. Thank you ... Ben Higgins—for your friendship and enthusiastic support of my book. Cara Meredith—for helping me make connections and believing in this project early on. Greg Boyd, Scot McKnight, Brian Zahnd, Bruxy Cavey, and Aaron Niequist—for your support through the years and for writing "pre-endorsements" for the book proposal. On this same note of gratitude, I also want to honor the memory of Rachel Held Evans, who in our last interaction before her tragic passing blessed me with a pre-endorsement too: "I'm eager to read his insights . . . and would be first in line to enthusiastically endorse." She made this world better.

Lastly, my family. Lauren's family—for accepting me as your own son or brother and for supporting us all in so many ways (including my mother-in-law, Ellenia, who cheers me on as a writer). My Penner side and my Willems side (including my uncles, aunts, and cousins)—for supporting and loving me through the years. I'm beyond grateful. Some of you feature in parts of the book, while others do not, but you *all* hold a unique place in my heart and story. Mom—for loving and celebrating me (and for all those times you sing "Happy Birthday" on my voice mail). Dad— for being a steadfast guide and an anchor in my life. Christina— for stepping into my story and embracing me as one of your own. My siblings—for memories that bring me joy and for a bond that goes beyond circumstance. Grandma—for being *more* than a grandma by contending for me during difficult times and believing in me throughout the journey. Also, you know how to have fun. Grandpa Corny and Uncle Dennis—for being heroes in my life. Until the day of resurrection, you will be missed.

My daughters, Chloe and Lydia—you are my greatest accomplishment. I love and treasure you both beyond words. And my dearest Lauren—for the kind of love that brings me to tears at the thought of writing your name in acknowledgment. These tears evidence the safety, support, passion, and friendship I've found in you. You are my best friend. You are my favorite. Isn't Jesus so good?

NOTES

*   *   *

Introduction: Jesus, Pain, and Becoming Human

1. Dietrich Bonhoeffer, *God Is in the Manger: Reflections on Advent and Christmas*, trans. O. C. Dean Jr., ed. and comp. Jana Riess (Louisville, KY: Westminster John Knox, 2010), 52. Thank you to Brian Zahnd for sharing this quote with me!

Chapter 1: Where Is Jesus?

1. James Martin, SJ, *The Jesuit Guide to (Almost) Everything: A Spirituality for Real Life* (New York: HarperCollins, 2010). See, especially, chapter 7: "God Meets You Where You Are: Ignatian Traditions of Prayer."
2. Martin, *The Jesuit Guide*, 130.
3. The website Orientations for Spiritual Growth, led by Jesuits in Canada, offers an example of this called "Healing of Memories for Oneself" at http://orientations.jesuits.ca/prayer.html#selfhealing. See also Dawn Eden, *Remembering God's Mercy: Redeem the Past and Free Yourself from Painful Memories* (Notre Dame, IN: Ave Maria, 2016).
4. Dictionary.com, s.v. "doubting Thomas," www.dictionary.com/browse/doubting-thomas.

Chapter 2: Just in Case You Haven't Noticed, Something's Wrong

1. Scot McKnight, *The Blue Parakeet: Rethinking How You Read the Bible*, 2nd ed. (Grand Rapids, MI: Zondervan, 2018), 78–81.
2. Cornelius Plantinga Jr., *Not the Way It's Supposed to Be: A Breviary of Sin* (Grand Rapids, MI: Eerdmans, 1995), 16. In the early part of his book, Plantinga brilliantly discusses the relationship of sin to shalom. I'm indebted to him for this connection.
3. Nicholas Wolterstorff, *Lament for a Son* (Grand Rapids, MI: Eerdmans, 1987), 91.

4. Dawn Eden, *Remembering God's Mercy: Redeem the Past and Free Yourself from Painful Memories* (Notre Dame, IN: Ave Maria, 2016), 47. With the help of Pope Francis, her fresh insights on this story, through the lens of trauma, opened up the Resurrection to me in a whole new way.

Chapter 3: Human . . . Like Jesus?

1. For an excellent and balanced argument for Jesus's divine portrayal in the gospel of Mark, see Timothy J. Geddert, "The Implied YHWH Christology of Mark's Gospel: Mark's Challenge to the Reader to 'Connect the Dots,'" *Bulletin for Biblical Research* 25, no. 3 (2015): 325–40. He rightly highlighted that even where Jesus is portrayed explicitly in human terms, there are clues in the text that alert us to his divinity as well.

   For an approach to the Synoptic Gospels that focuses on Jesus as an idealized human figure, see J. R. Daniel Kirk, *A Man Attested by God: The Human Jesus of the Synoptic Gospels* (Grand Rapids, MI: Eerdmans, 2016). While I am uncertain that I would go as far as Kirk on some points, I appreciate his attention to the humanity of Jesus in his study.
2. N. T. Wright, *How God Became King: The Forgotten Story of the Gospels* (New York: HarperOne, 2012), 56.
3. Michael Gorman wrote of Philippians 2, "In Christ's preexistent and incarnate kenosis [from the Greek word for "empty"] we see truly what God is truly like, and we simultaneously see truly what Adam/humanity truly should have been, truly was not, and now truly can be in Christ. *Kenosis is theosis.* To be like Christ crucified is to be both most godly and most human." Michael J. Gorman, *Inhabiting the Cruciform God: Kenosis, Justification, and Theosis in Paul's Narrative Soteriology* (Grand Rapids, MI: Eerdmans, 2009), 37.
4. I love John Mark Comer's reflection on Jesus's humanity: "If you want to know what a human being, fully awake and alive, ruling over the world as a conduit for the Creator God's love looks like in flesh and blood—then look at Jesus." John Mark Comer, *Garden City: Work, Rest, and the Art of Being Human* (Grand Rapids, MI: Zondervan, 2015), 139.
5. Gorman, *Inhabiting the Cruciform God,* 36.

Chapter 4: Why Suffering?

1. Eva M. Krockow, "How Many Decisions Do We Make Each Day?," *Psychology Today,* September 27, 2018, www.psychologytoday.com/us/blog/stretching -theory/201809/how-many-decisions-do-we-make-each-day.
2. "Current World Population," Worldometer, www.worldometers.info/world -population.
3. I used this illustration in a sermon series I taught a few years ago. I don't remember if I came up with the idea to multiply all the choices in this format

or not. If this formula came from another source, thank you and my sincere apologies for not knowing who to give credit to.

4. Several incidents are recorded within and beyond the New Testament about Pontius Pilate's cruel posture toward the Jewish people. Here are the accounts from outside the Bible: (1) Philo (*Embassy to Gaius* 299–305) tells us that Pilate tried to set up shields in the temple, which likely identified the emperor as divine; (2) Josephus (*Jewish War* 2.169–74, *Jewish Antiquities* 18.55–59) tells of a time when Pilate attempted to bring the military standards bearing the image of the emperor into Jerusalem (the issue is that it would be idolatry); (3) Josephus (*Jewish War* 2.175–77, *Jewish Antiquities* 18.60–62) records that Pilate stole money from the temple treasury to pay for an aqueduct; (4) Josephus (*Jewish Antiquities* 18.85–89) recounts Pilate's soldiers' attack on Samaritans at Mount Gerizim, where the death toll was significant. The ancient historian believed this was against God's will. For an introduction to these incidents, see Warren Carter, *Pontius Pilate: Portraits of a Roman Governor*, ed. Barbara Green (Collegeville, MN: Liturgical Press, 2003), 13–20.

5. See N. T. Wright, *Christian Origins and the Question of God*, vol. 2, *Jesus and the Victory of God* (London: Society for Promoting Christian Knowledge, 1996), 330–31.

6. In a book this size, I can't get into the biblical arguments as much as I would like to in this section. I highly recommend *Is God to Blame?* by Greg Boyd as a next step for those interested. Here's a helpful quote: "Behind every particular event in history lies an impenetrably vast matrix of interlocking free decisions made by humans and angels. We experience life as largely arbitrary because we can't fathom the causal chains that lie behind every particular event. In Christ, God's character and purposes are not mysterious, but the vast complexity of causal chains is. The mystery of evil, therefore, is about an unfathomably complex and war-torn creation, not about God's character and purposes in creation." Gregory A. Boyd, *Is God to Blame?: Beyond Pat Answers to the Problem of Suffering* (Downers Grove, IL: InterVarsity, 2003), 80.

7. Bonnie Kristian summarized the open future view (she has a chapter comparing popular perspectives): "The future is partly settled but also partly open. The settled parts are things God has determined will happen, like his final victory over evil. We don't have to wonder if that will come true, because God settled it.

"But the category of settled things is much smaller than the category of things that are genuinely open to multiple possibilities. In this bigger category, God has perfect knowledge of everything that *could* happen and is *likely* to happen, but he doesn't know what *will* happen, because that part of the future doesn't exist to be known." Bonnie Kristian, *A Flexible Faith: Rethinking What It Means to Follow Jesus Today* (New York: FaithWords, 2018), 31.

8. Kristian, *A Flexible Faith*, 32.

9. C. S. Lewis, *The Problem of Pain,* first paperback ed. (New York: HarperOne, 2001), 63, 65.

10. For a more thorough reflection, see Gregory A. Boyd, *God of the Possible: A Biblical Introduction to the Open View of God* (Grand Rapids, MI: Baker, 2000), 98–99.
11. My director was happy to have me share this insight but didn't want to be named when given credit for it.
12. Walter Brueggemann, *Praying the Psalms: Engaging Scripture and the Life of the Spirit*, 2nd ed. (Eugene, OR: Cascade Books, 2007), 3.
13. Soong-Chan Rah, *Prophetic Lament: A Call for Justice in Troubled Times* (Downers Grove, IL: InterVarsity, 2015), 21.
14. For a historical introduction to the basic "facts on the ground" of the Exile, see Walter Brueggemann, *Out of Babylon* (Nashville: Abingdon, 2010), 1–3.

Chapter 5: Vulnerable Courage

1. "Miscarriage," Mayo Clinic, www.mayoclinic.org/diseases-conditions/pregnancy-loss-miscarriage/symptoms-causes/syc-20354298.
2. Brené Brown, *Daring Greatly: How the Courage to Be Vulnerable Transforms the Way We Live, Love, Parent, and Lead* (New York: Avery, 2012), 34.
3. My friend Jer Swigart often speaks of helping others flourish. I adopted this language from him because it speaks to me.
4. Quoted in Richard A. Horsley, *Jesus and Empire: The Kingdom of God and the New World Disorder* (Minneapolis: Fortress, 2003), 23.
5. Quoted in Horsley, *Jesus and Empire*, 23–24.
6. Brown, *Daring Greatly*, 30. Later, I borrow her language and apply it to Jesus, who "showed up and let himself be seen."

Chapter 6: Embraced and Empowered

1. On this point, N. T. Wright gives some important context for understanding the word *repent* in *The Challenge of Jesus: Rediscovering Who Jesus Was and Is* (Downers Grove, IL: InterVarsity, 1999), 43–44.
2. N. T. Wright, *Mark for Everyone* (London: Society for Promoting Christian Knowledge, 2001), 4–6.
3. As Jonathan Martin wrote, "If Jesus really is the prototype for a whole new way of being human, and His way of functioning in the world is as revolutionary as I believe it is, if we will just show up, He'll take care of the heavy lifting." Jonathan Martin, *Prototype: What Happens When You Discover You're More Like Jesus Than You Think?* (Carol Stream, IL: Tyndale Momentum, 2013), 98.

Chapter 7: God in the Desert

1. Dallas Willard, *The Spirit of the Disciplines: Understanding How God Changes Lives* (San Francisco: HarperSanFrancisco, 1988), 101–2.

2. Willard, *Spirit of the Disciplines,* 102.

3. These reflections are inspired by Brené Brown, *Daring Greatly: How the Courage to Be Vulnerable Transforms the Way We Live, Love, Parent, and Lead* (New York: Avery, 2012), 18–30.

4. Jesus was led into the wilderness by God (Deuteronomy 8:2; Luke 4:1). Jesus spent forty days wandering, giving homage to the forty years Israel spent doing likewise (Exodus 16:35; Numbers 14:34; Deuteronomy 8:2, 4; Psalm 95:10; Luke 4:2; Acts 7:36). Jesus is God's Son and so is Israel (Exodus 4:22–23; Luke 4:3, 9; and many other places in the New Testament). Jesus was tested in this situation like Israel was tested (Deuteronomy 6–8). An important contrast, however: Jesus was full of the Spirit and followed the Spirit's leading, whereas Israel "rebelled and grieved his holy spirit" (Isaiah 63:10, NRSV). Many of the insights in this section are aided by Joel B. Green, *The Gospel of Luke,* The New International Commentary on the New Testament (Grand Rapids, MI: Eerdmans, 1997), 190–96.

5. Gregory A. Boyd, *The Myth of a Christian Nation: How the Quest for Political Power Is Destroying the Church* (Grand Rapids, MI: Zondervan, 2005), 20–22.

6. Green, *Gospel of Luke,* 194.

7. Boyd, *Myth of a Christian Nation,* 14.

8. Green, *Gospel of Luke,* 196.

9. Green, *Gospel of Luke,* 195.

Chapter 8: Normal Isn't Negative

1. Wikipedia, s.v. "sea legs," last modified February 17, 2015, 20:23, https://en.wikipedia.org/wiki/Sea_legs. This term can also be used in a positive sense to mean that a sailor is steady on the rocking deck of a boat. That wasn't true in my case after returning to solid ground.

2. Timothy J. Geddert, *Mark,* Believers Church Bible Commentary (Scottdale, PA: Herald, 2001), 56–57.

Chapter 9: Love in Advance

1. Dallas Willard, *The Divine Conspiracy: Rediscovering Our Hidden Life in God* (New York: HarperCollins, 1998), 41.

2. Jayson Georges and Mark D. Baker, *Ministering in Honor-Shame Cultures: Biblical Foundations and Practical Essentials* (Downers Grove, IL: InterVarsity, 2016), 40.

3. Georges and Baker, *Ministering in Honor-Shame Cultures,* 42.

4. Brené Brown, *Daring Greatly: How the Courage to Be Vulnerable Transforms the Way We Live, Love, Parent, and Lead* (New York: Avery, 2012), 69.

5. Georges and Baker, *Ministering in Honor-Shame Cultures,* 119–20.

6. On pride, shame, and humility, check out Dan Kent, *Confident Humility: Be-*

coming Your Full Self Without Becoming Full of Yourself (Minneapolis: Fortress, 2019).

7. Dallas Willard, *The Spirit of the Disciplines: Understanding How God Changes Lives* (San Francisco: HarperSanFrancisco, 1988), 7–8.

8. Dennis Edwards, *1 Peter,* The Story of God Bible Commentary (Grand Rapids, MI: Zondervan, 2017), 114. He added, "Godly slaves must submit to their masters no matter how kind or how harsh the treatment from those masters might be; Peter assumes it may be severe. . . . It must be seen, however, that Peter gives absolutely no validation of harsh treatment by slave masters. His advocacy of nonretaliatory behavior is not an endorsement of slavery and is also not an indication of the weakness of slaves. Peaceful submission to even the harshest of masters is evidence of genuine Christian faith. The point is to grasp what Christlike behavior looks like in one of the most difficult situations imaginable" (116).

9. I can't give a full defense of Christian nonviolence here. Check out: Preston Sprinkle, *Fight: A Christian Case for Nonviolence* (Colorado Springs: David C Cook, 2013); Brian Zahnd, *A Farewell to Mars: An Evangelical Pastor's Journey Toward the Biblical Gospel of Peace* (Colorado Springs: David C Cook, 2014); Scot McKnight, *Sermon on the Mount,* The Story of God Bible Commentary (Grand Rapids, MI: Zondervan, 2013); and Shane Claiborne and Chris Haw, *Jesus for President: Politics for Ordinary Radicals* (Grand Rapids, MI: Zondervan, 2008).

10. An important book on this topic is David Instone-Brewer, *Divorce and Remarriage in the Bible: The Social and Literary Context* (Grand Rapids, MI: Eerdmans, 2002).

Chapter 10: Trampling Fear

1. The following passages and observations are compiled by Pete Enns, "Yahweh, Creation, and the Cosmic Battle," Biologos.org, February 2, 2010, http://biologos.org/blogs/archive/yahweh-creation-and-the-cosmic-battle.

2. For a great study on the Greek word *pistis* (which can be translated "faithfulness" or "allegiance"), see Matthew W. Bates, *Salvation by Allegiance Alone: Rethinking Faith, Works, and the Gospel of Jesus the King* (Grand Rapids, MI: Baker Academic, 2017).

3. I can't recommend the following book enough: Latasha Morrison, *Be the Bridge: Pursuing God's Heart for Racial Reconciliation* (Colorado Springs: WaterBrook, 2019).

Chapter 11: The Process of Presence

1. For some good discussions of this text, see Timothy J. Geddert, *Mark,* Believers Church Bible Commentary (Scottdale, PA: Herald, 2001), 115ff and Ched

Myers, *Binding the Strong Man: A Political Reading of Mark's Story of Jesus* (Maryknoll, NY: Orbis, 1988, 2008), 190–94.

2. This point is adapted from a powerful sermon I heard years ago from Mike Pilavachi of Soul Survivor Church, called "See the One."

Chapter 12: Releasing the Stones

1. I recognize that some scholars believe this story may not belong in John 8, based on its style, which suggests it likely originated in Matthew, Mark, or Luke. I believe it belongs in the Bible, is authentic to Jesus, and is therefore a passage we should learn from. For a great discussion, see Marianne Meye Thompson, *John: A Commentary*, The New Testament Library (Louisville, KY: Westminster John Knox, 2015), 179.

2. For a compelling look at John 8 as a case against the death penalty, see Darrin W. Snyder Belousek, "Capital Punishment, Covenant Justice and the Cross of Christ: The Death Penalty in the Life and Death of Jesus," *Mennonite Quarterly Review* 83, no. 3 (July 2009): 375–403. Also see Shane Claiborne, *Executing Grace: How the Death Penalty Killed Jesus and Why It's Killing Us* (New York: HarperOne, 2016).

3. Joan Wallach Scott said, "Gender is a constitutive element of social relationships based on perceived differences between the sexes, and gender is a primary way of signifying relationships of power. . . . It might be better to say, gender is a primary field within which or by means of which power is articulated." Joan Wallach Scott, *Gender and the Politics of History*, 30th anniversary ed. (New York: Columbia University Press, 2018), 42, 44–45. For definitions of the terms discussed about the origins of the word *patriarchy*, consult a trusted classical Greek and Latin lexicon.

4. Dallas Willard has a few books in which he talks about guile. I honestly don't remember which one I was reading at the time, but this quote is from Dallas Willard, *The Divine Conspiracy: Rediscovering Our Hidden Life in God* (New York: HarperCollins, 1998), 231.

5. Miroslav Volf, *Exclusion and Embrace: A Theological Exploration of Identity, Otherness, and Reconciliation*, rev. ed. (Nashville: Abingdon, 1996), 123.

Chapter 13: When God Weeps

1. The Hebrew Scriptures call this place either the Valley of Ben Hinnom (Joshua 15:8; 18:16; 2 Chronicles 28:3; 33:6; Jeremiah 7:31–32; 19:6; 32:35, NIV) or the Valley of Hinnom (Nehemiah 11:30, NIV) or Topheth (Isaiah 30:33; Jeremiah 7:31–32; 19:6, 11–14, NIV) or, metaphorically, the Valley of Slaughter (Jeremiah 7:32; 19:6, NIV).

2. This is hard to prove from the historical data we have. It's something that has been in circulation for quite some time by scholars but may be nothing more

than an urban legend. Even so, the idea that it *may* have been a fiery dump isn't far-fetched. James connected it to a place of fire, for instance (3:6).

3. In addition to those listed in the main text, see Matthew 5:22, 29–30; 10:28; 18:9; 23:15; Mark 9:43, 45; James 3:6.

4. G. B. Caird said, "The gospel of Jesus was directed to Israel as a nation with a summons to abandon the road of aggressive nationalism and return to a true understanding of her historic role as the people of God." G. B. Caird, *The Language and Imagery of the Bible* (Philadelphia, PA: Westminster, 1980), 265.

5. N. T. Wright, *Christian Origins and the Question of God,* vol. 2, *Jesus and the Victory of God* (London: Society for Promoting Christian Knowledge, 1996), 326ff.

6. According to the World Health Organization, "Studies suggest that exposure to violence during childhood increases the likelihood of men perpetrating violence against intimate partners by 3 to 4-fold, compared to men who are not exposed to violence as children." "16 Days of Activism Against Gender Violence," World Health Organization, www.who.int/violence_injury _prevention/violence/global_campaign/16_days/en/index7.html.

7. To illustrate just how horrible the devastation truly was, the ancient historian Josephus gave an example of why Jesus warned that this time would be especially hard for pregnant and nursing mothers (Matthew 24:19; Mark 13:17; Luke 21:23). He recorded that due to starvation, at least one mother was found eating her child. We can imagine that the toll on women and children reached far beyond this one incident. Flavius Josephus, *The Works of Josephus: Complete and Unabridged,* trans. William Whiston (Peabody, MA: Hendrickson, 1987), 737–38, (*Jewish War* 6.201–13).

8. I owe "earth-shattering" to N. T. Wright, *New Heavens, New Earth: The Biblical Picture of Christian Hope,* Grove Biblical Series (Cambridge, UK: Grove Books, 1999), 9. Also, I'll note that Jewish hyperbole like this emphasized real-world shifts or judgments about to take place. Isaiah 13 uses various rhetorical devices (the stars, sun, and moon not giving light, land being destroyed, the earth shaking, and so on) to indicate that God would allow the Medes to destroy Babylon. Cosmic language has a point: something dramatic—and often political—is about to happen. Isaiah 34 uses cosmic language to describe something similar: the fall of Edom. Both of these cosmic-doom passages in the Hebrew Bible have already been fulfilled within history. See Caird, *Language and Imagery,* 110–14 and 133–44.

9. Josephus, *Works of Josephus,* 749, (*Jewish War* 6.420–220).

10. "They had [the dead] cast down from the walls into the valleys beneath." Josephus, *Works of Josephus,* 724, (*Jewish War* 5.518).

Chapter 14: The Cup and the Copeless

1. James Bryan Smith, *The Good and Beautiful God: Falling in Love with the God Jesus Knows* (Downers Grove, IL: InterVarsity, 2009), 64.

2. Gerald G. May, *The Dark Night of the Soul: A Psychiatrist Explores the Connection Between Darkness and Spiritual Growth* (New York: HarperOne, 2004), 67–68.

3. Richard Rohr, *Falling Upward: A Spirituality for the Two Halves of Life* (San Francisco: Jossey-Bass, 2011), xxvi.

4. Gerald G. May, *The Wisdom of Wilderness: Experiencing the Healing Power of Nature* (New York: HarperCollins, 2006), 34–35.

Chapter 15: *The Goodness of Friday*

1. The program is called Stewards of the Mystery. Check it out at https://paseo communities.com/direction.

2. James Bryan Smith, *The Good and Beautiful God: Falling in Love with the God Jesus Knows* (Downers Grove, IL: InterVarsity, 2009), 25.

3. Mark D. Baker, ed., *Proclaiming the Scandal of the Cross: Contemporary Images of the Atonement* (Grand Rapids, MI: Baker Academic, 2006), 22.

4. I have a seminary friend named Phil Schmidt who wrote an excellent paper on Mark 15 and Psalm 22 as his final project in our MDiv program. It was a deep dive into an argument that I had known only the basics of. I'm borrowing some of the research he so helpfully synthesized. Thanks, Phil, for your good work all those years back!

5. José Cárdenas Pallares, *A Poor Man Called Jesus: Reflections on the Gospel of Mark* (Maryknoll, NY: Orbis, 1986), 111.

Chapter 16: *Garden of Hope*

1. On this point, see Marianne Meye Thompson, *John: A Commentary,* The New Testament Library (Louisville, KY: Westminster John Knox, 2015), 413–18.

2. The idea of associating the eighth day with the first day of the week has several examples in the early Christian writings (those writings after the New Testament in the early centuries of the church). For a great discussion on this theme, see Jeannine K. Brown, "Creation's Renewal in the Gospel of John," *Catholic Biblical Quarterly* 72, no. 2 (April 2010): 275–90. I first heard this espoused by N. T. Wright years ago. Since then, I've preached and written about John 20 from this perspective in various forms. I also have heard Rob Bell adopt a similar approach in the past.

3. N. T. Wright, *Surprised by Hope: Rethinking Heaven, the Resurrection, and the Mission of the Church* (New York: HarperOne, 2008), 238.

4. If you want to dive into the book of Revelation, please go to two resources to get you started: Michael J. Gorman, *Reading Revelation Responsibly: Uncivil Worship and Witness—Following the Lamb into the New Creation* (Eugene, OR: Cascade Books, 2011) and N. T. Wright, *Revelation for Everyone* (Louisville, KY: Westminster John Knox, 2011).

5. Johannes Behm, "Καινός, Καινότης, Ἀνακαινίξω, Ἀνακαινόω, Ἀνακαίνωσις, Ἐγκαινίζω," in *Theological Dictionary of the New Testament,* ed. Gerhard Kittel and Gerhard Friedrich, trans. and ed. Geoffrey W. Bromiley, vol. 3 (Grand Rapids, MI: Eerdmans, 1964), 447.

6. Daniel Walker, *God in a Brothel: An Undercover Journey into Sex Trafficking and Rescue* (Downers Grove, IL: InterVarsity, 2011), 89.

7. Walker, *God in a Brothel,* 75.

8. Dennis R. Edwards, *Might from the Margins: The Gospel's Power to Turn the Tables on Injustice* (Harrisonburg, VA: Herald, 2020), 139.

Afterword

1. Dietrich Bonhoeffer, *Letters and Papers from Prison* (New York: Touchstone, 1997), 361.

ABOUT THE AUTHOR

KURT WILLEMS is a pastor, writer, and spiritual director. After several years working in church ministry with students and adults in Central California, he partnered with the Brethren in Christ to plant a Christian community called Pangea Church in Seattle. Kurt maintains a resource website called Theology Curator, which hosts articles and podcasts. He is passionate about taking dense ideas and communicating them in ways that are empowering for people in all walks of life. He holds a master of divinity degree from Fresno Pacific Biblical Seminary and a master of arts in comparative religion from the University of Washington (where he studied the historical life of Paul within Judaism and the Roman Empire). Kurt also completed a two-year training program, called Stewards of the Mystery, to become a spiritual director. His wife, Lauren, is a special-education teacher. They have two amazing young daughters.

CONNECT WITH KURT!

info@theologycurator.com

@KurtWillems

Kurt is available to speak at your next leadership, university, or church event or at your conference or camp.

Sign Up for Kurt's Newsletter
TheologyCurator.com/Newsletter

Theology Curator Podcast
Available on Apple, Spotify, and Google and also at
TheologyCurator.com/Podcasts

THEOLOGY CURATOR with KURT WILLEMS